Jonathan Grix
THE ROLE OF THE MASSES IN THE COLLAPSE OF THE GDR

Gunther Hellmann (*editor*)
GERMANY'S EU POLICY IN ASYLUM AND DEFENCE
De-Europeanization by Default?

Dan Hough, Michael Koß and Jonathan Olsen
THE LEFT PARTY IN CONTEMPORARY GERMAN POLITICS

Margarete Kohlenbach
WALTER BENJAMIN
Self-Reference and Religiosity

Charles Lees
PARTY POLITICS IN GERMANY
A Comparative Politics Approach

Hanns W. Maull
GERMANY'S UNCERTAIN POWER
Foreign Policy of the Berlin Republic

Christian Schweiger
BRITAIN, GERMANY AND THE FUTURE OF THE EUROPEAN UNION

James Sloam
THE EUROPEAN POLICY OF THE GERMAN SOCIAL DEMOCRATS
Interpreting a Changing World

Ronald Speirs and John Breuilly (*editors*)
GERMANY'S TWO UNIFICATIONS
Anticipations, Experiences, Responses

Henning Tewes
GERMANY, CIVILIAN POWER AND THE NEW EUROPE
Enlarging NATO and the European Union

Maiken Umbach
GERMAN FEDERALISM
Past, Present, Future

Roger Woods
GERMANY'S NEW RIGHT AS CULTURE AND POLITICS

New Perspectives in German Studies
Series Standing Order ISBN 0–333–92430–4 hardcover
Series Standing Order ISBN 0–333–92434–7 paperback
(*outside North America only*)

You can receive future titles in this series as they are published by placing a standing order. Please contact your bookseller or, in case of difficulty, write to us at the address below with your name and address, the title of the series and the ISBN quoted above.

Customer Services Department, Macmillan Distribution Ltd, Houndmills, Basingstoke, Hampshire RG21 6XS, England

---

The Left Party in Contemporary German Politics

Dan Hough
Senior Lecturer in Politics,
University of Sussex, UK

Michael Koß
Visiting Scholar,
Berlin Graduate School of Social Sciences,
Humboldt University
Germany

and

Jonathan Olsen
Associate Professor of Political Science,
University of Wisconsin-Parkside, USA

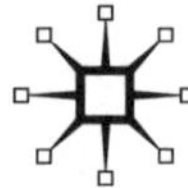

First published 2007 by
PALGRAVE MACMILLAN
Houndmills, Basingstoke, Hampshire RG21 6XS and
175 Fifth Avenue, New York, N.Y. 10010
Companies and representatives throughout the world

PALGRAVE MACMILLAN is the global academic imprint of the Palgrave Macmillan division of St. Martin's Press, LLC and of Palgrave Macmillan Ltd. Macmillan® is a registered trademark in the United States, United Kingdom and other countries. Palgrave is a registered trademark in the European Union and other countries.

ISBN-13: 978–0–230–01907–2   hardback
ISBN-10: 0–230–01907–2   hardback

This book is printed on paper suitable for recycling and made from fully managed and sustained forest sources. Logging, pulping and manufacturing processes are expected to conform to the environmental regulations of the country of origin.

A catalogue record for this book is available from the British Library.

Library of Congress Cataloging-in-Publication Data

Hough, Dan.
  The Left Party in contemporary German politics / Dan Hough, Michael
  Koß, and Jonathan Olsen.
      p. cm.
  Includes bibliographical references and index.
  ISBN 0–230–01907–2 (alk. paper)
    1. Linkspartei (Germany) I. Koß, Michael. II. Olsen, Jonathan, 1959–
    III. Title.

  JN3971.A98L5744 2007
  324.243'07—dc22   2007023309

10   9   8   7   6   5   4   3   2   1
16 15 14 13 12 11 10 09 08 07

Printed and bound in Great Britain by
Antony Rowe Ltd, Chippenham and Eastbourne

Contents

Acknowledgements   vi

Abbreviations   viii

Introduction   1

1 Unification and the Fight for Survival   12

2 Policies, Programmes and Personalities: The Post-1998 PDS   31

3 Aims and Ambitions: Policy, Office, Votes and the Left Party   47

4 Haven't We Been Here Before? Comparing the Left Party and
   the Greens   66

5 The Left Party in Mecklenburg-Western Pomerania   84

6 The Left Party in Berlin   99

7 The Left Party in Opposition   115

8 From the PDS to the Left Party   134

9 Conclusion   153

Notes   166

Bibliography   195

Index   211

Acknowledgements

The authors of this monograph, the first on Germany's new Left Party in the English language, make no apologies for admitting that they have found studying their subject a fascinating experience. We have thoroughly enjoyed speaking to Left Party politicians, researching their policy stances and trying to make sense of their public proclamations. Whether we have done so successfully will, of course, be for the readers of this book to judge. Yet, books, of course, only see the light of day not just because of the efforts of their authors, but also thanks to the support and assistance of many people and many institutions. This one is certainly no exception to that rule. First and foremost we would like to thank the Economic and Social Research Council for supporting our research through grant RES-000-22-0803. Second, we thank our academic institutions – the University of Sussex in the UK and the University of Wisconsin-Parkside in the USA – for the help and assistance they have provided. Third, we thank Professors William Paterson and Mike Butler of the University of Birmingham for having faith in us as authors and for agreeing to publish our book in Palgrave Macmillan's *New Perspectives in German Studies* series.

The institutional support enabled us to set out the parameters of our research and to get out into the field to collect data, talk with interview partners and to meet and discuss findings. But this is certainly not to neglect the smaller contributions from friends, family and colleagues who are, in their own way, just as significant. We would therefore like to thank, in no particular order, Ian King, for studiously reading significant parts of the manuscript and for pointing out some of our most heinous grammatical and conceptual failings. May the Scottish Premiership crown return to Ibrox sometime soon as a reward! Colleagues Tim Bale, Paul Taggart, Aleks Szczerbiak and Paul Webb were never slow to tell us what they thought of our work, and we thank them for their constructive criticisms and their thought-provoking analysis. Molly and the Olsen family also deserve a special mention for all of their help and support – to all of you, it really was very much appreciated.

We are also thankful to Felix Lange and Tobias Schulz for providing, as ever, roofs over our heads while we conducted fieldwork in Berlin. Felix proved that he knows more about Berlin's Indian restaurants than possibly anyone else alive, while Tobias never ceased to amaze us with his own culinary expertise! Both of these fine fellows also provided real food for thought on where the Left Party could, should, would or might go in the future; Sascha Brinkmann and the Messerschmidt family offered their hospitality in Dresden and Schwerin; Alister Miskimmon dealt admirably with anti-social working hours and persistent requests to borrow his laptop; the pub quiz team at Brighton's Lion and Lobster, under the skilful leadership of James Hampshire, offered a welcome escape route from the minutiae of documentary analysis on Monday nights; the people at Rounder Records inspired with their dedication to good music and well-thought-out listening suggestions and, finally, the commuters on the 06:53 train from Clapham Junction to Lewes also made their little contribution – not that they were ever aware of it, but many a paragraph was crafted while musing over, for example, why the slightly odd woman with the red coat never (ever) took off her woolly hat. One mystery that we'll probably never get to the bottom of.

Sometimes in academia it is easy to forget that what for us is a simple 'object' of study can mean much, much more to many others. This is something that we were reminded of every time we contacted members of the Left Party with questions and requests. We would therefore like to record our thanks to a number of people in, or near to, the party itself. Firstly, to Conny Hildebrandt and Michael Brie at the Rosa Luxemburg Foundation; they always showed an interest in our work and were always more than willing to help whenever they could. Secondly, to the many parliamentarians who agreed to speak to us – very few failed to reply to our letters and the vast majority generously gave of their time for no personal gain. Finally, we would also like to thank members of the Left Party such as the late Renate Vogt in Leipzig who spent so much time explaining to us how they thought 'their' party worked and where 'their' party was heading. To many of them it is, of course, more than a party. And we hope that our book will provide them with an outsiders view of the way it works.

Dan Hough, Michael Koß and Jonathan Olsen

Abbreviations

AG	Working Group (within the PDS)
AL	(Green) Alternative List (Berlin)
ALEKSA	Alternative State Development Plan (Saxony)
APO	Extra-Parliamentary Opposition
ASG	Initiative for Social Justice (forerunner of WASG)
B90	Alliance 90
Basis	The rank and file of a political party
BEWAG	Berlin's Electricity Company
BSR	The Berlin City Cleaning Department
BVG	The Berlin Public Transport Company
BWK	Association of West German Communists
CDU	Christian Democratic Union
CSU	Christian Social Union
DKP	German Communist Party
DVU	German Peoples Union
FDJ	Free German Youth (of the GDR)
FDP	Free Democratic Party
Fraktion	Parliamentary Party
FRG	Federal Republic of Germany
Fundis	'Fundamentalists' within the Green Party
GAL	Green Alternative List (Hamburg)
GDR	German Democratic Republic
Hartz IV	A package of welfare state reforms instigated by the last SPD-Green federal government
IG	Interest Group (within the PDS)
IM	Unofficial agents of the Stasi
KITA	Day care centres
KPD	Communist Party of Germany
KPF	Communist Platform within the PDS
LP	Left Party
MdA	Member of the Berlin *Land* Parliament
MdB	Member of the German Parliament
MdL	Member of a German *Land* Parliament (not Berlin, Bremen and Hamburg)
MEP	Member of the European Parliment
MV	Mecklenburg-Western Pomerania

NATO	North Atlantic Treaty Organisation
NPD	National Democratic Party of Germany
NRW	North Rhine-Westphalia
PDS	Party of Democratic Socialism
ÖBS	Publicly subsidised employment sector
OWUS	The Association of Small and Medium-sized Businesses and the Self-Employed in Saxony
Realos	'Realists' within the Green Party
REP	Republican Party
SAV	Forward with the Socialist Alternative
SED	Socialist Unity Party of Germany
SPD	Social Democratic Party of Germany
Stasi	The GDR's state security police
Ver.di	Public Sector Trade Union
WASG	The Electoral Alternative: Labour and Social Justice

Introduction

'A week' as former British Prime Minister Harold Wilson once said 'is a long time in politics'. If a week is a long time, then a year can sometimes feel like an eternity, a fact that would seem particularly true for the politicians, activists, members and supporters of the German Left Party (*Die Linke*) when they look back on 2005. The jubilant scenes at the post-election party in Berlin's Schlossplatz, just off Unter den Linden, on the evening of the federal election on 18 September would indeed have been hard for most of them to conceive of just 12 months previously. The event was the stuff of which politicians (and their supporters) dream. The enthusiastic, frequently ecstatic, party faithful had turned out in their hundreds, throngs of newspaper journalists queued for a word from the much sought after victors and TV camera crews lapped up every moment of the jubilant celebrations. At around 7 p.m. Oskar Lafontaine, Gerhard Schröder's former finance minister, long-time doyen of the Social Democratic Party's (SPD) left-wing and now leading light in *Die Linke*, and Gregor Gysi, the ebullient, sharp-tongued and quick-witted talisman of the old Party of Democratic Socialism (PDS), entered the victory tent to a cacophony of noise, striding confidently on to the stage to salute their supporters. *Die Linke* – all but non-existent on the national stage between 2002 and 2005 – had returned to the federal parliament (*Bundestag*) with an impressive 8.7 per cent of the popular vote. The Left Party became Germany's fourth largest political party, boasting 54 MdBs (MPs) and subsequently a stronger parliamentary presence than both the Green Party (51 MPs) and the Bavarian Christian Social Union (46 MPs). 'A serious political competitor to the left of the Social Democratic Party now exists in western Germany for the first time since the 1950s' boomed Gregor Gysi from the platform.[1] Few would argue that he did not have a point.

Twelve months previously the world looked a very different place. Gesine Lötzsch and Petra Pau, the PDS's only elected representatives in the 2002–5 *Bundestag*, cut a sorry sight, sitting at the back of the plenary hall in Berlin's *Reichstagsgebäude*. In what seemed curiously symbolic of the PDS's position in the German party system, they were deprived for most of the legislative period of tables (which the most prominent members of all parties possessed) and telephones (other MPs possessed them; Lötzsch and Pau had to leave the plenary hall to make a call as they did not, somewhat ironically, possess a table to place a telephone on)[2] as they no longer enjoyed the status of a 'parliamentary party'.[3] The PDS appeared to be slipping into an eastern German regionalist trough, rarely seen or heard at the federal level, largely insignificant in western Germany, with politicians who received precious little media attention and were, for the most part, hardly household names in their own households.[4] The PDS was dying, desperate to make a political impact, but devoid of enough electoral support or enough political imagination to be able to barge its way on to the political stage. The return, at the Potsdam conference of the PDS on 30–31 October 2004, of Gregor Gysi to the front ranks of the party following his partly self-imposed exile and his partly health-induced spell on the political sidelines represented the PDS's last throw of the electoral dice. Although the PDS had systematically failed to gain a foothold in western Germany under Gysi's tutelage through the 1990s, and with this the vital votes needed to hurdle the 5 per cent barrier for federal elections, delegates forgave his scandal-tinted resignation as Berlin's economics minister in July 2002 and hoped that the PDS's media star would be able to talk the party back into the *Bundestag*.[5] But they were only hopes, and the PDS rank and file realised that finding an extra 500,000 votes was a big ask even for Gregor Gysi working at full throttle.[6] Gysi's return and the next election (then still planned for autumn 2006) were, according to one well-informed source, 'going to be, come what may, our last chance'.[7]

A number of things happened in the intervening year that transformed the hopes of PDS/Left Party[8] members into hard and fast expectations. Several of these were outside the party's control. A battered and bruised Chancellor, Gerhard Schröder, continued pursuing policies of social and economic reform. Backed by a Christian Democratic Union (CDU)-dominated upper chamber (*Bundesrat*) he left clear (red) water to the SPD's left for new protest movements to take shape. In its pre-2005 guise the PDS was in no fit position to immediately lead any such movement; it was seen by many western Germans as too eastern, too dogmatic and, most significantly, as too attached to a failed state, the GDR.

But other forces could, and did, tap into the reservoirs of dissatisfaction that were deepening, giving the disaffected a political voice and, eventually, bringing them into the PDS's sphere of influence. Indeed, the emergence of 'The Electoral Alternative: Labour and Social Justice' (WASG) party, and subsequently the Left Party, was one of the key reasons for Lafontaine and Gysi's moment of victory in the tent on Schlossplatz on the 18th of September.

Other external influences also assisted the Left Party in finding its political feet. Gerhard Schröder's controversial decision to bring forward the date of the federal election by a full 12 months did not worry the Left Party unduly. On the contrary, it prompted the various parties and interest groups to the left of the SPD to channel their efforts into gaining parliamentary representation at the federal level. An extra 12 months would, given the traditional machinations and rivalries that are never far from the surface of left wing politics, have simply given the PDS and the WASG more opportunity to fall out with one another. The inevitable teething problems of forming a new party were subsequently postponed until the relative tranquillity of the post-election period.

Developments on the right of the political spectrum also played into the Left Party's hands. The CDU/Christian Social Union's (CSU) chancellor candidate, Angela Merkel, was, despite being born in Hamburg, an eastern German (she spent most of her youth in the Brandenburg town of Templin) and was previously leader of the CDU in Mecklenburg-Western Pomerania, in Germany's north-east. However, her eastern heritage never seriously looked like assuring her of any sort of *Ostbonus* (eastern bonus). On the contrary, the collaboration of the CDU with the SPD in pushing through the controversial package of social and labour market '*Hartz*' Reforms, or Agenda 2010, as well as ineffectual performance as a government-in-waiting through 2005 dismayed many eastern German electors.[9] Not enough to cost Merkel the chancellorship, but the members of her 'competence team' clearly flattered to deceive; one needlessly brought high-explosive issues such as hypothetical flat tax rates onto the political agenda (Paul Kirchhoff, Merkel's potential finance minister) while others bemoaned the fact that 'frustrated' eastern Germans could again vote in silly ways that might cost the CDU/CSU the election (Edmund Stoiber, Bavarian prime minister and federal economics minister designate). Jörg Schönbohm, CDU-deputy prime minister in the eastern state of Brandenburg, further claimed that easterners were 'proletarianised' by the pre-1989 GDR state in which they lived and were therefore more likely to accept violence as legitimate behaviour and generally behave in more wayward fashion. On message, Messrs

Kirchhoff, Stoiber and Schönbohm certainly were not. A familiar story of 'Left Party against the rest' was developing; the nuances may have been slightly different – there was no 'red socks' or 'red hands' campaign, as there had been in yesteryear, and there was little attempt to undermine the Left Party's democratic credentials – but the Left Party was certainly not unwilling to let a picture of it as (once again) a persecuted party be painted all the same.

The Left Party's success in 2005 was nonetheless not all down to being in the right place at the right time. Political opportunity structures abound, yet parties and politicians are frequently unable and/or unwilling to make the most of them. Gregor Gysi and Lothar Bisky – the enigmatic and sharp-tongued campaigner allied with the cool-headed and competent party manager – steered the PDS through tricky negotiations with a new and largely unknown set of western German WASG leaders. Managing (frequently without actually looking like they were trying to do so) complex processes of alliance building, while avoiding legal pitfalls, and keeping a vocal array of ideological '*Querdenker*' onside was not straightforward. Bisky and Gysi, Bodo Ramelow (the Left Party's election manager) and WASG executive board members Klaus Ernst, Axel Troost, Thomas Händel and Sabine Lösing could not have conducted this process much better.

Of protest and anti-capitalism, extremism and milieus

That the 2005 federal election was a great success for the Left Party is therefore indisputable. The election result speaks for itself. Yet understanding how the party got to this point, and what the future may hold for the 'new' party, divides, often starkly, academics and practitioners alike. Through the 1990s the PDS's successes were certainly explained in strikingly different ways, with varying emphasis placed on particular facets of the party's make-up. One thing is clear; there has been no lack of literature on the PDS, and it has become one of the most-studied parties in contemporary Germany. Through the 1990s, most analysis generally fell into one of two main schools of thought. The first saw the PDS (and it will no doubt see *Die Linke*) as a dysfunctional, disruptive element within the German political system, often bordering on the extremist fringe, contributing to a destabilising of political life; the second saw (and is also likely to continue to see) the PDS more as a stabilising, reforming, corrective influence, stressing its integrative and representative functions. It would nonetheless be a mistake to view these schools of thought as individual and distinct; significant degrees of overlap and co-ordination exist, even if core assumptions may differ. When analysed more closely, there tend to be four key strands within these schools of thought.[10]

For many, the key element of the PDS's success was the post-unification protest that it gave voice to. The party was subsequently viewed as a representative of diffuse and uncoordinated protest movements.[11] A complex mixture of economic, political and socio-psychological dissatisfaction was perceived to be the basis of a vote for the party, and it was widely felt that as the eastern *Länder* became further integrated into German society, and as, in particular, the economic environment there improved, the reasons for protest voting would subside. Yet protest voters are generally viewed in the political science world as volatile swing voters. 'Protest parties' are, by their very nature, seen as transient phenomena that citizens only turn to in extraordinary conditions of political, economic or social dissatisfaction. In the case of the PDS, voter loyalty is strong and sustained. In fact, the PDS has traditionally had the most loyal supporters of any party in eastern Germany – a trait that fits uneasily with the protest party thesis.[12] Although the PDS played on its reputation as a protest party in the early and mid-1990s in particular, it is now clear that if Easterners wish to protest at the political level, then they tend towards the parties of the far right, principally the German Peoples Union (DVU) and the National Democratic Party (NPD). Hence, although the PDS profits from feelings of general dissatisfaction in the eastern states, characterising the PDS as a 'protest party' does not help explain the successful mobilisation of votes by the PDS in eastern Germany *over a sustained period of time*.[13]

Commentators keen on putting the PDS's ideology and self-perception under the microscope tended to adopt an altogether different mode of analysis. The 'left-wing politics' approach was only invoked by a minority of authors, many of whom appeared to hold principles near to those which the party espouses. The PDS was viewed as a renewed, democratic-socialist party that grew out of the reforming wing of the SED. Rather than treat the party as a transitory 'protest' phenomenon, the emphasis shifted to the important long-term role that the PDS could/should play as the heir to the long-established socialist tradition in Germany. Through the 1990s this approach remained in stark contrast to the hostile responses that the party generated across the majority spectrum of academic literature, as well as in most journalism – left wing newspapers *Neues Deutschland* and *Junge Welt* excepted – covering the party's activities. The PDS could, for these observers, contribute to the 'ideological rearmament' of the German Left, pressuring and cajoling the SPD to remember its socialist conscience.[14] Decidedly unpopular through the 1990s, this approach gained ground as the PDS (and particularly *Die Linke*) stabilised itself in the German party system at the beginning of the 21st century.

Through the early 1990s most of the literature produced on the PDS took a(nother) completely different line to that of the protest and left-wing-politics approaches. A group of scholars, centred primarily in and around the conservative Hanns Seidel and Konrad Adenauer Foundations, saw the PDS as nothing short of a threat to Germany's democratic order, dismissing its commitments to democracy as shams covering up much more sinister aims. As time has passed, the anti-system approach has gradually lost its dominant position, even if authors such as Viola Neu and Jürgen Lang still insist on viewing the PDS through the prism of extremist politics.[15] The PDS allegedly polarised and destabilised the German party system, 'ideologising' polit-ical discourse and broadening the political spectrum to include 'left-wing extremists'. Jürgen Lang, for example, claimed that the PDS's parliamentary orientation and commitment to representative democ-racy were purely functional.[16] Attempts to sideline elements such as the Communist Platform (KPF), the *AG Junge GenossInnen* (the party's youth wing in the early 1990s) or the *Westlinken* (a group – long since defunct – of radical western Germans) were, above all, tactical steps, assisting the PDS in achieving its anti-democratic aims.[17] Now, in the mid-2000s, this approach appears quirky at best. In truth, it was – once the PDS had got through the initial 12–18 months after the fall of the Berlin Wall and had begun to stabilise itself – quirky for most of the 1990s as well. Put another way, those who go hunting for witches will, sooner or later, eventually find them. The all-encompassing Marxist–Leninist ideology of the SED has long since been replaced and the PDS now attempts to portray itself more as a broad church of leftward leaning opinion, hav-ing denied the importance of the leading role of the working class and chosen to accept – however begrudgingly at first – the democratic rules of the game.[18] The (in)coherence of this socialist alternative is irrelevant (such things are for voters to pass judgement on); the party has adapted to the system, and now adheres to the rules of the political game like every other democratic party.

A final group of commentators saw the PDS as a representative of a distinct 'milieu' in eastern Germany.[19] The party remained specific to both its social environment and its culture, maintaining elements of a particular form of self-help group. These authors highlight how the party united different groups, characterised by relatively high levels of education, secularisation and urbanisation while sharing similar cultural and political orientations.[20] These groups may have been quite diverse, but they were united within a broad cultural milieu whose interests and problems in coming to terms with life in the FRG were articulated by the PDS within the political arena.[21] Throughout the 1990s this approach clearly had something to offer and it was only in the late 1990s that non-milieu members moved towards the PDS with any sort of enthusiasm.[22] By the turn of the 21st century this approach had metamorphosed into a slightly different beast, stressing the PDS's skill at articulating and representing (largely self-defined) eastern German interests in the political process. The PDS became an expression of the east–west value conflict, attracting not only those who saw themselves as critical of capitalism, but also those who were suspicious of western (German) culture and who saw their 'eastern German-ness' as something to be (reasonably) proud of.[23] The PDS flourished in an eastern German community that needed political representation at the local, regional and national levels.

It is with these wide and diverse analyses of the PDS in mind that this book attempts to bring some clarity to our understanding of what sort of party its successor, the *Linkspartei*, or *Die Linke,* as it has been known since June 2007 is and where it is going. Is the coalition of disparate forces that have come together in the new party sustainable or will the tensions and (considerable) potential areas of conflict prove to be the death of it? How is it likely to come to terms with the practical and programmatic dilemmas that its (apparently) more established position in the German party system will bring? And how will the rest of the party system react? The book begins, in Chapter 1, by mapping out the PDS's development since the collapse of the GDR in 1989/90 up to its triumphant performance in the 1998 federal election. During the 1990s the PDS was consistently underestimated and frequently written off. Chapter 1 illustrates how it nonetheless managed to survive the implosion of the system (the GDR) with which it was, for many, indelibly linked. It moved away from its dogmatic, and at times positively Stalinist, past and reinvented itself as both left-wing protest movement and skilful articulator of eastern German distinctiveness. It possessed an ideological diversity unique among German parties. Skilful leadership prevented too much internal rancour, as the more or less universal climate of derision that surrounded the party spawned a backs-to-the-walls mentality which helped foster a spirit of solidarity between activists with divergent agendas and the party and its voters. Through the 1990s the PDS remained a broad church of left-ward leaning opinion, and the merger of WASG and PDS in

2007 ensures that managing heterogeneous sets demands from actors with at times strikingly different understandings of where the *Die Linke* should progress from here remains one of the new party's biggest challenges.

Whereas Chapter 1 explains how the PDS stabilised itself in the German party system, Chapter 2 illustrates how – between 1998 and 2005 – it very nearly threw all of this good work away. Polling 5.1 per cent of the popular vote in the 1998 election looked like it was going to be the high watermark of the party's success, ensuring full parliamentary rights, and the apparent end of the PDS's transformation into a democratic party. Perceptions can, however, be deceptive of course. The failure of the party to repeat this feat in 2002 – when it polled just under 600,000 fewer votes than it did in 1998 – and the internal wrangling and indiscipline that followed pushed the party into an existential crisis. No matter that at least some of the reason for the party's difficulties in 2002 were external and largely unique to the time; the party's pacifist credentials were undermined by Gerhard Schröder's anti-Iraq War rhetoric in the summer of 2002 and the floods in significant parts of eastern Germany gifted the then Chancellor an opportunity to look dynamic and in touch with an area of the country where the PDS has traditionally polled very strongly. Factional battles within the party's executive, weak and disjointed leadership and the virtual disappearance of the party from federal politics led the party to the edge of the political abyss; something that, perhaps more by luck than by judgment, it was only able to pull away from in the months running up to the September 2005 election.

In order to make sense of the ups and downs of the PDS and Left Party's development in recent times, the third chapter introduces an analytical framework that should help us to understand a little more about how the party works and how it may develop in future years. Political parties, as has been well documented in the literature on party behaviour, are faced with a number of strategic dilemmas. The 'policy, office, votes' trichotomy developed by Kaare Strøm illustrates that parties can and do attempt to trade off these different aims against one another without ever (completely) neglecting any one of them.[24] They may, firstly, stress the need to participate in government. Parties who expressly emphasise this aim seek, above all, concrete advantages for themselves and their clientele that result from governing. They therefore tend to stress the importance of manoeuvring themselves into an advantageous position within the party system, and with other actors, so as to gain significant ministerial portfolios. A genuine influence on governmental outputs remains important, but office-seeking parties do not tend to stress ideological consistency and programmatic purity in the way that other actors may choose to do. Secondly, they could place a stress on policy-seeking. Policy-seeking parties are in many ways the antithesis of office-seeking parties. They have particular programmatic goals and aims and seek to do all they can to implement them in as 'pure' a form as is possible. These parties are likely to have a coherent political agenda stemming out of core ideological beliefs that have been developed over many years. Alternatively, they may be individual issue-orientated parties who seek to profile themselves on a much narrower policy base. Office-seeking remains important to policy-seeking parties – but it does not become an end in itself. Such parties may subsequently find decisions on when, and under what conditions, to enter government particularly testing. Thirdly, parties may place most emphasis on simple vote maximisation (vote-seeking). The principal aim that these parties adopt is that of maximising the number of votes they achieve in elections. Again, policy-seeking and office-seeking are not completely insignificant, but the initial emphasis remains one of expanding a voter base. Party programmes are likely to be less ideologically rigid and office-seeking may be either implausible or unwanted – the emphasis therefore moves to embedding the party's position within the electorate.

Although this framework is ultimately derived from deductive, rational choice reasoning, it can still function quite easily as a framework or a heuristic. It helps us to throw light on processes and deeper meanings without purporting to provide law-like generalisations about the ways that politicians make tough decisions. Indeed, Müller and Strøm actively seek to confront formal modellers with the ways that real actors deal with tough choices in real-world situations.[25] They seek to do this at the level of the party. We take this a step further and look at how inner-party democracy is affected by such choices. Territorial groupings (i.e. *Landesverbände, Fraktionen* in *Land* parliaments), ideological platforms and working groups within the Left Party do not believe, just as is the case within other parties, that the party should seek to pursue any of these three aims independently of the others. Linkages, and trade-offs, therefore inevitably exist between all three. However, over time the federal party has the ability to stress particular strategies, just as do individual *Landesverbände*. And this can lead to frictions, as happened with the PDS/Left Party post-2002. Chapter 3 therefore introduces an analytical tool with which we can analyse these frictions, pinpointing the different aims and strategies that the PDS/Left Party (at federal and *Land* levels) has used before honing in on where these relationships might take the party in the years to come.

Chapter 4 brings another dimension to the Left Party's development by bringing in an overtly comparative element. The Left Party is not, of course, the first party to rise up and challenge the traditional cartel of institutionalised actors. Challenger parties on the far right and far left have periodically risen and fallen. The one party that grew from radical roots to successfully challenge the established actors and find a niche for itself in the German party system was, however, the Green Party. The Greens were, at least in their early stages, every bit as dismissive of capitalism and the dynamic of party competition in Germany as is the Left Party. Yet, as is widely known, they proceeded to march through the institutions of German government to eventually take up positions of power not just in *Land* governments, but also as a junior partner in Gerhard Schröder's two SPD-led administrations between 1998 and 2005. The processes of institutionalisation that the Greens have undertaken can be seen either as evidence of selling out at the expense of their radical ideals or as proof that parties develop their ideas over time and learn how to 'play the political game'. Either way, there are clearly distinct parallels with the development of the PDS through the 1990s and early 21st century. Yet, as Chapter 4 illustrates, there is no guarantee that the Left Party will ultimately become coalitionable at the national level and that 'institutionalisation' is an inevitable process. This might happen, but there is certainly no incontrovertible logic that says that it has to. This chapter concludes by illustrating that there is not, as yet, a fully developed red-red model of government and it is for this reason that the Left Party has some way to go before it genuinely establishes itself as preferred coalition partner for the SPD. Thus far, and this is illustrated in more detail in Chapters 5, 6 and 7, coalitions have come to bear for largely pragmatic reasons centring around personalities and practical politics. A concerted red-red style of governance and pro-grammatic agenda appears to us to be some way from fruition.

Chapters 5, 6 and 7 turn the focus on the Left Party itself. They illustrate that factions within the Left Party are indeed able to articulate particular wants and needs over and above those of the federal party. There is, indeed, plenty of institutional wriggle-room available for a *Landesverband* that actually wants to make use of it. Chapter 5 illustrates that in eastern Germany's northernmost *Land*, Mecklenburg-Western Pomerania, the Left Party has followed the Green path closer than is the case elsewhere. But, even then, the reasons for this are unique to Mecklenburg-Western Pomerania. The Left Party in Schwerin concentrates on developing and implementing specific policies that might help to solve the (many) socio-economic problems that exist in Germany's north-east. This is in contrast to the Left Party in other eastern German states (including Berlin), where policy-seeking goals play a much less significant role. The party subsequently entered the coalition with the SPD in 1998 with a clear set of programmatic aims and concrete proposals – a situation that was not in any way replicated in Berlin, for example. Governing has therefore not changed the Left Party in Mecklenburg-Western Pomerania as much as we would originally have hypothesised.

The Left Party entered government in Berlin (in 2001) for altogether different reasons. Berlin remains a domain of modern socialism (defined in Chapter 1) within the party. For many in the party the importance of a long-term strategic vision comes into play. Gregor Gysi and the modern socialists saw the German capital as a test bed for persuading western Germans (in the shape of West Berliners) that the Left Party was not the eastern German demon frequently portrayed in the media and that effective, non-dramatic performance in government was of fundamental importance in doing this. The lack of a coherent socialist programmatic profile was abundantly evident both to Left Party insiders as well as to those (both critical and sympathetic) looking in from the outside. The Left Party in the German capital is evidently willing and capable of articulating goals and aims that go well beyond those of its rank and file, and also arguably beyond those of its most loyal electorate, mainly as it wants to increase its ability to exert influence on the western part of Germany – no matter how small the steps are towards this goal – through competent and coordinated behaviour in the Berlin sub-state government.

Chapter 7 moves the microscope away from eastern *Länder* where the Left Party has governed over to those where it has been in permanent opposition. It throws light on the heterogeneity of aims and strategies within the Left Party, illustrating that there is most certainly not a clear route to pro-government attitudes, stances and aims within the party. The Left Party remains a diverse and at times contradictory political actor. And it is for this reason that the merger with the WASG that took place in the spring of 2007 is such a challenge; Chapter 8 illustrates how the merger actually took place and what different beasts were entering into it. The Left Party may indeed be the first socialist party to the left of the SPD that has established itself in the *Bundestag*, but, as the old adage goes, the road to hell can still be paved with good intentions. The conclusion therefore explains the challenges that lie ahead for the party and where possible potholes may lie.

1
Unification and the Fight for Survival

Introduction

Had they been given prior warning of the 2005 election result, observers of German politics in the late 1980s and early 1990s would have been astonished at what they were being told. No doubt they would have found the idea of Germany's first female Chancellor intriguing; that she should be a Protestant from the East would also have prompted considerable interest; the failure of the two main parties to genuinely mobilise support around their programmes for reform would also have prompted comment and observation, as would the discussion of 'traffic light' and 'Jamaica' coalition options.[1] The real astonishment would, however, have come when they heard that the Socialist Unity Party's (SED) successor party, the Party of Democratic Socialism (PDS), had metamorphosed into a left-wing protest movement capable of persuading over four million electors to vote for it and entering the federal parliament with 8.7 per cent of the popular vote. What on earth, they may well have asked, had 'gone wrong' with German democracy to facilitate such a strong performance by a party that should be out of democratic bounds? How on earth had such a party survived that long? How had the PDS/Left Party pulled off the (apparently) unthinkable and (apparently) stabilised itself as a respectable force in the German party system?

The Left Party's strong showing in 2005, as well as the PDS's – if only in eastern Germany – through the late 1990s, should not disguise the traumatic and, at times, positively schizophrenic early period of the party's development. The path to that 2005 success has been characterised by as many stops as starts, and, even now, its position in the German party system is not completely secure. The threat of the SPD moving back leftwards to tempt back some of its old voters, the danger of internal splits and general discord within the newly created *Die Linke* and the perennial worry about slipping towards the 5 per cent trapdoor out of parliament ensure that it has plenty to keep it honest. Compared to where it was in 1989, however, the Left Party is facing a completely different set of challenges, and conquering them would appear to be child's play when compared with what the PDS's immediate predecessors had to come to terms with.

The PDS, and the SED before it, grew out of a dictatorial and inherently anti-democratic predecessor – the GDR's Socialist Unity Party. Its starting position as Communism began to crumble was, therefore, anything but advantageous. Over 40 years the SED had proved itself to be one of the most hard-line and dogmatic Communist parties in central and eastern Europe, and, as the GDR collapsed, it was only at the last moment that its leaders appeared to realise the true severity of the crisis affecting their party and their state. As the GDR imploded in the weeks and months after the fall of the Berlin Wall, the party leaders began to grasp that radical changes in ideology, organisation and policy were necessary if the SED were to survive in post-unification Germany. Indeed, survival – nothing more – was the name of the game, and in late 1989 and early 1990 the SED set out on an uneasy and disjointed process of reform with precisely this aim in mind. Parties naturally become conservative beasts, reticent to set out on new programmatic paths, never mind slaughter sacred cows. It takes skilful leaders, mixed with advantageous opportunity structures, to carry party members along and to coax and cajole them into reinvigorating their party. The stumbling nature of the SED's reform process stemmed not only from the traditional reticence of party members, but also from the nature of the dilemma which the leadership faced. Once it became clear that unification was highly likely to take place, the party needed to make rapid and quantifiable progress in aligning itself with the structures enshrined in the West German Basic Law. The key pillars of a society that SED leaders and members had pilloried for years suddenly had – in a plausible way – to be accepted and internalised. A new programme was needed, new leaders were required and a new raison d'être had to be crafted. A couple of million voters needed to be persuaded (of something as yet undefined) too.

Yet, at the same time, the leaders of the SED realised that wholesale reforms were completely out of the question. If the SED was too quick to condemn the GDR, or too keen on embracing western German 'bourgeois democracy', then its truest supporters – the believers who had stayed loyal to socialist ideals through thick and thin in the GDR – would most likely be appalled at the hypocritical behaviour of a party that they had served, and believed in, for, in some cases, over 40 years. The SED needed to reform without reforming too much. It needed to stay true to the core of its rapidly shrinking membership base, without defending the indefensible (such as the human rights abuses that took place in the GDR, the lack of anything approaching party democracy and the hapless economic management that it had overseen). If it got this balancing act wrong, then there was a strong chance that the party would not have even made it to the first all-German election in December 1990.

Of names and leaders

Following the breaching of the Berlin Wall on 9 November 1989, the SED quickly called an extraordinary conference from 8–9 December to discuss the future of the party. Even though the vast majority of delegates believed in socialism in the GDR, perceived it to be reformable and, indeed, believed that the GDR itself had some sort of socialist future, it was clear that the SED in its then form almost certainly had no chance of survival. Wild thoughts that the SED might act as a counterweight to Helmut Kohl's Conservative Coalition were far removed from reality as the SED's unpopularity – now that GDR citizens were able to articulate their thoughts free of any worries that they would be punished for them – became clear for all to see. The rapidly shifting societal dynamics within the GDR, as well as the new movements and political parties that were springing up, left a rigidly conservative SED faced with little option but to move (as best it could) with the times. The morale of party members – dwindling as it had been for several years following the leadership's reaction to (or, more specifically, a lack of any sort of reaction to) Gorbachev's perestroika and Glasnost – reached rock bottom, and there seemed to be very few attractive and viable options on offer for turning the party's fortunes around.[2] Longtime party secretary Erich Honecker's resignation on 18 October (three weeks before the Wall actually fell) was a start, but it was nothing more than a symbolic gesture. Honecker's crown prince and subsequent successor, Egon Krenz, could do nothing about the 900,000 members who gave back their party membership books in the last months of 1989 as the calls for a complete overhaul of all the party stood for grew ever louder.[3] The resignation of the entire Politbüro and the exclusion, following an extraordinary meeting of the central committee on 3 December 1989, of all Politbüro members from even being members of the party was quickly followed by the central committee disbanding itself and being replaced by a working group with the specific aim of preparing the forthcoming congress. The SED was in chaos and the aim of the congress was nothing more than to prevent the party from imploding.

The extraordinary congress could not deal with every one of the (many) pressing questions with which it was faced. Delegates subsequently reconvened the following weekend, 16–17 December, to try and continue mapping out a path to survival. Amidst all of the confusion, one question rose above all others in importance and came to dominate discussion: should the SED disband completely and reconvene as a different organisation, under another name, as free as possible from the ideological ballast of the GDR, with new, fresh and untarnished democratic structures or should it reform itself (again perhaps under another name) in an attempt to act as a bridge of continuity between the 'old' GDR and the 'new' GDR that many believed was developing? The majority of delegates opted for the latter option. The ever-worsening membership drain and the internal crisis of confidence did not prevent the same question from arising again in January 1990 as groups of party intellectuals once again called for dissolution and a clean break with the past. The Party Executive resolutely rejected this (on 20 January), claiming that it would be, on the one hand, a dereliction of duty to try and dissolve the party of both its historical responsibilities and its obligations to its (shrinking, but still loyal) membership base and, on the other hand, the way to financial and organisational ruin as the substantial assets that the SED owned would have to be sacrificed and 44,000 party workers would be instantaneously sacked (and most likely lost to the SED cause from then on).[4] In purely practical terms, it also made clear sense: without the advantages of maintaining the SED's connections, networks and resources,[5] it is doubtful that any new version of the party would have been able to survive beyond the initial months of the unification period.

On 17 December 1989, therefore, tired and dispirited delegates chose to adopt a new, transitional name – the SED/PDS.[6] This compromise solution came about mainly as the congress was split down the middle on whether the term 'SED' should be abandoned; it was never meant to be a permanent solution, more a temporary way of buying time to consider further options. Gregor Gysi – the witty, telegenic and charismatic East Berlin lawyer who had defended political prisoners in the 1980s – was elected leader of the SED/PDS, while the former SED leader in Dresden and the (last, as it turned out) prime minister (he took over from Krenz on 13 November) of the GDR, Hans Modrow, and a former mayor of Dresden, Wolfgang Berghofer, became deputy chairmen. Gysi came to epitomise like no other the attempt to drag the 'new' party forward – at times kicking and screaming – into the Federal Republic's democratic system. Gysi never tired of appearing on talk shows and was always willing to fight unwinnable fights with western German politicians who rapidly came to understand that if they underestimated his polemical skills and charming mannerisms then it was they who would come off worst. Gysi's relationship with his party was also no walk in the park; he frequently challenged party members in ways that many found uncomfortable. It was Gysi who pushed the party to deal – as best it could – with the GDR past; it was Gysi who challenged party members to engage with the FRG's democratic system with a view to using it to achieve their own socialist aims. Gysi – frequently alongside Lothar Bisky, who was soon to become party chairman, and André Brie (chief party strategist through the 1990s) – coaxed and cajoled the PDS forwards, at times dragging the grumpy party rank and file with him.

Following the formation of the SED/PDS, Gysi continued to champion a further name change that would lead to 'SED' being dropped altogether. He hoped that this would signal a clear and definitive break with the past (regardless of whether such a thing had genuinely occurred or not). These moves were not enough to placate members of the party who strove for more unequivocal steps forward; Berghofer, for example, left the party in January 1990 (along with 39 other members of the Dresden SED/PDS) over the foot-dragging that continued to plague party discussions.[7] The lifespan of the SED/PDS was nonetheless short: at the Executive meeting of 4 February 1990 the party was renamed (again) – this time simply as the PDS. This, so the leadership hoped, would bring such discussions about the PDS's previous life as the SED to an end; they were very much mistaken, and very few neutral observers genuinely regarded the PDS as a new, democratic, political actor that could be treated like a 'normal' party. Unsurprisingly, the vast majority of Germans also saw through the smokescreen and remained unconvinced by the PDS's apparent metamorphosis. Only in later years, and largely for reasons that few envisaged in early 1990, did the PDS genuinely begin to gain acceptance in the German political system.

Organisationally, the PDS certainly did develop a diversity that never existed in its predecessor. Democratic centralism was rapidly discarded as an organisational paradigm and many of the draconian policy preferences from GDR times (such as the need for a secret police) vanished more or less overnight. The overwhelming top-down dynamic of SED organisation was quickly shelved and the SED-PDS/PDS became a party where voices and opinions were heard, and welcomed, from all sorts of different directions. Working and interest groups were created (with some vanishing almost before they ever contributed anything substantial in policy terms) on issues and topics ranging from lesbian and gay rights, to communal politics and '*Sportpolitik*'. Some, such as the party's nominal youth wing, the *AG Junge GenossInnen*, verged on the extremist in their dismissals of German democracy, while others, such as the *AG Christinnen und Christen*, defended the interests of relatively narrow sections of the membership in much less confrontational ways. Ideological 'platforms' were also created (and were given particular rights in terms of sending delegates to party conferences), the most well known and vociferous of which became the Communist Platform (KPF), headed as it was by the glamorous and eloquent Sahra Wagenknecht. A plethora of other platforms also existed (or have existed at some point in time), and currently 36 working groups, interest groups and platforms are affiliated to the party.[8] Pluralism was certainly adopted in practice just as much as in theory, and PDS leaders have long since had to act diplomatically in finding compromise policy solutions that placate the diverse interests stemming from this complex web of internal pressure groups.

Of programmes and policies

If questions of the future party name dominated early debates in the party, issues of ideological orientation, programmatic purity and policy detail soon took them over. The PDS was – and its successor, the Left Party, still is – the most political of all Germany's established political parties. Once the overtly undemocratic parts of the SED's programmatic profile had been axed, programmatic questions – and the policy questions that led out of them – dominated discourse in most party fora. Programmes were fought over and discussed in impassioned debates, ensuring that policy development was both piecemeal and, for the most part, disjointed. Programmatic development subsequently took place in a series of waves; it remained quite rigid and focused on distancing itself from the GDR in 1990, before offering more space to ideological conservatives in the years between 1991 and 1998. This was the era of formulaic compromises before the modern socialists came out on top in the run-up to the 1998 federal election. Thoughts of reviewing and renewing the party programme following that election prompted more introversion and introspection, leading to eventual crisis post-2002 as the party slipped out of the *Bundestag*. Programmatic debates were always fiercely contested and factions from across the whole spectrum never failed to fight their respective corners, ensuring that the PDS's programmatic development was anything other than linear.

At the beginning of the 1990s, the PDS – despite the attempts to start afresh in late 1989 and early 1990 – could not disguise the fact that it remained tied to much of the ideological rhetoric that its predecessor had espoused in the GDR.[9] The party embraced the democratic structures of the Federal Republic, but only as it had no choice but to do so. It was quick to criticise weaknesses and problems inherent in contemporary Germany, but was slow to admit that it had contributed to many of them, thanks to the SED's economically illiterate stewardship of the GDR. As indicated above, it was in its attitude to the recent past that the party experienced the most difficulties in creating a coherent line. Indeed, it was only in the late 1990s that the PDS genuinely attempted to come to terms with what the GDR was, what it stood for and what exactly was wrong with it; the PDS (and the Left Party) is now prepared to admit that socialism in the GDR was fatally flawed.[10] The lack of democratic accountability, the dogmatic economic planning[11] and the huge contraventions of human and civil rights have all been condemned by the PDS.[12] The role of the SED in these crimes has also been unambiguously admitted.[13] Yet, the Left Party does still have work to do in this area; the reticence of Berlin's then culture senator, Thomas Flierl (as well as other PDS politicians), to condemn the rowdy behaviour of former Stasi officials at a conference on the subject of the former Stasi prison at Hohenschönhausen in March 2006 illustrated that PDS politicians can still be far too slow to condemn aspects of the GDR, and far too ready to give 'the benefit of the doubt' where it clearly is not warranted.[14]

The PDS also needed to redefine its whole raison d'être: what exactly did it want to achieve? If this was to be a form of socialism, what would it look like? How would the PDS avoid the mistakes made in socialism's name in the past? The intellectual thrust of the PDS's programmatic development centred around the '*Plattform Dritter Weg*' ('Third Way Platform'). The Third Way Platform, of course, had nothing in common with the Third Way brand that Bill Clinton and Tony Blair marketed in the late 1990s. Intellectuals such as the current leader of the PDS-near Rosa-Luxemburg-Foundation, Michael Brie, his brother André, the late Michael Schumann and Dieter Klein had started to discuss the future of socialism in and around the Humboldt University in Berlin in the late 1980s. They were reformers who believed in the socialist ideal but did not believe that the GDR in its current form was in any position to help realise it. Post-1989, they saw that the SED had no future and campaigned for its dissolution. They wanted to give the socialist cause room to breathe and citizens the opportunity to develop answers to society's many problems. In recent times, they have continued to accept and applaud the death of real-existing socialism and they now campaign for a fundamental reform of the social-market economy, of Germany's democratic structures and of the international system to increase levels of democratic accountability and social justice. This includes a strong link to international pacifist movements. The aim of the modern socialists is to stabilise *Die Linke* into a genuine socialist alternative to the left of the SPD.[15]

An altogether different group of realists also existed (and continues to exist) within the party. A group of pragmatic reformers interested primarily in realpolitik and finding solutions to the problems which face German society today began, in the early to mid-1990s, to establish itself in and around the PDS's parliamentary groups in eastern German *Landtage*. They normally have some sort of semi-political career in the GDR behind them and they tend to be driven mainly by the wish to shape and craft practical answers to specific policy problems. They subsequently tend to shun the (at times) heavyweight intellectual discussions that interest the modern socialists. The most prominent of these pragmatic reformers are Helmut Holter in Mecklenburg-Western Pomerania, Petra Pau in Berlin, Roland Claus in Saxony-Anhalt and Christine Ostrowski in Saxony.[16]

Other significant groups, such as the KPF and, in more recent years, the Marxist Forum, on the other hand, were completely different beasts; these 'restorative ideologues' were much more reticent to break with the past and many KPF members were dismayed at the compromises (or 'sell-outs', as they saw them) that the modern socialists were prepared to commit to in order to be accepted into the bourgeois democratic game.[17] At the extremes, some members still refuse – even now – to condemn the excesses of Stalinism and are prepared to defend the building of the Berlin Wall.[18] The KPF was never numerically strong, but it has always been treated with respect by the leadership and the rank and file alike, mainly as it recalls the founding anti-capitalist ideals that many older PDS members embodied in the early years of the GDR. The KPF's influence has, however, always been much less than it would like everyone to believe. KPF members such as Uwe-Jens Heuer, Michael Benjamin, Ellen Brombacher and particularly Sahra Wagenknecht have always attracted publicity for their strong, anti-capitalist views. A KPF member (or someone who is seen as being close to them) is also normally in the Executive committee. But on issues of substance, the KPF (and other far-left groups that may support it) nearly always loses out to a leadership that has traditionally been dominated by the modern socialists. It is the modern socialists who shape the programmatic and policy orientation of the party, and it is the modern socialists who have forced the KPF into being a sulky group on the far outskirts of the PDS's power centres.

Dominant though the modern socialists have traditionally been, the PDS nonetheless remained unique among political parties in Germany in that it was home to an almost impracticably broad church of members. Communists, as was indicated above, are still welcome, and more or less the only group on the far left for whom the door is fully closed would be self-proclaimed Stalinists.[19] The non-Communist members of the PDS also come in quite different shapes and sizes, and as members of the *Aufbaugeneration* (literally translated as the 'generation that began to build' the GDR) die away, this diversity within the membership is becoming ever more evident.

There is also evidence of what Michael Brie terms a 'radical-alternative wing'. The main antagonists of this faction are normally to be found in the extra-parliamentary and anti-authoritarian groups within the party that attract younger members of the party to their cause. They tend to place much more emphasis on the importance of opposition to prevailing systemic structures and much less emphasis on socialism as an ideology. They tend to differentiate themselves from other groups by rejecting all forms of dogmatism and by dismissing much of what they saw (or have read about) in the GDR.[20] Until recently the most well known representatives of this wing were Angela Marquardt and the circle of like-minded individuals that formed the *AG Junge GenossInnen*.

The PDS's initial programmatic aims were therefore twofold; on the one hand it sought to open itself up to all progressive radicals and to offer a prospective home to all elements of the anti-capitalist left. Inclusion – stretching from Communists to Social Democrats (around the short-lived 'Social Democratic Platform') – was the aim. On the other hand, the PDS realised that it would have to come to some sort of programmatic accommodation with the structures and processes of Germany's social-market economy in order to be allowed to exist by the constitutional watchdog, the *Bundesverfassungsschutz*. It could no longer condemn capitalism as being purely evil, and it subsequently accepted the rule of law and parliamentary democracy, and rejected the democratic sham that had existed in the GDR. It had to find a way of being constructively critical, while being unambiguously clear about not wanting to overthrow Germany's constitutional settlement. No easy task.

By the February 1990 conference the PDS was starting to have to prepare for its first experience of free and fair elections (to the GDR parliament, the *Volkskammer*, in March 1990). Many of the programmatic motions that had been passed in December were done so without any real attempt to build a party with a new and coherent programmatic identity; time was simply too short. Many of the delegates were overwhelmed by the severity and complexity of the issues before them, and questions of how the party would survive were too salient to allow detailed discussions of such issues from taking place. It would take the PDS many years to genuinely work through its own ideological and programmatic contradictions and, as in all political parties, dividing lines still exist within the party today over many significant programmatic questions. The PDS's first party programme – passed in February 1990 – was a reflection of this; it was rushed, defensive and a product of its time. It was not the outcome of years of discussions and internal wrangling; it was created to fill a hole before the rapidly approaching *Volkskammer* election. What it did do, however, was confirm that the PDS was no longer the SED and it offered a broad, imprecise and suitably vague set of ideals that a significant number of PDS members could mobilise around. It encouraged a pluralist conception of what it meant to be socialist, stressing the need to avoid dogmatic understandings of what socialism is or was. The programme made a conscious effort to say something to everyone. Quite how, for example, Bernstein and Lenin – two of the names that came up in the document – could ever consistently be worked into one coherent political outlook was not something that concerned the party at this point in time.[21] The PDS was scrambling for legitimacy wherever it might conceivably lay its hands on it and at times the party looked positively anarchical in the way that it developed ideas and agendas. The PDS did, however, clearly accept enough of German democracy's key tenets (the rights of the individual vis-à-vis the state, the formal structures of democratic competition etc.) to pass the watchful eyes of those who were looking for evidence of the PDS's alleged extremist nature. This pattern, as Franz Oswald has perceptively observed, was to be a recurring theme in PDS discourse through the 1990s; the PDS criticised the facelessness and coldness of capitalism, while at the same time acknowledging that its achievements (democracy, rule of law, individual rights) needed to be incorporated into any future socialist state.[22]

Of elections and voters

In the months and years immediately following unification, the PDS was consequently written off as an anachronism that, over the course of time, would disappear from the party political map.[23] It had no coherent political agenda, its programme was both vague and contradictory, and it appeared unable to influence the wider political environment around it. Furthermore, who, apart from a small band of disaffected SED stalwarts, was ever likely to support a party that had presided over a state with a moribund economy, a state that had consistently trampled on the democratic rights of its citizens and a state that had shown a blatant disregard for human life – as the shootings at the Berlin Wall and other border crossings amply testified? The answer, surely, would be hardly anyone.

The March 1990 *Volkskammer* election was the first test of such a hypothesis. For the first time in its history the PDS had to present itself to the electorate at large. It did not do so with much enthusiasm, mainly as it knew that it was destined to end up, again for the first time in its history, in opposition. The 16.4 per cent that it polled was, in many ways, a very good result for the party. Given that just about everyone thought that the party would fade into oblivion, it is worth noting that over 1.8 million people still put their cross next to the PDS's name.[24] Yet the result was still seen as disappointing by many party strategists, although quite who else they expected to vote for the party is unclear. Helmut Kohl's Conservative Coalition won a clear mandate to push on with the process of unification and the PDS suffered further electoral setbacks in the 6 May local elections (14.6 per cent of the vote) and *Land* elections on 14 October (polling barely 11 per cent).

Despite doing better than many expected in the last election to the GDR parliament, the PDS was still in a tailspin – and not just in the electoral arena. The 'Independent Commission for the Investigation of the Property of Parties and Mass Organisations in the GDR' that was created in May 1990 soon started to challenge the PDS about its assets, threatening to bankrupt the party by demanding it return much of what it said it owned back to the state. If such a demand had been deemed legal, then the PDS could well have been erased from the party political map completely. Moreover, in June and July 1991 the *Treuhandanstalt* (the holding company responsible for restructuring and selling off assets once owned by the East German state) actually took control of all the real estate that the PDS owned in Berlin and Brandenburg (including its present-day headquarters at Karl Liebknecht House, in central Berlin) and it was only in August 1992 that the Berlin Administrative

Court ruled that Liebknecht House should be returned – without any restrictions – to the party.[25] More or less all financial activity of significance by the PDS in 1991 had to be approved by Treuhand officials as the German authorities tightened the financial noose around the PDS's neck. At one point, the Independent Commission even decreed that membership subscriptions paid to the SED before 1989 were not legitimate, putting yet more doubt on the PDS's claims on SED property.[26] For its part, the PDS willingly gave away most of the assets it had inherited – such as printing works, most of its 16 publishing houses, many administrative buildings, vehicles and residences – realising that any attempt to retain them would be both legally impossible and politically unfeasible. The PDS also gave 3041 million GDR marks to the GDR government in an attempt to show goodwill and generate support for itself within eastern German society. In this it failed. Financial scandals involving prominent PDS stalwarts Wolfgang Langnitschke, Karl-Heinz Kaufmann and most notably former treasurer Wolfgang Pohl, who admitted moving the colossal sum of DM 107 million to a bank account in Moscow, further fuelled suspicion that the PDS was being anything but open about what it possessed.[27] By the time that all three had their convictions quashed and the defendants were subsequently acquitted (in June 1995), such questions had long since lost their salience.[28] The PDS fought tooth and nail – using the legal system of the '*Rechtsstaat*' that its predecessor had been so utterly scornful of – to retain what it felt legitimately belonged to it, as well as enough funds to allow it to function as a normal party. Proving such a case took time (and many appeals) but eventually the PDS was allowed – in mid-1995 – to retain enough of its assets to remain a viable organisation.[29]

As unification day came and went, the PDS also started to think about the first all-German election, scheduled for 2 December 1990. Again, the Conservative Coalition – and particularly Helmut Kohl – came out victorious. The Social Democrats, led by a future leader of *Die Linke*, Oskar Lafontaine, came a distant second. The PDS slid even further than it had done in previous elections; it managed 11.1 per cent in the eastern states and a paltry 0.3 per cent in western Germany. Nationally, the PDS/Left List (as it was known in an attempt to appeal to left-wing western German voters) managed 2.4 per cent, well below the traditional barrier to parliamentary entry of 5 per cent. For this one election, however, the PDS received an institutional lifeline. As long as a party polled over 5 per cent of the popular vote in *either* eastern or western Germany, then it was guaranteed parliamentary representation. Seventeen PDS MPs therefore took up seats in the parliament in Bonn.

The PDS knew, however, that this get-out clause would only save it once as come the 1994 election it would have to double its vote share, win three seats outright (it won one in 1990) or face vanishing from the federal stage. The likelihood of either of these life-saving scenarios happening seemed far-fetched at best. Observers and politicians alike realised that something dramatic and unforeseen would have to happen if the PDS was going to save itself in national politics.[30]

1990 and 1991 were probably the blackest years in PDS history. There was a systematic campaign by the other parties – and not to mention the federal administrative authorities – to ostracise the PDS and they treated it as a party that was far beyond the democratic pale. PDS politicians were treated with disdain in national and regional parliaments, the CDU/CSU and Free Democratic Party (FDP) members painting a picture of an extremist and anti-democratic relic of the past that had no place in a democratic polity while the SPD and Greens – although not quite as scathing – made no attempt to hide their scorn for the Democratic Socialists. Even as late as 1998 – by which time the PDS had slowly established itself as a democratic (if still very much unloved) actor – CDU spokesman Otto Hauser poured scorn on the PDS's participation in a regional government in Saxony-Anhalt by claiming that 'it is roughly the same as if the National Socialists had, under another name, played a role in governing post-1945 Germany'[31]. Periodic Stasi problems kept returning to haunt the party as a steady stream of members were revealed to have worked either as full-time Stasi operatives or unofficial agents (*Inoffizielle Mitarbeiter* – IMs). This image as a 'Stasi-party' was to plague the PDS for years to come. These negative images – when coupled with plummeting membership numbers and poor performance in the elections through 1990 – left very little room for optimism in Liebknecht House.

It certainly seems plausible that had eastern Germany blossomed into the 'flourishing economic landscape' that Federal Chancellor Helmut Kohl had promised, the PDS would have drifted, as the cadre gradually died away, into non-existence. Yet, by the end of 1991, and increasingly thereafter, the fallout from unification was beginning to disillusion many eastern Germans, and new and unexpected electoral potential was developing for the PDS. The perceived arrogance of western politicians, the apparent annexation (although initially approved of) of eastern Germany and the blatant lack of regard for most things 'East German' led many to feel like strangers in their own land.[32] The PDS sensed that things might not be as bleak as was first believed, and sought to develop a new role for itself as the articulator of dissatisfied sections of the eastern German electorate.[33] The PDS remained anchored in eastern

German society, entrenched in welfare organisations such as the *'Volkssolidarität'* and at the core of a myriad of interest groups in civil society. The PDS became – perhaps more through luck than judgement – the representative of disgruntled citizens in eastern Germany, of which there were surprisingly many. The effects of having lived under state socialism as well as having experienced the difficult transition from socialism to capitalism prompted a significant number of Easterners to re-identify with both eastern Germany and with other eastern Germans – and with the PDS as a, albeit rather peculiar, political voice. The enduring material and psychological differences between eastern and western Germany ensured that the PDS was able to develop and expand on its steady bedrock of former functionary support.

Internally, the PDS sought to maximise this protest potential at the same time as it redrafted its 1990 programme. This took time, but was eventually completed in 1993 – and it remained valid for over a decade, until October 2003. The 1993 programme differed considerably from the 1990 document and represented the first genuine evidence of a change in PDS self-understanding. In many ways, it also represented a step backwards, illustrating how the KPF and other left-wing orthodox forces were still able to influence party policy. It discussed in great detail why the 'real-existing' socialism of the GDR had been a defensible attempt at creating a new society, why socialism was still a legitimate aim in itself and how a state built on socialist principles would solve the many ills of the (capitalist) world.[34] Relatively little time was spent discussing what actually went wrong in the GDR, why this happened and what lessons socialist parties could and should take from this. Similarly, the PDS spent barely five sides explaining what it would do should it ever regain the reins of power: primarily as (1) the PDS was simply fighting to justify its existence and thoughts of government participation were nothing more than pipe dreams and (2) the PDS had neither the time nor the expertise to develop convincing policy preferences. The 1993 programme therefore contained vague claims that broadly fitted with socialist doctrine: 'Germany needs to undergo a radical democratisation of political and economic life', 'the rightward drift of German society needs to be halted', 'culture, education and science needs to be "set free"' and 'the relationships between employers and employees needs to be altered in favour of employees'.[35] The only clear aim was the abolition of capitalism and the creation of some sort of vague socialist republic. Quite what this socialist republic would look like, the PDS was not sure. But that was, again, largely irrelevant. The PDS was positioning itself as a protest movement, mopping up support from those who were unsatisfied with the fallout from unification, as well as voters from the social and cultural milieu that had been close to the ideological aims of the GDR state. The PDS still had not found a way to make an electoral breakthrough in western Germany, but its position in eastern Germany was stabilising. Despite the orthodox undertones in the new party programme, the (first) period of existential crisis had come to an end and the seeds for an unexpected revival had been sown.

The super election year of 1994

1994 was a peculiar year in German politics, mainly as it was completely dominated by elections. In addition to a federal and European election, there were eight *Land* elections, as well as local elections to a significant number of councils. The year was, in effect, one long election campaign – and, in terms of election results, it marked a qualitative jump forward for the party. The PDS attempted, unsurprisingly, to broaden its appeal; its election manifestos made nods to the western German left, the pacifist movement, environmentalism, feminism and eastern German interests. The PDS possessed precious few activists and resources to push its ideas forward in the western states, but it was well anchored in eastern Germany and was hopeful, at the very least, of improving on its performances of 1990.

The PDS also hit upon the clever idea of persuading leading (socialist) personalities to front its campaigns; some of whom were anything other than supporters of the SED. This sent out signals that the PDS was no longer a party for defenders of the status quo ante, but rather for any and every eastern German. Stefan Heym, the dissident author and long-standing critic of the GDR, was the most famous of these (he became the *Alterspräsident* – the German equivalent to the Father of the House – in the 1994–98 *Bundestag*), although seeing Otto von Bismarck's great grandson, Count von Einsiedel (another vehement critic of the GDR), on the ticket also raised a few eyebrows. The first genuine test was the election to the European parliament in June 1994, where the PDS polled 4.7 per cent of the votes. This was not enough to register any seats, but 1.6 million votes was a real sign that the PDS was bouncing back. The local election in Mecklenburg-Western Pomerania that was held on the same day was even more encouraging – the PDS polled 24.3 per cent – while the polls in Saxony (16.3 per cent) and Thuringia (15.7 per cent) were also encouraging. The major test was, however, the 1994 federal election, which took place on 16 October. Given the first-order nature of the poll, registering more than the 4.7 per cent that it achieved in the

European election was always likely to be a tall order – and so it proved. The PDS could only poll 4.4 per cent of the votes, thereby missing the opportunity to enter parliament as a full parliamentary party. The PDS was saved – much as it had been in 1990 – by a quirk in the system; it still qualified for parliamentary representation as it won four eastern Berlin constituencies outright. This rather opaque law had been introduced in 1949 to placate claims that the electoral laws disadvantaged smaller, regionally concentrated political parties – mainly those representing national minorities such as the Danes in Schleswig Holstein and the Sorbs in a number of eastern German states. The rule stipulates that if a party managed to win three (or more) constituencies outright, then it can forgo the need to poll 5 per cent of the vote to be eligible for distributed seats. Rarely do small parties do this. The FDP, for example, have been represented in every *Bundestag*, but have only once won a constituency outright since 1957, when Uwe Lühr won Halle in the exceptional election of 1990. The Greens have only ever managed to directly win seats twice – when the charismatic Hans-Christian Ströbele won Friedrichshain-Kreuzberg in Berlin in 2002 and 2005. This rule subsequently remained a permanent footnote in election rule books until 1994, as the mainstream parties achieved 5 per cent of the vote (if sometimes only just) while concurrently never registering three directly elected MdBs. In 1994 the PDS won four constituencies in its heartland of eastern Berlin. It therefore entered parliament with 30 MdBs, 26 of whom came from its party lists. Eight years later in 2002 the experience of the PDS illustrated how fine the line is between success and failure – it polled more or less the same number of second votes as it did in 1994 (4.0 per cent) but, crucially, won only two constituencies in eastern Berlin. The PDS was therefore represented in parliament purely by Petra Pau and Gesinne Lötzsch as it failed to gain that one, crucial, extra constituency.

The years of recovery: 1994–98

The election result in 1994 marked the beginning of a new chapter in the PDS's development. Its solid position in the six eastern *Landtage* and its return to the federal parliament were reassuring to the party faithful who had been battered from pillar to post since 1989. The PDS was by no means loved by all, but it was slowly being accepted – by some – as a legitimate political force.

The electoral successes of 1994 prompted – perhaps unsurprisingly – much discussion of where the PDS should attempt to go now. In the run-up to the 1995 Schwerin party conference, the Party Executive put forward ten 'theses' that should shape the PDS's future direction. They were clear and unambiguous in condemning the neo-liberalisation of Germany under Helmut Kohl and in calling for radical alternatives to overcome the dominance of capital. They also used terminology that, for some in the party, was worrying. There was talk of 'reforming majorities' on the left of the German party system; there was an acceptance of Germany's social-market economy that seemed to suspiciously play down the importance of creating an overtly socialist alternative model and there was talk of a 'new social contract' that also appeared (to some) to be suspiciously non-socialist in rhetoric.[36] The left of the party, and particularly the KPF, felt that this was a recipe for a sell-out and they sensed that some PDS politicians might be getting very keen to sit in ministerial offices and enjoy the comforts of ministerial limousines. The Schwerin conference was the scene of open conflict between the two groups – the KPF saw the PDS's whole identity as an oppositional force being put on the line, while the reforming leadership saw the theses as the first step to making the PDS genuinely relevant in post-unification Germany. That the KPF (and other left-wing groups that supported it) were defeated marked a sea change; the PDS clearly distanced itself from the hardest of the hard-core left and it marked a clear move away from being purely a party of opposition to one that could, in specific circumstances, enter governments.

The increasing normality of the PDS became more apparent through the mid-1990s when both the Social Democrats and Greens started to toy with the idea of bringing the PDS into positions of responsibility at the *Land* level. The personalisation of local politics meant that PDS politicians there had long since been brought into everyday political affairs, and PDS mayors – tacitly supported in some places by politicians from other parties – were not an uncommon sight across eastern Germany. Bringing the PDS into the *Land* coalition equation was a more difficult task. Social Democrats in the eastern states had realised that ostracising the PDS was doing the SPD no good at all at the polls; the PDS could portray itself as the victim of western German bullies and consistent claims that the PDS was either extremist or too linked to the GDR (or both) were not the trump cards that they were back in 1990. The exclusion strategy of the SPD and Greens therefore needed some intellectual overhaul.

The first fruits of this actually came in the months *before* the 1994 election, when Reinhard Höppner's SPD in Saxony-Anhalt was tempted to take the PDS up on its offer of acting as a support party to the

SPD/Green coalition. Höppner had expressly ruled out such an option in the election campaign, but the closeness of the results – and the PDS's position as the third-largest parliamentary party – prompted him to take the plunge. Höppner did insist that his government would, on occasion, seek support from the CDU in crafting majorities – in truth, more of his programme appealed to the pragmatists in the PDS than it did the centre-right parties. Contrary to the dire warnings of the Christian and Free Democrats, Saxony-Anhalt did not lurch into chaos. Political life continued on very much as normal. Whether the SPD/Green, PDS-tolerated government was successful in its policy aims is a moot point; what is beyond doubt is that political life continued much as it had done before.

These events were watched particularly keenly in Germany's northeast, in Mecklenburg-Western Pomerania. Relations between Berndt Seite, leader of the CDU, and Harald Ringstoff, leader of the SPD, had reached breaking point. The two were hardly on speaking terms and personal relations between politicians of both parties were poor and getting worse. The CDU/SPD coalition was treading water. The SPD was subsequently eyeing up a way out – and the only one available came in the shape of the PDS. Officially, Rudolf Scharping, the leader of the SPD at the national level, stressed – in the so-called Dresden Declaration – that the Magdeburg Model of toleration was a one-off. There was to be no repeat. However, Scharping's removal as SPD party leader in November 1995 appeared to open up a new window of opportunity, particularly as new leader Oskar Lafontaine was known to be much more on the left of his (then) party. A coalition crisis in April 1996 in Mecklenburg-Western Pomerania subsequently seemed to offer the perfect opportunity for Ringstoff to jump ship and set up the first red-red coalition. Lafontaine – still wary of the suspicion of the PDS in many Social Democratic *Landesverbände* – eventually spoke out against this, claiming that he could not support it as the Greens (who weren't represented in the Mecklenburg-Western Pomerania *Landtag*) were needed as a buffer between the two parties. Red-red-green was an option; red-red was, at that time, not.

The failure of the Mecklenburg-Western Pomerania PDS to enter government did not hinder the momentum towards such an event happening in the future. Lafontaine's support for such an idea in principle was clear; the time nonetheless needed to be right. The publication of the Erfurt Declaration in January 1997, calling for a working alliance of all parties to the left of the SPD, was further – incontrovertible – evidence that the SPD had not ruled the PDS out as a prospective coalition partner. While critical voices from the eastern German civil rights movement such as those of Brandenburg MdBs Stephan Hilsberg and Markus Meckel were strong, the SPD knew that it had to bide its time – and this is was prepared to do, knowing that the electoral cards dealt out in 1998 might provide for a more advantageous political climate.

The run-up to the 1998 election was therefore one of genuine excitement within the PDS. The party hoped to poll 5 per cent of the votes (while being confident of winning enough constituencies to re-enter parliament even if it was unable to) and it eagerly awaited the *Land* election in Mecklenburg-Western Pomerania, which was to take place on the same day. This was a time of great anticipation. Internal dissent was still evident, particularly towards the PDS's attitude to government participation, but the party had nonetheless stabilised itself as a serious actor that had at least a medium-term future. The 1998 election would give a much clearer indication of whether the PDS could expect to achieve anything more than that in the long term.

2
Policies, Programmes and Personalities: The Post-1998 PDS

Introduction

The 1998 federal election was a milestone in the PDS's short history. On 27 September over 2.5 million voters put their cross next to the party's name. Just over 2 million (2,054,773) were resident in the eastern states (21.6 per cent of eastern voters), and 460,000 in western Germany (1.2 per cent of all western voters). The slightly improved performance in the West (the PDS polled 91,000 votes more than it did in 1994) was enough to push the PDS's national percentage of the vote over the crucial 5 per cent mark. The margin for error was small; had 55,000 PDS voters opted to support another party on election day, then the PDS would – once again – have been entering the *Bundestag* as a parliamentary group rather than a fully fledged parliamentary party.[1] That the PDS now enjoyed *Fraktionsstärke* (the status of a parliamentary party) entitled it to more money (to fund the activities of its *Fraktion*), granted its politicians more time to speak in parliamentary debates (important in terms of gaining visibility and publicity) and to representation on significant parliamentary committees. The PDS was also able to fund a political foundation, which it duly did, the Rosa Luxemburg Foundation, based at Franz-Mehring-Platz, in eastern Berlin.[2]

The 27 September was also a milestone in another way; Mecklenburg-Western Pomerania held its *Landtagswahl* on the same day and the PDS increased its share of the vote by 1.7 per cent to 24.4 per cent. The SPD, no doubt benefiting from the national wave of support that was to sweep Gerhard Schröder into the *Kanzleramt*, also performed well, increasing its vote share by 4.8 percentage points to 34.3 per cent. The SPD therefore had the option of leading a government with either the CDU (that polled a disappointing 30.2 per cent) or with the democratic socialists. SPD *Ministerpräsident* designate, Harald Ringstorff, had long since signalled his interest in forming Germany's first red-red coalition with the PDS and although there remained a minority within the SPD who were unhappy with the idea, Ringstorff's invitation to Helmut Holter shortly after the results came through was a clear statement of intent. The PDS was set, for the first time in post-unification Germany, to be given responsibility in a *Land*-level government.

The PDS's electoral successes in 1998 were carefully planned. The modern socialists around Gregor Gysi, Lothar Bisky and André Brie had brought the party (occasionally kicking and screaming) to the verges of political respectability. Party conferences in the mid-1990s were dominated by this small group of influential politicians as well as like-minded supporters at lower levels of the party, ensuring that ideologues on the far left were skilfully marginalised without ever being totally ignored. The failure of Sahra Wagenknecht to be elected to the Party Executive at a fiery Schwerin conference in 1995 was the first clear signal that the PDS was moving on; there was to be no 'grand showdown' with the KPF and, in subsequent years, the Marxist Forum, but they were to know their place – at the fringes of the PDS's power centres.[3] The PDS continued to remain critical of capitalism and of the profit maximisation that it saw as being so detrimental to the quality of life in contemporary Germany (and beyond its borders), but it did not, and had no plans to, overcome such things through revolution. It accepted the democratic rules of the game and planned to use them to create a more egalitarian society based on (rather abstract) notions of social justice and radical democratisation. The PDS had also shown that as and when it was given responsibility – even if this had not, as yet, amounted to much in practice – it could deal with it. Saxony-Anhalt survived the 'Magdeburg Model' with the minimum of fuss. The PDS had made a start at coming to terms with its past in the GDR. For some in the party the need to critically engage with the failed state would always be a bridge too far; their biographies were too interlinked with East Germany and any attempts at dealing with the crimes, misdemeanours and failures committed in its name would simply smack of the 'victors' of history (i.e. western Germans) imposing their ideas on the 'defeated' (i.e. eastern Germans). For the modern socialist leadership of the party this task was also not unproblematic, but it was more straightforward for them than for many of the *Altgenossen* (older generation of members) and those on the far left. Crucially, public discourse ensured that the PDS could now paint itself as a victim of a witch-hunt by vindictive opponents; in 1990 Easterners had no truck with the PDS's complaints, but by the middle of the decade attitudes were changing.

Of policies and promises

The PDS's voters did not support the party in 1998 (or in 2005 for that matter) because they were convinced that the PDS had a policy package that would radically transform Germany for the better. They did, however, find something in the PDS's rhetoric and criticisms of other parties and politicians that rang true with their own dissatisfaction at post-unification German politics. One consistent theme has been the PDS's willingness to profile itself as the representative and voice of eastern Germans in the political process. It did this explicitly in the run-up to the 1998 election by publishing, in April, the 'Rostock Manifesto' and specific proposals aimed to revitalise the eastern German economy.[4] In 1998 it was *the* issue that divided all the other parties from the PDS the most.[5] This was not so much in the area of economic and social policy (although differences clearly did exist), but rather in interpretations of the extent and causes of eastern Germany's economic and social difference.[6]

The PDS traditionally articulated eastern German interests in two specific ways: first, in the *Bundestag*, as well as across the parliaments of the eastern *Länder*, it tabled motions (that were nearly always rejected) and adopted policy approaches that sought recognition of lived existences in the GDR. Second, the PDS sought (and still seeks) 'a better deal' in economic and political terms for the six eastern *Länder* now. In practical terms, the first strategy saw the PDS table initiatives between 1994 and 1998 aimed at securing, for example, more protection for officials who worked in the public sector in the GDR, the equal recognition of teachers' qualifications and achievements from both East and West Germany and an amnesty for spies.[7] As Lothar Bisky once put it, 'we are continuing to fight for fair recognition of eastern German biographies' and the PDS 'demands an end to the political isolation (*Ausgrenzung*) of Easterners'.[8] In the late 1990s the PDS subsequently grew to voice complex feelings of collective memory towards the now defunct GDR – something that only it, as a product of the eastern German political environment, was in a position to do plausibly.

The PDS also developed a unique (when compared with other parties) foreign policy agenda. The PDS unambiguously (not to mention completely impractically) sought to demilitarise international relations and to insert a civilian dimension to global conflict prevention.

These pacifist themes were never far from the forefront of every speech a PDS politician made in the run-up to both the 1998 federal election and the 1999 election to the European parliament. PDS politicians argued that NATO should be abolished and Russia incorporated into a new European security framework, just as the *Bundeswehr* should be reduced in size and scope.[9] Foreign policy took on even more of a pivotal role in PDS discourse through 1999 as NATO bombs rained down on a Slobodan Milosevic-led Serbia.[10] The PDS's populist touch was also evident in its claims that expensive projects such as the creation of the Eurofighter jet and new attack helicopters should be dumped.[11]

Another core tenet of the PDS policy agenda was that of placing the slippery issue of social justice on the political map. Claims of 'social injustice' rang particularly true in eastern Germany where many citizens were dissatisfied with their allegedly shabby treatment at the hands of the new republic. The emphasis in speeches and policy papers on social justice became even more pronounced after the 1998 federal election when Gerhard Schröder's SPD/Green government took over the reins of power and found itself faced with the need to make tough decisions in government. The PDS sensed a perfect opportunity to (continue) exert(ing) *Druck von Links* (pressure from the left) and it attempted to portray the SPD as selling out to rich, capitalist interests (who also happened to be mostly resident in western Germany). Eastern Germans seemed to be receptive to these claims; the extent of this was shown by an Allensbach survey that was carried out in the eastern states in April 2000 revealing that 56 per cent of Easterners perceived the PDS as the 'party of social justice', while only 23 per cent thought that the SPD was the party that would most effectively strive for this (albeit fuzzy) ideal.[12] Despite the persistent refusal of the PDS to define what it understood by the term, it remained highly prominent in all PDS literature published in the late 1990s.[13] The PDS sought to guarantee lower rents and better quality housing, and it stressed labour market policies that maximised employment through the creation of more jobs in care work and social assistance, as well as active support for single parents, the unemployed and the (again fuzzily defined) 'working classes'. And it appears that this rhetoric hit home; in the October 1999 state election in Berlin, for example, 77 per cent of Easterners who voted for the PDS did so in the hope that the PDS would be able to create a more socially just society.[14]

Over time the party created working groups looking at specific issues and problems and – as and when they reported back – the PDS was able to build-up a broader spectrum of hard and fast policy proposals.

The PDS broadly took on Keynesian doctrines of economic demand management, with the state having a fundamental responsibility both in stimulating demand and providing its citizens with employment. Like a number of socialist parties across Europe the PDS aimed to counter high levels of unemployment by advocating policies such as legally enforceable reductions in the number of hours that employees are allowed to work (in weekly and yearly terms) and drastic reductions in the amount of overtime.[15] In concrete terms, this meant a maximum working week of 35 hours and, in the long-term, a five-day week of just 30 hours. The PDS also claimed that drastic reductions in the 1.8 billion hours of overtime that are worked yearly in Germany could create a further 600,000 jobs.[16]

The PDS had no qualms about demanding the return of full employment.[17] Through the late 1990s the PDS argued that government participation in the economy was vital in achieving this aim and the PDS had very specific ideas on how to do this. These included the creation of a non-profit sector (the so-called *öffentlich geförderter Beschäftigungssektor* (ÖBS) – publicly subsidised employment sector) and programmes to support the expansion of the industrial and service base.[18] The ÖBS was intended to offer the opportunity of bypassing the profit-making imperative. The SPD/PDS coalition in Mecklenburg-West Pomerania was the first state government that was faced with putting the PDS's employment policies into practice and, unsurprisingly, implementing these ideas proved highly problematic (see Chapter 5). Nevertheless, Helmut Holter was still insistent that 8000 extra jobs could be created.[19]

The (im)practicality of implementing these policies is not something that the PDS worried about unduly. Even the most cursory of glances at the wish list above reveals that such schemes are only viable if the PDS enters *national* government, and even then the PDS would have to be remarkably successful in its negotiations with – one would presume – the SPD if it were to achieve even a modicum of them. But in 1998 and 1999 the PDS simply used its increasing acceptability and its populist policy agenda as a battering ram to (so it hoped) attack Gerhard Schröder's coalition from the left and, most importantly, to cement itself as a serious actor in the federal parliament.

Of disputes and disagreements

The fundamentals of the PDS's post-1998 political strategy were therefore simple and intuitively logical. It was extremely unlikely that the PDS would govern at the national level, so many of its policy proposals were almost certain to remain untried and untested. As Schröder's government made mistakes, it would be the PDS's job to point them out and to act as a left-wing corrective on the *Genosse der Bosse* (the 'comrade of the bosses', as Schröder was not altogether affectionately known).[20] The PDS expected that its traditional supporter base in eastern Germany would remain loyal to it and it therefore set out its stall to win over disillusioned left-wing Social Democrats and Greens to its cause, slowly expanding into western Germany in the process. The PDS believed it was on the way to becoming a left-wing *Volkspartei* and took the 'vacuum thesis', stating that a genuine gap to the left of the SPD would enable the PDS to embed itself in the German party system, at face value.[21]

Initially, the PDS's strategy did appear to be working well as, in 1999, the PDS performed admirably in a number of eastern German *Land* elections; it replaced the SPD as the second largest party in both Saxony and Thuringia, improving its vote share by 5.7 and 4.7 percentage points respectively, and it improved its position by 4.6 percentage points in Brandenburg. Further controversies over possible government participation were also side-stepped; the poor performance of the Social Democrats in Thuringia and particularly Saxony (where it polled a mere 10.7 per cent of the vote) ensured that the CDU could govern on its own in those states, while the reluctance of Brandenburg's prime minister, Manfred Stolpe, to form a coalition with the PDS meant that a Grand Coalition with the CDU came into being in Potsdam.

The first major public hiccup in the post-1998 period did not come via the ballot box; it came at the PDS's first party conference in western Germany – in Münster, North Rhine-Westphalia, in April 2000. Party conferences are usually of great significance for members and activists, and little or (more frequently) no importance to the everyday voter. Important decisions can indeed be taken, significant messages sent out and/or new political figures make their entrances, but this normally only filters through to the world outside – if ever it does at all – at times when politics is high on the public radar (i.e. election time) or if major gaffes are made. The PDS's conference in Münster fell into the second category; what should have been a run-of-the-mill event turned into nothing short of a major crisis for two specific reasons.

Firstly, delegates chose to express their pacifist credentials in a way that surprised both the leadership and watching observers, subsequently limiting the party's room for manoeuvre in foreign affairs. The fact that the PDS was a country mile away from actually having any genuine say in Germany's foreign policy was irrelevant – the symbolism of a party out of kilter with significant currents of popular opinion was still significant. Two-thirds of the delegates voted against a motion that would have allowed the PDS to support German troops being stationed abroad, providing that a UN mandate for the mission had been obtained. The party leadership had wanted the conference to allow it to assess each proposed mission on a case-by-case basis, and although it remained very critical of the use of force in international affairs, it (sensibly) believed that it would be foolish to reject on principal the use of force *on every occasion*. Delegates disagreed. The original motion was replaced by one adopting a much more black and white understanding of foreign policy; it called for the dissolution of NATO, criticised the militarisation of the EU and forbade the PDS leadership from supporting any mission (including peace-keeping missions) that would involve German troops stepping outside the territory of the Federal Republic.[22] The PDS was beginning to look dangerously dogmatic and a little too far-removed from reality.

Secondly, the problems over foreign policy brought another simmering issue to the forefront of political debate; the PDS had a leadership crisis to deal with. The tried and tested troika of Gysi, Bisky and Brie was looking to hand over the leadership mantle to a new generation.[23] All three politicians had been active within the party from the beginning (Bisky had been Party Chairman since 1993, Gysi the public figurehead since late 1989, Brie election strategist for almost as long) and they felt that 10 years at the helm was enough; both for themselves as individuals and for the future good of the party.[24] The public announcements by Bisky and Gysi at Münster that they would be standing down at the next conference (in Cottbus, in October 2000) did not therefore come as a particularly great surprise, even if the timing did catch some delegates on the back foot. The frosty debates over foreign policy undoubtedly accelerated their decision, but the stubborn refusal of the hard left in the party to countenance programmatic renewal or structural modernisation meant that it had been on the cards ever since the 1998 federal election.

The question now turned to who their successors should be. There were no obvious replacements. Gysi was in many ways irreplaceable; it is impossible to create a quick-witted media-star, and parties have to hope that such personalities simply evolve. The then 58-year-old Bisky was more of a fatherly figure: a well-respected professor of film studies from GDR days, expert in smoothing through controversial decisions and placating fiery comrades. The significance of these two politicians in leading the PDS away from the political abyss to a degree of political respectability should not be underestimated. The next generation of PDS leaders was, however, going to have to be different. They were going to be people who were not at the forefront of 'saving' the party in 1989–91; they were likely to be people who had made their name in post-unification German politics and they were not going to immediately enjoy the stature and respect that both Gysi and Bisky had.

After a summer of drift and internal confusion, the Cottbus conference saw a new group of politicians step up to the political plate. Most had come through the ranks of *Land* politics, although there were also a number of outsiders who entered the revamped Party Executive for the first time. The new leader was Gabriele Zimmer from Thuringia. She had been one of the party's deputy leaders since 1997 and was widely seen as a rising star. She had led her *Land* party between 1990–98 and had also been leader of the parliamentary party in Thuringia for two years; the Thuringia *Land* party had made steady progress in terms of election results and it was seen as a thoughtful, constructive and forward-thinking *Landesverband*. Three new deputy leaders were elected. Petra Pau, the leader of the strategically significant Berlin PDS and MdB since 1994 was an uncontroversial choice for one of the positions. Peter Porsch, then 'Germanistik' professor in Leipzig and leader of the feisty Saxon state party was also a popular option.[25] The third deputy leader was altogether more controversial; Dieter Dehm, former SPD member, western German singer-songwriter and alleged millionaire was much more of an unknown quantity. Dehm left the SPD in 1998 (after being a member for 33 years) to join the PDS, and within a matter of months he rose to the position of Zimmer's deputy.

The new leadership of the party ran – more or less immediately – into a number of serious problems, many of which it inherited from the end of the previous era. Zimmer failed to set out a clear and coherent set of strategic goals and in her public appearances she rarely made any genuine impact on the national political scene. Affable and reasonable though she was, she did not possess the rhetorical ability of Gysi and failed to impress when quizzed on national television. The team around her (and particularly Roland Claus as leader of the parliamentary party and Dietmar Bartsch as General Secretary) also remained largely unknown to the wider world. Executive committee members had extremely wide and varied backgrounds and finding consensual solutions to the challenges that the party faced rapidly became very difficult. On the one hand there was a group of *Realpolitiker* who either already had experience of taking part in sub-national government (such as Helmut Holter; deputy prime minister of Mecklenburg-Western

Pomerania as well as (the grandly named) minister for Employment, Construction and Development), had been on the fringes of governmental responsibility (Petra Sitte; a member of the Saxony-Anhalt state parliament during the Magdeburg Model years), were soon to become government members (Thomas Flierl, who in late 2001 was to become Culture Senator in Berlin) or who had been active in the reformist section of the party for a number of years (Pau). Although these four Executive members by no means agreed on everything, they did bring real-world experience of dealings with the SPD to the table and realised the need to address questions of programmatic renewal, government participation and strategic planning in rather more pragmatic, flexible and arguably realistic fashion than did those to their ideological left such as Rouzbeh Taheri (who eventually left the PDS in the run-up to the 2005 federal election to become a founding member of the troublesome Berlin branch of the WASG), Harald Werner (an ex-German Communist Party (DKP) member from western Germany) and Sahra Wagenknecht (long-standing doyen of the Marxist left).

This loss of profile was facilitated by an increasing feeling that complacency was setting in concerning the PDS's ability to perform well in elections. The unspoken assumption appeared to be that more or less regardless of its own performance the PDS would continue to do well in elections, largely on account of the mistakes and errors that other parties made and the weak alignments that (eastern) German voters possessed. The PDS's excellent showing in the 2001 state election in Berlin, where it polled 47.9 per cent of the vote in the city's eastern districts (as well as winning all of the *Direktmandate*) and 22.6 per cent in the city as a whole did not help to rectify this.[26] The PDS did well in Berlin because of the wretched performance of the Grand Coalition, subsumed as it was in a banking scandal which was on the verge of financially ruining the city.[27] But what would happen when the PDS had to compete in elections where the major parties could portray themselves in a more positive light? How would the PDS sell its message when other competing messages were no longer as dreadful as they had been in Berlin? Zimmer and her executive appeared to have very few answers to these questions.

Personal differences between Executive members were beginning to further undermine Zimmer's internal authority. As time went on, the Executive itself appeared to be breaking into antagonistic factions and becoming ever more unleadable – largely as different Executive members appeared to have fundamentally different understandings of the PDS's position in German society, the party's position in the

German party system and even in the way that politics itself should be conducted.[28] These differences were rarely visible in public, and the only real evidence of this was the lack of anything substantial coming out of Executive meetings. Zimmer, for her part, was keen to push on with reforming the party's programme and its organisation to enable it to look to the future with both a clear programmatic agenda and a coherent electoral strategy. She was, however, rarely able to convince all of her colleagues of the necessity of doing this in anything like a systematic fashion. Hopes that the party would have a new programme in place before the 2002 federal election were quickly dashed and the PDS's election was described by some young internal critics as 'an inconsequential collection of individual statements from previous years'.[29] Others in the Executive – most noticeably Dieter Dehm – preferred a much more straightforward oppositional approach, mobilising extra-parliamentary forces to create pressure from below and foot-dragging on issues such as programmatic reform. Relations between Executive members became ever more tetchy and communication with party members and activists patchy and unconvincing; the party therefore appeared to be drifting towards the 2002 election without any clear message or any clear strategy. Even as the election beckoned different factions could not find common ground, presenting different motions to the floor at the pre-election conference in Rostock. Unsurprisingly, this sent a confusing and contradictory message to the population at large.[30] Public relations gaffes also kept on occurring; the worst of which was the public apology that the new leader of the PDS's parliamentary party in the *Bundestag*, Roland Claus (who had replaced Gysi in 2000), made to the US President, George Bush, after PDS politicians had walked out of parliament while he was making a speech there. Why on earth was the PDS apologising to a President who, so many in the party felt, was a war-monger? What message did this send out about the PDS's commitment to the pacifist movement? The PDS was looking – largely because it was – rudderless. And rudderless parties normally perform poorly in elections.

For the first time since the early 1990s, the PDS also had to deal with exogenous variables that were not in its favour. Through the 1990s the parties of the centre right systematically hammered away at the PDS's dubious past, its alleged extremist nature and its apparently unconvincing acceptance of democratic norms and ideals. To no avail. The PDS skilfully portrayed itself as a poorly treated and persecuted victim – sentiments that drew enough support for it to be able to survive. By 2002 the PDS was faced with a much more powerful challenge; it was being ignored. And not as other parties continued to reject and scorn it; there were simply other more significant issues to be discussed in eastern Germany and the PDS simply slipped off the party political radar.

Two very particular events in 2002 illustrated this perfectly; first, during the early summer months of 2002 torrential rain fell in central Europe, prompting severe flooding in Hungary, Slovakia, the Czech Republic, Bavaria and particularly eastern Germany. By mid-summer large parts of Saxony and Brandenburg were under the very real threat of being swamped. This played very much into the hands of then Chancellor Gerhard Schröder. Although he clearly could not do anything to stop the waters rising, he was able to look extremely active and dynamic in his attempt to clear up the damage once the floods had subsided and once the need to plough money back into infrastructure projects arose. Schröder was in his element and as the waters dropped in mid-late August, the SPD was able to strongly pick up in the opinion polls. The PDS suffered primarily as the waters lay in areas where it is likely to have done better than average and in an era when personalities and specific issues are of particular importance in swaying voting preferences.

More or less at the same time, as the floods were hitting eastern Germany and Bavaria, the spectre of a second war in Iraq began to loom large. Schröder, playing what many regarded as an overtly populist set of cards, rejected German participation in such activities out of hand, playing up his 'anti-war' credentials and concomitantly robbing the PDS of one of its core mobilising issues. The PDS, traditionally seen as a party that rejected German military intervention abroad, found the SPD moving leftwards and usurping the role it had fostered for itself as Germany's 'peace party'. Hence its support steadily petered away from mid-June onwards. Schröder's unequivocal rejection of US-led intervention took whatever wind that was left out of the PDS's sails, rejuvenating the left wing of the SPD and stumping a dangerous eastern German competitor.

Of scapegoats and sob-stories: The 2002 federal election and its aftermath

By late August, PDS politicians therefore sensed that the party was heading for a big fall. The final results illustrated this starkly. The PDS polled 598,000 votes fewer that it had done in 1998, 4.0 per cent of all votes cast. Perhaps unsurprisingly, the PDS suffered its most heavy losses in eastern Germany (its share of the vote was down 4.6 per cent, from

21.6 per cent to 17.0 per cent, a worse electoral performance than it had achieved there in 1994). It remained strongest in eastern Berlin (21.2 per cent – down 4.1 per cent on its 1998 performance), followed, at a considerable distance, by Brandenburg (17.2 per cent – down 3.1 per cent) and Thuringia (17.0 per cent – down 4.3 per cent). It managed to maintain its (weak) presence in western Germany (1.2 per cent of the vote compared to 1.1 per cent in 1998), even slightly improving on 1998 in the Saarland (up 0.4 per cent to 1.4 per cent), but the party's failure to win more than two East Berlin constituencies outright ensured that it would to all intents and purposes be forced off the federal stage. Even though there was precious little movement of PDS supporters to the Greens, CDU/CSU or the FDP, 290,000 former PDS voters did opt for Gerhard Schröder's Social Democrats, while most of the rest moved to the non-voter category.[31]

The PDS had not convinced electors of why it was needed in parliament. The PDS campaign had neither appealed to voters nor scared them off; the PDS's programmatic agenda had neither struck fear into people's hearts nor inspired them. The party had simply failed to prompt any sort of reaction at all. The PDS was too passive, too reactive and eventually too ineffective in getting its (mixed) message(s) across. The departure of Gysi had indeed been a crushing blow; the party no longer possessed any household names and no PDS politician had the ability to make an impact on public discourse. In short, the PDS had drifted into the election without a clear programme and without a clear message; the party subsequently drifted out of parliament and into (another) existential crisis.

The PDS's difficulties with the SPD and with coalition options in the *Länder* had undoubtedly contributed to this situation. As will be discussed later in this book, the PDS has a number of different faces in *Land* parliaments and the federal party never managed to shape this diversity into a broad, but nonetheless coherent, line on when, and under what conditions, the PDS was prepared to work with the SPD. Every party needs to stress red lines over which it will not go as well as a particular set of demands that it will insist upon if it is to be a coalition partner. Taken together, the two illustrate both what a government that it participates in will not (under any circumstances) do, as well as what it clearly does hope to achieve. The PDS failed, perhaps for understandable reasons, to find forms of words that mixed these two things and in a block-party system such as that in Germany, the price for equivocation is often high.

The challenges that the PDS faced in the autumn of 2002 were therefore clear. It needed, firstly, to (somehow) find personalities who had the style, charm and charisma to get its message (whatever it was to be) across to a wider audience. Secondly, it needed a more straightforward and understandable programmatic agenda – no more mixed signals, rather a recognisable and digestible set of practical policies. Thirdly, it needed to develop a more accessible image and identity that had a much more positive resonance than was the case in 2002. Fourthly, and finally, the PDS needed to sort out its strategic options in terms of taking part in *Land*-level governments; regional politicians could take decisions on a case-by-case basis, but the federal party needed to structure and shape the contours of these decisions so that blatant contradictions (or the perception that such things existed) could be eradicated.[32]

2002–5: Picking up the pieces

The disappointing result in 2002 prompted, perhaps unsurprisingly, another round of PDS obituary writing.[33] Few commentators claimed that the PDS's poor performance was the result of one-off issue-based or personality factors that, all being well, the party would be able to resolve/overcome by the time of the next election; virtually all academic analysis pointed to deep-seated problems that were more than likely to lead to the end of the party as a national force. The PDS had been drawn into sub-national government and had lost its oppositional edge; its membership was getting ever older and new recruits were few and far between;[34] the PDS had little convincing to offer in programmatic terms; it had also proven manifestly unable to set down roots in western Germany, ensuring that it remained an eastern German regional party.[35]

That the PDS returned to parliament in 2005 had, as indicated in the introduction to this book, much to do with the behaviour of other political actors as well as coherent leadership of the party. In March 2003 Gerhard Schröder's red-green coalition introduced a package of welfare reforms under the rubric of 'Agenda 2010'. Needy though they undoubtedly were, the cuts in welfare spending brought howls of despair from vested interests on the left and, of course, from the PDS itself. Yet it was only in the summer of 2004, after the so-called 'Hartz Reforms' to the labour market were introduced, that the PDS started to see any sort of movement in its opinion poll ratings; even then, the rise was hardly meteoric and the PDS's slightly increased popularity remained limited to eastern Germany.[36] As is analysed in Chapter 8, a group of disaffected western German social democratic trade union members started to express dissatisfaction with 'their' party and 'their' government and, when the government made a point of stressing that it was not for turning on Agenda 2010, they began to leave the party in order to form what became the WASG. The WASG was expressly anti-neo-liberal and directly opposed to the specific sets of reforms that the SPD/Green government was seeking to implement. That they were predominantly based in western Germany initially worried the PDS, who saw them as a serious competitor for the votes of disaffected Social Democrats. It soon became apparent, however, that the two parties were moving in different circles and that, as Schröder brought forward the 2006 election by 12 months, both parties had much more to gain (parliamentary representation) by working together and forging what they hoped would be a broad left-wing alliance that would enjoy popular resonance across the whole of the Federal Republic.

The PDS was also able to bring a little clarity to its confused and contradictory internal affairs. Gabi Zimmer's unhappy period as party leader came to an end in March 2003 when she announced that she would not seek re-election, and she was replaced at a Berlin party conference in April 2004 by (a reluctant) Lothar Bisky. Fortunately for the PDS, Bisky made it clear that he would only return as party chairman if he could install a team around him with whom he knew he would be able to work. Bisky made it clear that he was stepping back into the front line of practical politics to do a very specific job: to lead the party out of its internal crisis, to complete the process of writing a new programme and to give the party clear lines of strategic orientation in the run-up to the next election. There were a number of changes in the Executive committee; all three of the deputy leaders changed. Dehm was replaced, and both Peter Porsch and Heidemarie Lüth (who had replaced Petra Pau in 2002) also left the Executive. One of the three new deputy leaders was a rising star from Dresden, 25-year-old Katja Kipping. A former 'Miss Bundestag', Dagmar Enkelmann, joined her as another of Bisky's deputies, while the third slot was filled by Wolfgang Methling, Mecklenburg-Western Pomerania's environment minister since 1998. None of these politicians were Bisky clones, but they did share his belief that the party needed to make genuine progress in reforming itself before going to the polls again. Bisky's integrative style and combative internal agenda was made more feasible by the return to national politics of Gregor Gysi at the Potsdam conference on 30–31 October 2004. Gysi's exile had been partly self-imposed (he resigned as economics minister in the state of Berlin in 2002 when it became public that he had used air miles gained when flying on business for private flights; it was not exactly a heinous crime, particularly given that a number of other politicians who were also uncovered doing the same thing remained in their respective positions, but the scandal was enough for Gysi to choose to take his leave) and partly health-induced, but by late 2004 it seemed clear that – love him or hate him – he represented the PDS's last chance to bounce back from the 2004 debacle. As is discussed in much more detail in Chapter 8, the PDS found a set of issues (welfare and labour market reform) around which it could effectively mobilise, it drafted and passed a new party programme in Chemnitz in October 2003 and the positive relationship that developed between WASG and the PDS gave it the opportunity to paint an image of itself as rejuvenated actor. The final pieces of the PDS's pre-election jigsaw came when the party symbolically changed its name to the Left Party and Oskar Lafontaine agreed to run alongside Gregor Gysi as the spearhead of the party's anti-Schröder election campaign (see Chapter 8). The pieces for an election recovery were, finally, in place.

The 2005 election: The return of the dead

Over 4.1 million electors voted for the Left Party on 18 September 2005, 8.7 per cent of those who went to the polls. The party doubled its share of the vote and was able to send 54 MdBs to the federal parliament in Berlin. One in four eastern Germans (25.3 per cent) voted for the newly re-named party, while 4.9 per cent of all western Germans put a cross next to *Die Linke's* name. The 2005 election was undoubtedly the best result in the party's short history.

The party's excellent performance in the West had much to do with Oskar Lafontaine's talismanic presence; his anti-capitalist rhetoric appealed to disgruntled socialists and Social Democrats alike and it was no surprise that over a quarter of all of *Die Linke's* supporters in 2005 had voted for the SPD in 2002. Ten per cent of all *Die Linke* supporters had not voted at all in 2002. The Left Party therefore successfully managed to build on its core strengths; it maintained a clear presence among those possessing university degrees, civil servants, the unemployed and those with strong connections to the GDR. It also managed to appeal to more workers with a strong belief that more social justice – over 60 per cent of *Die Linke* supporters stated this as their primary reason for supporting the party[37] – was needed in German society as well as those with lower levels of formal education.

However, if the 2002 debacle taught Left Party politicians anything, then it made them aware that successful elections do not simply repeat themselves ad infinitum. The losses that the Left Party suffered in *Land* elections in 2006 in Mecklenburg-Western Pomerania and particularly

Berlin further illustrated how electoral successes can change into defeats in remarkably short periods of time. Issues come and go, politicians' stars can rise and fall quickly and independent voters may opt to support other parties next time around. Add in the difficulties of two parties merging, new leaderships emerging and the Left Party's opponents putting up a much more robust performance in the future and a repeat performance at the federal election in 2009 is therefore anything but self-explanatory.

The next chapters of this book will not be able to foresee what will happen in the future but they will offer pointers as to how the newly formed Left Party may seek to deal with the main challenges that it is likely to face. Before this can be done Chapter 3 attempts to develop an analytical framework suitable for putting the Left Party's pre-2005 progress in context.

3
Aims and Ambitions: Policy, Office, Votes and the Left Party

As Chapters 1 and 2 have illustrated, the Left Party went through a challenging and decidedly unpredictable first 15 years in existence. By 2005 it appeared, in spite of its inglorious past in the GDR, to have found a place in contemporary German politics, and it is undoubtedly becoming an ever more 'normal' part of the German party system. Thus far we have mapped out the roller coaster ride that the Left Party has experienced in everyday practical politics. We have also illustrated that the Left Party's successes and failures have been analysed by political scientists in different ways; some have persisted in seeing it as a dangerous, populist, extremist party on the fringes of democratic acceptability, others as a milieu-based protest party articulating fuzzily defined eastern German interests, while yet more have, as we have seen, concentrated on analysing the party's progress through the prism of left-wing politics. While all have had some merit, the results of the 2005 federal election, the merger of the PDS and the WASG into *Die Linke* and the establishment of the new party as a serious actor with genuine long-term prospects indicate that an approach based on the latter may now have the most mileage. Finally, thus far we have also concentrated primarily on the past rather than the future, avoiding any analysis of what problems, predicaments and dilemmas the 'new' Left Party is likely to be faced with. This chapter makes a start in rectifying this.

This chapter attempts to do three specific things; firstly, given that *Die Linke* began life as a radical, anti-establishment party, this chapter develops an analytical framework suitable for assessing how such parties have tried to come to terms with the institutions and processes of parliamentary democracy and the transition from purely oppositional politics to one involving some sort of governmental role. Looking, briefly, at the literature on how left parties in general have attempted to deal with a 'system' that they either reject completely or have fundamental problems with should give us some idea of how the Left Party has slowly moved away from a position of outright opposition to the political system towards a more constructive, even governmental role. More specifically, it asks whether radical left parties inevitably set out on a steady path of (uneasy) accommodation with the institutions and processes of parliamentary democracy, followed by progressive pragmatism, and (eventually) total acceptance of a system they had initially rejected/had major reservations about. Is the Left Party simply doing what the Greens did 15/20 years before it? Where is this process of institutionalisation likely to leave the Left Party's more radical elements? Some sort of dissent, at both the national and *Land* levels, would appear to be pre-programmed; how, given the experiences of others, is the Left Party likely to deal with this? A review of the literature reveals that institutionalisation processes are indeed common in radical parties, leading to either more radical sections breaking away to form their own organisations and/or the party distancing itself from its previous doctrines (discussed in more detail in Chapter 8). The vertical and horizontal 'wriggle-room' that parties in federal states (although also, if to a lesser extent, in unitary states too) enjoy also facilitates territorially distinct interpretations of a radical party's role in contemporary politics – a fact amply illustrated by the ideological and strategic diversity evident across the Left Party's territorial units.

Secondly, having established that while there is no inevitability about such processes (even if there is a strong likelihood of them taking place), this chapter develops some analytical tools suitable for understanding the Left Party's ideological, programmatic and strategic complexity. Only if we understand how the Left Party works will we be able to speculate on how it is likely to fare in the future. Germany's federal system offers territorial units within parties, as well as politicians representing different ideological streams, the opportunity to exert significant influence on political life. Diversity within the Left Party, much as in other parties, can, and is, channelled into the political process through a number of different avenues. Pre-2000, Left Party politicians expressed a wide range of divergent political opinions and attempted to try to achieve their aims in noticeably different ways. The salience of this diversity in both aims and methods nevertheless remained low as the national party – and particularly the parliamentary party – proved strong enough to centre attention on to its own political goals. Divergent *Land* or ideological preferences remained important for party activists, but largely irrelevant to the wider world. This changed, initially at a pedestrian pace, when the

Left Party was evicted from the *Bundestag* in 2002. The parliamentary party in the *Bundestag* vanished and the coherent message from the Party Executive became fuzzy and contested. Although the return of the Left Party to the *Bundestag* in 2005 will assist the national leadership in co-ordinating the activities of the sub-ordinate *Land* branches – largely as the parliamentary party will become a central point of reference in debates about national politics – it is by no means clear that this will lead to a return to the pre-2002 status quo.

In order to make sense of both why the Left Party struggled at the turn of the decade and how it will attempt to avoid such pitfalls in the future, we argue that it is best to analyse the different goals that can be pursued not just by the federal party but also by different factions/ streams/territorial units within the Left Party. The debates that surrounded, for example, the Berlin state branch's office-seeking strategy, Saxony's and Brandenburg's zigzagging between vote maximisation and policy-seeking and Mecklenburg-Western Pomerania's policy-specific approach (see Chapters 5–7) provide ample evidence that the sub-national level does matter. This takes on even greater importance when the groups/units adopt radically different positions towards issues such as government participation – and there is no issue that has proved as problematic for the Left Party in recent times as this one.

Political scientists have, however, traditionally struggled to make sense of the intra-party diversity evident within *the vast majority of* parties; the differing positions and attitudes of groups within political parties, territorial or otherwise, has therefore been systematically ignored. Parties have tended to be seen, if mainly for reasons of simplicity rather more than genuine conviction, as unitary actors. German parties clearly are no such things. Where strong direction from the national party is lacking, internal groups stressing different aims and ambitions can extenuate frictions and tensions as well as articulate territorial distinctiveness. On a good day this can lead to unity in diversity; on a bad day it can lead to bitter disputes and internal splits. In other words, if a party is both organisationally flexible and programmatically pragmatic, then these tensions can be dealt with relatively painlessly. If a party is not able to institutionalise tensions by defusing their high-explosive character then, again, trouble will inevitably lie ahead. This comes down to the different aims that groups within a party possess. The goals of important factions within the Left Party as well as the organisational ability to manage conflict smoothly is therefore highly significant in understanding where *Die Linke* goes from here. This is particularly true if more left-wing orthodox groups were ever to gain the policy-orientated higher ground in one or other of the party's factions. Put another way, are the varying agendas (discussed in greater detail in Chapters 5–8) expressions of vibrant intra-party democracy and therefore very much within the spirit of Germany's federal system, facilitating regionally specific answers to regionally specific questions? Or are they the root of future fault-lines which the decidedly heterogeneous *Die Linke* will not be able to master when the political going gets tougher? If that is indeed the case, then the happy glow of electoral success that permeated the party in the autumn of 2005 may not last long at all.

Thirdly, and linked with this second aim, we discuss how the performance of the Left Party (and the perception of that performance) in *Land*-level governments will fundamentally influence the Left Party's progress within the *Länder* where it governs (or has governed), in other (eastern) *Länder* where it does not (and never has) govern(ed) and also at the national level. The Left Party (much like the Greens before it, see Chapter 4) has found itself torn between the role of principled opposition and responsible party of government. The party, again much like the Greens before it, has entered into coalitions with the SPD in two states with significant hesitation and with mixed policy and electoral results. Should a coalition with the SPD at the federal level ever be a real possibility, then these coalition experiences at the *Land* level will be instructive for the Left Party, again just as they have been for the Greens. Given these similarities, this chapter explores in theoretical terms how such red-red coalitions have come about. We finish the chapter by investigating whether a red-red model of government could be developing, and if so, what the core elements of such a model could be. We offer two models of red-red coalitions, the first dealing with coalition formation and the second with coalition maintenance. These models are then compared with the experiences of the SPD and the Greens in the 1990s before being put under the empirical microscope in Chapters 5–8. The concluding chapter of this book then analyse what implications the red-red governments at *Land* level will have on both the Left Party's relationship with the SPD and their future prospects as viable coalition partners as well as assessing what lessons the Left Party can learn for the future.

Selling your soul or playing the game?

Left-wing parties, no matter whether they declare themselves to be social democratic, socialist, communist or some other variant on this, have periodically wrestled with the question of how to 'deal with' parliamentary democracy. Should they reject it as a bourgeois, capitalist charade that in reality represses the working classes and exists to serve the interests of rich paymasters? Or should they work within the system, seeking either to undermine capitalism from within (a position advocated by more radical groups) or 'play the game' to achieve the best deal possible for their own vested interests (a position adopted by less ostensibly radical factions). In the early 1990s these debates could frequently be heard across all levels of the Left Party. Should the Left Party oppose a socio-economic system that it fundamentally rejected (and with this refuse to take part in governments at all levels) or should it seek to do what it could to shape German capitalism in the most socially acceptable way? Even now in the middle of the first decade of the 21st century, sections of the party, most noticeably around the Marxist Forum and what is left of the Communist Platform, prefer more outright opposition to any sort of compromise and, fewer though their voices are, they have not yet become completely insignificant.[1] That having been said, Tim Bale and Richard Dunphy persuasively argue that the no-nay-never faction on the far left of Europe's far left parties have still not been able to prevent any of their parties from accepting, when asked, invitations to join governing coalitions in any western democracy since 1989.[2]

The Left Party was not, of course, the first German party to have to deal with such questions. The SPD and the Greens both began life as movements that sought radical social change. Both contained significant sections that had little (if any) faith in capitalism to achieve social justice, to avoid (apparently unnecessary) wars and to avoid being hijacked by the capitalist classes. Both, however, eventually began not only to accept the system within which they were forced to work, they became integral parts of it, entering governments, talking in non-revolutionary language and actively defending the system against its critics. The most recent of these two cases, the Green Party, is put under the microscope in more detail in the next chapter in order to aid us in understanding one of the possible evolutionary paths of the Left Party.

Such a de-radicalisation of the anti-capitalist (or at least capitalism-critical) left would hardly surprise many writers on political parties through history. At the turn of the 20th century Robert Michels famously argued that an 'Iron Law of Oligarchy' existed and that even the most radical of parties would sooner or later be led, defined and eventually controlled by groups of (parliamentary) elites. Michels was particularly dismayed by his finding that even parties that had an explicit commitment to inner-party democracy at the forefront of their agendas could also be dominated by small leadership cliques. Although his study was based primarily on the German SPD, he nonetheless concluded that once the initial excitement of the founding phase of a party had passed, every party, no matter how radical and system-challenging, would inevitably need direction and leadership. Michels's understanding of human nature, perhaps unsurprisingly given that his own intellectual mentors were the well known elite theorists Vilfredo Pareto and Gaetano Mosca, remained expressly elitist and he argued that a political class would inevitably develop, just as a (much larger) group of followers was also inevitably bound to crystallise beneath them. 'Organisation' he observed 'implies the tendency to oligarchy [and] the aristocratic tendency [will] manifest itself very clearly'.[3] This suits the leaders and the led alike as the need for both an efficient party bureaucracy and some form of delegation naturally prevents grass-roots democracy from being workable in practice. The choice for every overtly radical party was therefore a stark one – remain anarchical beasts that lack the organisational capability to articulate coherent political ideas or organise, in whatever way, or professionalise in order to progress in every day political life. Michels is unlikely to have been surprised by Left Party moves towards government participation in the late 1990s. He is likely to have stressed that the Left Party's parliamentary elites, both in the *Bundestag* and in the eastern German *Landtage*, will naturally have subsumed the interests of the party as a whole with their own interests in parliament(s). And that would mean a move, perhaps slowly at first, but a move nonetheless, towards conservatism, risk-avoidance and eventually a lunge for the reins of power.[4]

In spite of not insubstantial methodological and substantive criticisms, Michels's arguments remain influential today.[5] Richard Katz and Peter Mair's controversial cartel party thesis, for example, builds on similar ideas about the party in public office inevitably dominating political parties' daily affairs.[6] One particularly controversial part of the Michels argument is, however, his dismissal of party organisation as a tool with which to prevent such elitism and conservatism from creeping in. Michels has no time for formal checks and balances on power; they are, in his mind, cosmetic tools that may give the impression of flourishing internal democracy and democratic control by the masses but, in reality, are never likely to be sufficient in preventing party leaders manipulating party life to suit their own interests.[7] The need for specialisation and hierarchy facilitates domination of the masses. Whether this is quite as true in expressly decentralised states remains a lot less clear than Michels appears to claim. Where sub-national politicians can shape their activities to the demands of the sub-national political and electoral arenas, and where parties recognise this and shape their organisations accordingly, it is likely that different programmatic and ideological preferences will – at least theoretically – develop. If parties are aware of the need to allow their *Land* branches to act upon regional sentiment and to react to territorially specific issues and cleavages, then there is no reason why a diversity of political opinion cannot develop across *Land* boundaries.

Party members may indeed be very aware of the dangers of leadership elites manipulating the party to suit their own interests. Members may organise their parties, perhaps by overtly democratising decision-making processes through party conferences, specifically to throttle such processes.[8] Theoretically, members clearly can create rules and regulations that should shape the behaviour of their elected representatives. Yet the very nature of the parliamentary system of government, and particularly the stress on *parliaments* as the key loci of power, influence and attention ensures that that is where the public gaze inevitably settles. The party in public office will be at the forefront of the general public's understanding of what the party does, who leads it and what it stands for.[9] All politicians (bar anarchist ones) see getting into parliament, whether it be national, sub-national or local, as one key goal. If a party wishes to influence political life it has no choice but to place this aim high on its political agenda. This leads, sooner or later, to some emphasis on vote-maximising goals and a corresponding de-emphasis on ideological purity. Politicians may dispute this, but poor performance in elections means little (or no) representation in parliament meaning little (or no) influence on policy outputs. The parliamentary system of government demands that gaining votes remains paramount in having a political say. The challenge for a radical left-wing party is therefore clear; it is faced with the choice between incompatibles – between forwarding and protecting clear principles and compromising them so as to manoeuvre itself into a position where it actually has the power to get something done.[10] Viewed like this, there is little future for the ideologically pure and politically consistent (left-wing) party. Given their electoral track record, there also appears to be little chance of ideologically consistent radical left parties ever gaining a parliamentary majority. Parties such as the Left Party will, inevitably, adapt to the rules of the parliamentary game. This will lead not only to parliamentarians dominating party life but also to an inevitable move towards acceptance of 'bourgeois' norms and values. Contemporary politics is more integrative than ever before and agitating outside the generalised norms of the political game is only possible in the extreme short-term. Authors such as

Michels would also not be surprised to see the Left Party governing in Mecklenburg-Western Pomerania (1998–2006) and Berlin (2001–); he would be likely to argue that such processes of institutionalisation are only logical and to be expected and that the radical currents in the party should not be surprised to find themselves marginalised.

Aims and ideals: Policy, office and votes

Obtaining parliamentary representation has therefore become a non-negotiable aim for all radical parties. Parties that reject parliaments as a key forum for activity slip, sooner or later, off the political radar. Eventually, obtaining parliamentary representation becomes paramount. Once parties accept this, different questions are asked. Members, activists, politicians and voters can expect vastly different things from political parties and consequently they have radically different political aims. They may also stress different methods and means in attempting to achieve them. In order to make sense of the multitude of different wants and needs that are placed on modern-day parties, scholars need to situate parties institutionally, culturally and contingently. Put another way, party researchers accept that one of the best ways of exploring political phenomena is to trace and to take seriously (if not necessarily at face value) the narratives and self-understandings of those involved in the political process.[11] They are the ones who (think they) know what they are doing, why they are doing it and how they plan to proceed in given sets of circumstances. Only by throwing light on these processes can we genuinely deepen our understanding of why politicians (and therefore parties) behave as they do both within parliaments and within society at large. This is something we do in Chapters 5–8 of this book.

Given this, and despite the significant number of radical-left parties in existence across western Europe, political scientists of all persuasions have shown a surprising lack of interest in studying their behaviour.[12] The reasons for this are not immediately obvious. Even though the electoral performances of virtually all radical left parties have been either poor or in decline (or both), they have continued to play an important role in helping social democratic parties form governing coalitions in states as diverse as Cyprus (from 2003), Finland (1995–2003), France (1997–2002), Greece (1989–90), Ireland (1994–97), Italy (2006–), New Zealand (1999–2002) and Norway (2005–). They have also taken on support party status in Denmark (1993–2001), France (1989–93), Italy (1996–99), Spain (2004–) and Sweden (1998–2006).[13] To say that they are an unworthy object of study would therefore be considerably wide off the mark. One framework that may help us to make more sense of the behaviour of radical left parties, and the Left Party in Germany in particular, is the schema that was famously developed by Kaare Strøm concentrating on a party's aims.[14] He contends that parties have three main aims:[15]

- Parties exist to obtain office. Parties who expressly emphasise this aim seek, above all, concrete advantages for themselves and their clientele that result from taking part in governments. They therefore tend to stress the importance of manoeuvring themselves into an advantageous position within the party system, and with other actors, so as to gain significant ministerial portfolios. A genuine influence on governmental outputs remains important, but office-seeking parties do not stress ideological consistency and programmatic purity in the way that other actors may choose to do so.
- A stress on policy-seeking. Policy-seeking parties are in many ways the antithesis of office-seeking parties. They have particular programmatic goals and aims and seek to do all they can to implement them in as 'pure' a form as is possible. These parties are likely to have a coherent political agenda stemming out of core ideological beliefs that has been developed over many years. Alternatively, they may be individual issue-orientated parties who seek to profile themselves on a much narrower policy base. Office-seeking remains important to policy-seeking parties, but it does not become an end in itself. Such parties may subsequently find decisions on when, and under what conditions, to enter government particularly testing.
- A stress on vote maximisation (vote-seeking). The principal aim that these parties adopt is that of maximising the number of votes they achieve in elections. Again, policy-seeking and office-seeking are not completely insignificant, but the initial emphasis remains one of expanding a voter base. Party programmes are likely to be less ideologically rigid and office-seeking may be either implausible or unwanted – the emphasis therefore moves to embedding the party's position within the electorate.

None of the three aims is pursued by any party independent of the others. Linkages, and trade-offs, inevitably exist between all three both within the national party organisation and (at least in federal states) between and within state party organisations. However, individual factions (particularly if they dominate in one *Landesverband*) do have the ability to stress particular aims, particularly as there is frequently direct and indirect conflict between the three of them. This tends to lead to one strategy gaining the dominant hand, even if that need not be constant over time. A party may, for example, seek to maximise vote share expressly in order to take part in government. Government participation would, in this case, be the dominant aim with vote maximisation serving as an instrumental tool to assist in achieving it.

The picture is further complicated in that actors with different and potentially conflicting interests exist across all levels in political parties.[16] Due to these conflicting interests, parties lack a commonly accepted set of organisational rules that could facilitate a homogeneous perception of reality. For party activists as well as for party members there remain many realities and therefore many prospective courses that their parties could or should seek to take. This is aggravated by the voluntary nature of membership in political parties which ensures that they frequently resemble what Peter Lösche famously termed 'loosely coupled anarchies'.[17] According to Elmar Wiesendahl, there are four ways to manage these functional problems: vagueness, loose coupling, hypocrisy and fragmentation.[18]

- Problems that simply cannot be resolved may be settled by the use of deliberately ambiguous compromise formulas (*vagueness*), allowing different actors (whether they be *Landesverbände*, ideological streams or interest groups) to pursue conflicting goals that still pull in the same ideological direction.
- Alternatively, *loose coupling* between different units ensures that groups can take decisions semi-independently and prevents explicit contradictions from developing in the first place. 'Loose coupling' thus indicates that there is no intention of creating any sort of meshing between groups, rather they tend to co-exist alongside zones of strong coupling where harmonised and co-ordinated collective action does take place.[19]
- *Hypocrisy*, meanwhile, may also be accepted and tolerated, as the actions of leaders can never completely reflect their members' differing thoughts and ideas. As Nils Brunsson has observed, 'hypocrisy is a fundamental type of behaviour in the political organisation: to talk in a way that satisfies one demand, to decide in a way that satisfies another, and to supply products in a way that satisfies a third'.[20] We should expect hypocrisy to occur only at the vertical level, primarily as there may well be a gap between actions at the national level and talk at the state level since the national party is made up of state branches.

- Finally, *fragmentation* represents an attempt to reconcile differing intra-party goals through creating different organisational sub-units. Maintaining cohesion amidst internal ideological and programmatic diversity, even to the extent where some factions within anti-establishment parties reject the prevailing constitutional and/or political consensus, is therefore difficult, but not impossible.

The most important variables that influence a party in deciding what its key aims will be are threefold. First, external shocks that occur outside of the party's control. Such shocks may prompt wide and diverse reactions within parties, including a shifting of the party's main goals. Pinpointing what type of shock will lead to what type of change will depend on the previous aims of the party; vote maximisers, for example, are likely to see election defeats as existential crises while parties that are office-seekers by nature will view the loss of their main potential coalition partner in much the same vein. Policy seekers, on the other hand, are likely to react most dramatically to the loss of one of the central tenets of their policy platform (in the case of the Left Party this could feasibly have happened if some sort of economic and political-cultural assimilation of eastern Germany had occurred in the 1990s).[21] Second, a change in the internal balance of power within the party itself can also prompt strategic changes of direction by either a 'new' dominant faction or a re-modelled leadership hierarchy. Changes in national and *Land* leaderships can alter the political balance within a party as it is the leadership that reacts to internal and external challenges and it is the leadership that has the job of thinking strategically.[22] Finally, the nature of the relationship between the leadership of the party and the rank and file can also be of considerable significance.[23] Parties that strive for ideological consistency tend, for example, to have higher levels of inner-party democracy and a well-developed '*Streitkultur*'.[24] The party is likely to be organised in a decentralised way with party conferences playing an influential role in developing and, at times, dictating programmatic orientation. The rank and file therefore have considerable influence over those that they elect to lead them. Parties that prefer to stress strategies of vote maximisation tend, on the other hand, to develop organisations that enable effective electoral campaigns and party profiling to take place. The party leadership subsequently has more independence in internal affairs and has the ability to shape their party's activities more than would be the case in policy-seeking parties. The leadership uses the stick of possible negative media portrayals of their policy agenda to overtly influence the style and substance of the parties that they lead, frequently choosing to stress media attractiveness above programmatic consistency providing that this does not in itself cause problems in marketing the party to the wider public. Office-seeking parties, meanwhile, are the most difficult group of parties to identify. According to Stephen Wolinetz, they are best recognised by their aversion to high-risk politics and particularly high-risk political campaigns. Their leaderships also tend to have the highest degree of independence from the party rank and file. They seek to remain palatable as a coalition partner to as many other parties as is necessary while also maintaining a degree of independence. Office-seeking parties also tend to make very good use out of patronage structures and can be characterised as parties with very low numbers of non-paid party workers.[25]

Such a neat framework intuitively seems more applicable to parties that are not placed at either extreme of the political spectrum. The ability to trade-off these three aims is seen as being more viable for parties that can make a genuine claim to actually being able to plausibly pursue all of them. To assume that left parties such as *Die Linke* are devoid of these pressures would nonetheless be a mistake. Their chances of gaining office may be smaller, as could be their bases of support, but that does not mean that they are not presented with tough decisions to make in each of these areas. Müller and Strøm's framework helpfully throws light on complex processes and developments rather than providing law-like generalisations about the way politicians make 'hard choices'.[26] Indeed, one major merit of their approach is its desire to confront formal models (the type of which are discussed below in terms of coalition theory) with the ways in which real actors in real situations conceive their dilemmas.[27]

The picture is further complicated by the fact that the same party can pursue completely different strategies in different electoral arenas. As indicated above, this is more or less completely ignored in the current literature, mainly as bringing in multiple electoral arenas across space and levels adds complexity to already complicated areas of study. Put another way, pinpointing why political parties behave as they do in the national arena is difficult enough without bringing in the supranational, sub-national and local levels of party political competition. This is particularly true in the case of the Left Party: through the 1990s at the federal level the Left Party remained a policy-seeking, regionalist party with a clearly socialist profile.[28] It possessed (and still possesses now) no viable coalition options and concentrates almost exclusively on policy-orientated politics. At the sub-state level in the six eastern German *Länder* the situation is altogether different. The Left Party's vote share can differ considerably from *Land* to *Land* (in the last round of sub-state elections the Left Party polled as little as 16.8 per cent in Mecklenburg-Western Pomerania and as much as 28 per cent in Brandenburg), it possesses a heterogeneous electorate giving the party some of the core characteristics of a traditional *Volkspartei* and it is – in one state at least – a member of a governing coalition.[29] National and sub-national party systems differ considerably and the Left Party exists, to all intents and purposes, in a number of different political worlds. A classification of which goals the Left Party pursues in which political arenas is therefore not immediately forthcoming.

In order to conceptualise the differences between individual units within a party we also need to be aware that aims will change. We subsequently need to develop indicators that offer pointers towards understanding when, how and why different units appear to be heading in different directions. Angelo Panebianco has described internal party changes – defined as changes in the leadership of a party – as occurring in three particular ways. First, 'co-optation' involves a generational change within the leadership, largely leaving other structures intact. The balance that exists between other personalities and wings therefore remains stable and unchanged and this is therefore the most non-dramatic form of change. Second, an 'amalgamation' involves a gradual change in the relationship of the different wings of the party. Internal battles and, eventually, a change in the composition of the leadership that has kept the wings together/apart then occurs. Although change is taking place, it is normally well controlled and relatively stable – although not as stable as co-optation. The most unstable form of change takes place, thirdly, when what Panebianco describes as 'circulation' occurs. These changes can take place rapidly and dramatically as party leaderships are challenged and either quickly manoeuvred out of key positions of power, or simply dethroned altogether.[30]

In terms of their political aims, we should, therefore, expect to find a degree of horizontal and vertical diversity across the Left Party's organisational units. Parties have long since ceased to be homogeneous, unitary actors, and party leaders are required to manage diversity in a nuanced way so as to avoid splits and disagreements in public. German federalism and the decentralised organisation of German political parties therefore offer different units within the Left Party ample opportunity to forward their own agenda. Müller and Strøm's heuristic offers a simple and logical framework for conceptualising this and for making sense of what this diversity across *Länder* means for the future of the Left Party project.

When and under what conditions to govern?

Within the Left Party one particular question has proved of particular salience in recent years. When, and under what conditions, should the Left Party enter sub-national governments? The intellectual elite of the party has traditionally tried to be all things to all men when answering this question, claiming that the Left Party moved within a 'strategic triangle' of political options. In one corner were those articulating protest and dissatisfaction with prevailing societal circumstances. In appealing to this section of the party (as well as similar sections of society at large) the emphasis was clearly on opposition to the prevailing socio-economic order. In the second corner were politicians and members who wanted the Left Party to shape and defend the weak and needy from, if possible, within government (*'Gestaltungsanspruch'*). This part of the Left Party's strategy saw the party attempt to implement policies suitable for ameliorating some of society's problems alongside preventing 'neo-liberal' competitors from wreaking yet more damage. The final corner of the triangle saw the Left Party attempt blue-sky thinking; the aim was to develop new, innovative and different solutions to the 'bigger issues' that all politicians faced.

The stress that Left Party politicians put on the various components of this strategic framework has much to do not just with the aims that they personally want to pursue, but also their very understanding of how politics should be conducted. As was touched upon in Chapter 1, ideologues on the left of the party see politics as overtly confrontational and they view deal-making with Social Democrats as verging upon a treasonable offence. They tend very much towards protest and opposition. The emancipated left takes a rather mixed approach towards government participation with some of its members being (at least rhetorically) much more oriented towards social movements than towards other political parties and their prospective roles in governments. They are subsequently good at 'big picture' thinking, even if the practicality of their answers is sometimes in doubt, and less well made for actually implementing policy. Both groups nonetheless argue that too strong an emphasis on governing for the sake of governing will lead to too many compromises and a betrayal of the ideals that they see as lying at the Left Party's core. The pragmatists within the Left Party are not opposed to government participation, but they cautiously look at the conditions under which it takes place and stress the importance of 'carrying' the membership along and in actually being able to achieve some of their aims when in government. This is certainly a much more 'realist' approach than that of the utopians on the far left. The fourth faction within the Left Party, the modern socialists, is the only group that openly and almost unconditionally favours government participation as a means to increasing the Left Party's profile and stabilising it as a serious political actor. Significant groups in the Left Party still therefore have worries that the party will be de-radicalised and de-mystified. Others, meanwhile, see little point in talking radically and claiming to be fighting for the interests of the weak and oppressed if the party persistently refuses to enter governments to attempt to alleviate some of the problems that it pinpoints. Finding common ground on these questions has, perhaps unsurprisingly, been one of the most difficult and divisive issues in the Left Party in recent years and it is for this reason that it is worth taking time to conceptualise and, in later chapters, analyse empirically the Left Party's behaviour in the eastern German *Landtage*.

These questions are not, of course, unique to the Left Party in Germany. Other parties on the radical left (as well as the radical right) across Europe have had to deal with similar questions. Such questions may of course take years, decades even, before they seriously have to be addressed. They may also remain largely theoretical in nature as other parties refuse point blank to bring radical leftists into coalition discussions. Election results, institutional rules and coalition dynamics will all help shape when the (perhaps no longer so) radical left is brought into the coalition equation. It goes without saying that in coalition governments some form of pragmatic deal-making is necessary between all coalition partners.[31] It is also clear that even in centralised states such as the United Kingdom, parties are not always able to implement the programmatic agenda on which they have been elected, no matter whether they rule in conjunction with another party (or other parties) or alone. The practicalities of everyday politics may render ideas too utopian or unworkable; the compromises that party members struck in the name of getting elected may not hold once power is in a party's grasp, prompting infighting and programmatic dispute, or unforeseen external shocks may prevent parties from implementing policies that they genuinely intended to when initially elected.

The study of coalitions nonetheless offers plenty of opportunity to speculate on when, and under what conditions, the Left Party will seek to enter coalition government in the six eastern *Landtage*. Moreover, analysing the successes and failures of the Left Party in *Land* government will help us understand whether the possibility of national-level coalitions with the SPD exists and what sort of beasts these coalitions are likely to be.[32] In essence, coalition theory can be divided into three issue areas which have their own distinct logic and sets of dynamics: the study of coalition formation, the study of coalition maintenance and the study of coalition termination. All of these areas have traditionally been dominated by rational choice approaches to understanding political behaviour that have tended to invoke game-theoretical models in attempting to understand more about how coalitions come into existence, are maintained and eventually collapse.[33] Coalition formation in particular is seen as forcing parties to bargain with each other, prompting clear 'winners' and 'losers' and can therefore be best understood by creating models based on sets of assumptions that the actors involved are perceived to hold.[34] Over and above this, traditional coalition theory tends to split in two clear directions. One set of authors seek to explain coalition formation in terms of office-seeking motivations (so-called minimal-winning coalitions), others stress more policy-orientated dynamics ('ideologically connected' coalitions), while a final group seeks to merge the two.[35]

There are however major problems with both of the traditional variants of formal coalition theory. For one thing, they are remarkably poor at predicting real-world coalition outcomes.[36] Allied to this are methodological critiques that question the entire relationship between 'new' theories and the same somewhat limited dataset.[37] These important caveats aside, it is still clear that both office-seeking and policy-seeking motivations are important in helping us to get near understanding how coalitions come into being. Out of this synthesis has come the notion that parties seek 'minimal-winning connected' coalitions. In other words, in multi-party parliamentary systems parties seek to maximise the number of ministries that they control in a government by keeping the number of coalition partners to the minimum required to reach a mathematical majority. Yet not any old mathematical majority will do: parties seek to maximise the offices that they hold but only in a coalition where ideological/policy differences are also kept to a minimum.

Although most scholars believe that the 'minimal-winning-connected' model of coalition formation has a great deal of validity, it has been criticised for (among other things) still being a very poor indicator of what actually happens in practice, mainly as it more or less wholly ignores context. There are institutional constraints on coalition formation (some being linked, for example, to the electoral system), the history of relationships between parties (which could preclude coalition formation between parties where the leading politicians simply do not get on, even if such a coalition were mathematically possible and ideologically opportune), and regional/national political cultures that can immediately black-ball theoretically attractive coalition options. As noted above, this is not an abstract issue since minimal-winning-connected models fail to predict coalition formation a significant amount of the time. Consequently, rational-choice-inspired factors of coalition formation have frequently been supplemented with factors that attempt to capture these kinds of particularities. Further attempts have been made to model coalition bargaining on the basis of, for example, two or more policy dimensions. Concepts of 'core parties' that attempt to make themselves unavoidable coalition partners have been introduced, as have models based on portfolio allocation, where parties attempt to control the median legislator for the policy portfolio in question.[38]

The vast majority of this research has been conducted, perhaps understandably, with the national level of party political competition in mind. The one major exception to this is William Downs's excellent contribution from 1998 that explicitly investigated how coalitions worked at the sub-national level across Belgium, France and Germany.[39] He uses measures such as the volatility of sub-national election results over time and the deviation of sub-national election results from national ones (what he terms 'localisation') as well as survey data to test a number of hypotheses on which coalitions come into existence when, how long they tend to last and why they might conceivably fail. His key hypothesis is that the coupling of high volatility in election results with high levels of localisation 'heightens risk and accountability' within sub-national coalitions.[40] He finds significant evidence that in this situation sub-national parties act more cautiously, do not allow national parties to intervene and do not tend to use the sub-national political arena as a 'proving ground' for prospective national coalition models.

In the German case, Downs's survey illustrates that decisions on who coalesces with whom are taken at the *Land* level. Ninety four per cent of the *Land* parliamentarians whom he surveyed claimed that sub-state politicians took the main decisions in German sub-national coalition negotiations.[41] National politicians and national party machines are much more likely get involved in such decision-making processes when volatility (of election results across time in that *Land*) is high and the party system in that *Land* arena closely resembles that of Germany as a whole (i.e. 'localisation' rates remain low). Downs contends that the potential for conflict between the levels rises when volatility and localisation are high, and that the less hierarchical a party is, the bigger the deviations from national coalition patterns will be. He also finds some evidence in the German case of bottom-up strategic learning in parties and of a form of spillover between national and sub-national politics. Importantly, Downs concludes that much more effort needs to be made to overcome the prevailing notion that parties in Germany are still unitary actors and that the *Land* level is an important, significant and under-researched level of analysis.[42]

Downs's call to arms has become even more relevant in recent years. His (very thorough) research was conducted in the mid-1990s, so before the Left Party had entered any *Land* coalition government and before the processes of regionalisation in the German party system had genuinely taken root.[43] Given that the sub-national level can give important insights into how complex parties work and also guidance as to how future national politics may (theoretically) function, any analysis of the Left Party's position in the coalition equation is more than overdue. The behaviour of a party that campaigns on an overtly radical political agenda in coalition negotiations and then within the coalition itself has been strangely overlooked thus far. While the deals that centrist parties strike with one another undoubtedly affect political outcomes significantly, the nature of deals struck with a party that wants to, for example, fundamentally re-structure the tax system can take on completely different dimensions.

The Left Party's dilemmas of government

Given that formal coalition theory appears unable to predict in any consistently meaningful way when coalitions will come into being and how long they will last, it would seem futile to attempt to create a deductive model of red-red government at the sub-national level in Germany. For one thing, the available data set is far too small to allow generalisable conclusions to be drawn. Yet there would appear to be a number of indicators allowing us to speculate on where and when such coalitions are likely to come to fruition and how they will behave once in office. Where only three parties are present in eastern German *Landtage* the coalition potential of the Left Party inevitably rises. It is therefore not unreasonable to hypothesise that when either the Greens or the FDP, or ideally (from the prospective of proponents of government participation within the Left Party) both, fail to gain parliamentary representation then the chances of red-red increase. Secondly, the electoral strength of the coalition partners over time is also likely to be significant. In concrete terms this means that when the SPD increases its vote and seat shares from the previous *Land* election – a development that will frequently involve a decrease for the CDU – the SPD will be more favourably disposed towards a coalition with the Left Party. When, on the other hand, its vote and seat shares decrease, then the SPD is much more inclined to go into a Grand Coalition (regardless of total percentage of the vote). Finally, effective policy-making for client groups of the Left Party also remains an important consideration.

On top of this, Chapter 4 will offer pointers likely to help us in answering a number of other questions raised in this chapter. We have seen that the decentralised nature of the German party system leaves, at least theoretically, *Land* parties with plenty of opportunity to shape their own aims. Under what conditions do *Landesverbände* choose to pursue which goals? Can an analysis of the Left Party, and the Greens, throw any light on whether particular types of sub-national party organisation choose to pursue which goals and why? Furthermore, does there appear to be a relationship between changes in the aims of parties and their organisation? More specifically, are changing aims a means to deal with specific (organisational and/or political) problems? Is it the case, as the discussion above would appear to indicate, that the looser the organisational structures and the more organisational room for manoeuvre a sub-national party branch has, the more diverse the goals the branches will inevitably pursue? Finally, can an analysis of the behaviour of *Die Linke* tell us anything about the dynamics of leadership change – is there evidence to suggest, as Angelo Panebianco has inferred, that the more frequently and fundamentally that leadership hierarchies are changed, the more likely we are to see changes in party goals?

Before elaborating in more detail on these questions as well as on the tenets of a framework for understanding when and where we may see more red-red coalitions, it makes sense to look in more detail at one party (the Greens) and one relationship (that of the Greens and the SPD) that offers a distinct parallel to that of the Left Party and the SPD. As indicated earlier, the Greens fostered an anti-system image but eventually marched through the institutions to establish themselves as a normal party that was even able to govern at the national level. There are therefore clear and unambiguous similarities between the routes that the Greens and the Left Party appear to be taking. Chapter 4 analyses the Greens' trajectory in more detail before attempting to draw lessons that may be helpful in understanding where the Left Party is likely to go from here.

4
Haven't We Been Here Before? Comparing the Left Party and the Greens

If any German party has gone down a similar path to that of the Left Party, then it is the Green Party. Much like the Left Party, the Greens have had a profound effect on party political competition in Germany – increasing the number of effective political parties, widening the party system's ideological scope and (at least theoretically) increasing parties' coalition options. Yet, also like the Left Party, at their birth the Greens were an 'outsider' party, considered extremist by some, uncoalitionable by most, and largely shunned by the established political parties. Also initially, both the Greens and the Left Party – or at least important players within them – revelled in this outsider status, preferring the role of principled opposition to constructive partner in government. However, it did not take long before both parties found that they could have significant political clout as a prospective potential coalition partner for the SPD. The practical possibility of taking part in coalitions, while emboldening the more pragmatic elements within these parties, subsequently set the stage for some dramatic inner-party conflicts over the identity of both the Greens and Left Party.

In this chapter, we seek to push this comparison between the Greens and the Left Party a little further by tracing the processes of institutionalisation and 'normalisation' that the Greens have undergone.[1] We are not aiming to write a detailed history of the Green Party. This has been done very adequately elsewhere.[2] Rather, two sets of questions concern us here. First, what was the Greens' experience in developing *Politik-* and *Koalitionsfähigkeit* in the *Länder?* How did the Greens' attitudes towards government participation evolve at the *Land* level, and, following this, at the national level? Second, how and why did the Greens move from being principally a party of opposition to a party of government? What ideological and organisational changes were involved in this transformation process?

In order to answer these questions, we briefly examine the *Länder*-level coalition experiences of the Greens, with five cases serving as our prime examples – an initial, but ultimately unsuccessful, attempt at co-operation in Hamburg in 1982; toleration and then a coalition in Hesse from 1983–87; the SPD-Green government in Berlin from 1989–91; the red-green coalition in Lower Saxony from 1990–94 and the red-green government from 1991–98 once again in the state of Hesse. We then turn to our analytical framework of party goals in order to analyse the evolution of the Greens from a party of opposition to a party of government. Our framework takes as its point of departure a view of the Greens as originally a radical (new) left, anti-political-establishment party whose primary party goals at the national level in the 1980s were limited to vote maximisation and policy-seeking.[3] In some states (such as Hesse), however, office-seeking goals came to the fore in the mid-1980s, a situation that contributed to a significant amount of tension within the Greens as a whole. In 1990–91, in the wake of the disastrous 1990 federal election, the Greens moved away from their anti-establishment identity by altering policy positions, reorganising internally and, in general, muting their previous pure politics of opposition. The transformation of the Greens had various causes and various effects which we will briefly explore. In the next section, we attempt to understand the specific conditions under which red-green coalitions have come about, and what factors make these coalitions shape their success or failure. Here we draw on Charles Lees work on 'red-green models' of coalition government.[4] Finally, we offer some observations on the similarities and differences between the development of *Politik-* and *Koalitionsfähigkeit* for the Greens and for the Left Party. This last section is, of course, preliminary: it will serve as an introduction to the empirical examination of the Left Party at the state level in either coalitions with the SPD or in opposition in the following chapters.

Red-green co-operation at the state level, 1977–98

The history of the German Greens is well known. The Green Party emerged from diverse strands of the peace, anti-nuclear and women's movement during the late 1960s and early 1970s. At first, the Greens were a very broad church combining left-wing activists from a 'post-APO world' (the young leftist 'extra parliamentary opposition') with disillusioned 'value-conservatives' from the CDU. There was also a smattering of extreme right-wing groups which tried early on to harness the nascent party for their own ends thrown in as well.[5] The extreme right groups were expelled before too much time had passed, while conservative ecologists left *en masse* after the founding party conventions in Karlsruhe and Saarbrücken in 1980.[6] Nevertheless, up until 1990, the Greens – while decidedly leftist – were very diverse in terms of both ideology and the political strategy they favoured. Media commentators generally divided the party into two broad camps based on ideology and strategy – the 'Realists' (*Realos*) and the 'Fundamentalists' (*Fundis*). The *Realos* were less ideologically dogmatic, more reform-orientated, and clearly favoured parliamentary over extra-parliamentary politics. For them, participating in government was not out of the question completely. The *Fundis* were farther to the left and gave priority to extra-parliamentary work. Indeed, for *Fundis* parliaments were simply stages for public 'consciousness-raising', and the idea of taking part in coalitions was very unpopular.[7] Although this broad typology did not correspond completely with the reality of the factions and ideological disputes within the Greens in the party's formative period, it certainly did capture the broad differences over the question of governmental participation.

While candidates from environmental and anti-nuclear groups ran for office and won representation in local elections as early as 1977, in 1979 a Green political group won representation at the *Land* level for the first time, in Bremen. After its founding party meetings, the newly formed Green Party contested the 1980 federal election. While it polled only 1.5 per cent, state elections in Baden-Württemburg in 1980 and in Berlin in 1981 gave the party representation in these states with 5.3 per cent and 7.2 per cent of the vote respectively. At this point, the Greens in these states were politically marginalised, considered uncoalitionable and merely one, relatively powerless, opposition party in states ruled by the CDU. In contrast, the years 1982–83 saw Green influence begin to rise as *Land* election results in Hamburg and Hesse made red-green coalitions at least mathematically possible.[8] Still implausible in practice, but theoretically viable.

By the time of the first red-green coalition at the federal level, there had been a number of red-green coalitions in the *Länder*: Hamburg (1997–2001), Hesse (1985–87, 1991–99), Berlin (1989–90), Lower Saxony (1990–94), North Rhine-Westphalia (1995–2003) and Schleswig-Holstein (1996–2004). In addition, there had been 'traffic light' coalitions of the SPD, Greens and FDP (in Bremen from 1991–95 and in Brandenburg from 1990–94), Green toleration models (i.e. the Greens reaching co-operation agreements with the SPD, in Hamburg in 1982 and in Hesse from 1983–85) and a red-green minority government with toleration by the Left Party (Saxony-Anhalt from 1994–98).

The Hamburg state election in June of 1982 provided the first theoretical possibility for red-green co-operation to take place.[9] In the wake of an impressive result for the Green Party there (called in Hamburg the 'Green Alternative List', or GAL) and the failure of either of the two big parties to achieve an absolute majority, the only feasible alternative to a Grand Coalition would be some kind of arrangement between the SPD and GAL. After GAL helped to defeat a no confidence motion in the SPD government, the Social Democrats invited GAL into formal negotiations. For its part, GAL offered a 'co-operation' agreement, by which it meant neither a coalition nor a (more) formal toleration model, but rather issue-by-issue conditional support of an SPD-minority government in return for an emergency programme against unemployment, an annulment of all budget austerity measures, and an immediate exit from nuclear energy. Despite several provocative media 'events' staged by GAL – the participation by high-ranking GAL representatives in house-squatting actions and GAL's proposal to declare Hamburg a 'nuclear-free zone' being just two of them – SPD leader Klaus von Dohnanyi, with support from his party's left wing, nonetheless continued to seek agreement with GAL. But the parties' impasse over atomic energy as well as an SPD plan to extend Hamburg's harbour doomed his efforts and von Dohnanyi subsequently called new elections. The result of this poll was that the SPD garnered enough votes to govern alone. The first tentative attempt at red-green co-operation therefore failed before it had even really begun.

Seeing itself as the defender of the left wing of the Greens against the *Realos*, the leadership of GAL continued to see co-operation with the SPD as a betrayal of its principles and aggressively pursued a vote-maximisation strategy. Initially, this proved successful. However, in the 1987 state election GAL suffered a considerable setback, its vote share dropping to 7 per cent. Sensing an opportunity, the *Realo* faction within GAL began a long struggle with the left wing of the party, making the argument that GAL's refusal to reach a *modus vivendi* with the SPD was hurting it electorally. The immediate result of this was an intense power struggle within GAL from 1987–90, a situation that led to a decidedly absurd splitting of the party into five separate party organisations. By late 1991, however, leftists and fundamentalists within GAL had departed in droves and the moderate/realist wing of the party had triumphed and merged (almost) all of the factions back into GAL. GAL became just another 'regular' state unit of the Greens, with a moderate left tilt, which pursued office-seeking aims.

In contrast to the situation in Hamburg in the 1980s, red-green co-operation in Hesse enjoyed a more sustained existence, providing the first instance of a fully fledged red-green coalition. Elections in September 1982 left both parties in a similar situation to those in Hamburg, with a strong showing by the Greens yielding a mathematical majority for red-green. Declaring that the Greens included 'a lot of thoughtful young people', Hesse SPD leader and later leader of the Friedrich-Ebert Foundation Holger Börner – someone who had earlier sworn to 'take care of' Greens with a *Dachlatte* (lath) – offered to co-operate with the new party.

The co-operation/toleration agreement between the two parties functioned without incident until the autumn of that year when a dispute over the licensing of two nuclear projects (NUKEM and ALKEM) began to poison the climate between the two parties. Proponents of red-green co-operation within both the Greens and SPD argued that the only way that such co-operation could continue would be if *Realos* could have something tangible to show for their efforts in compromising on such controversial issues – namely a formal coalition agreement. In May 1985, Börner finally offered such an agreement, and at a party conference the Greens affirmed the coalition experiment with some 80 per cent of the delegates present approving the document.[10]

The relatively brief red-green coalition government had some notable policy successes, including new legislation that forced chemical companies (in particular, Hoechst AG) to install new technology in order to meet lower permitted limits of industrial waste discharge into the Main River. However, the SPD grew frustrated by the Greens' often contradictory desire to take government responsibility while still trying to preserve the image of an opposition or 'anti-establishment' party. The coalition's collapse in 1987 came quickly in the wake of the Chernobyl disaster in 1986 as well as pressure from Green fundamentalists in national leadership positions to leave the coalition, *Flügelkämpfe* within the national and state Green organisations that limited effective policy-making[11] and a decision by the SPD to issue an operating permit for the aforementioned nuclear facilities. At a Hesse Green Party conference in February 1987, fundamentalists managed to push through a motion stating that continuing in the coalition government would be contingent upon a retraction of the nuclear plants' permits. In response, Börner fired Fischer, dissolved the coalition and, for good measure, then retired from political life shortly thereafter. Despite its ignominious end, however, the red-green coalition in Hesse was nevertheless taboo breaking, if only for the simple reason that the Greens had made the jump from a pure opposition party to one that was prepared to actually enter government.

Not even a 'co-operation' or toleration model of government (let alone a formal coalition) looked likely in Berlin in the 1980s. This was not only because of the weakness of the SPD vis-à-vis the CDU, but also because of the perception that the Berlin 'Alternative List' (AL) was dominated by fundamentalists.[12] For its part, the SPD and its mayoral candidate, Walter Momper, rejected the idea of a red-green coalition, arguing that the Greens were not competent to govern (*regierungsunfähig*). Yet this situation changed dramatically after the 1989 *Land* election. The SPD increased its share of the vote dramatically (up 9.3 per cent from the previous poll) while the CDU's preferred coalition partner, the FDP, failed to clear the 5 per cent hurdle. Meanwhile, the AL won 11.8 per cent of the vote, giving it 17 seats in the new parliament. Just as importantly, coalition arithmetic was thrown into further confusion by the election of the far-right Republicans (REP) who secured 11 seats in parliament. The CDU's post-election strategy was one designed to publicly hem in the SPD by comparing co-operation with the AL to co-operation with the REPs, thus leaving – in the CDU's mind – the SPD no option but a Grand Coalition. The Social Democrats were in many ways ideologically closer to the CDU than they were the AL, but the SPD and AL did share a number of common concerns, from welfare policy and social provisions to issues of women's rights and law-and-order/policing issues. Thus the SPD had options.[13]

After the SPD's negotiations with the CDU collapsed, the Social Democrats opened formal negotiations with the AL. Just as in Hesse, the AL was unprepared for governing, yet tempted by the possibility.[14] That power was thrust upon the AL nonetheless gave the resulting coalition something of a desperate feel to it that undoubtedly damaged its long-term prospects.[15] At the end of coalition negotiations, the two parties agreed that AL should receive a women's issues post – which included a large number of other portfolios attached to it. Yet, the new coalition in Berlin found itself in an uncomfortable position almost immediately. In early March 1989, groups of *Autonomen* (autonomous groups) took over a number of buildings in Berlin, daring the AL and SPD to act against them. Because the AL had enjoyed a good relationship with *Autonomen* – both could be seen as having their origins in a similar 'alternative' milieu – it was reluctant to move against them. But the AL finally relented after coming under pressure from SPD Interior Minister Erich Pätzold and agreed to the police moving in to clear the squatters.

Other conflicts between the two parties emerged: regarding an agreement to supply the local city-owned power company, BEWAG, with power from 'Preussen Elektra' in the GDR; the question of how to handle a strike by workers at the city's day care centres (KITAs) and the sale to Daimler-Benz of some 61,000 square metres of real estate on the edge of Potsdamer Platz. The strike by the city's day workers damaged the AL because KITA workers had earlier been important supporters of the party and the AL lost one of its key parliamentary leaders, Heidi Bischoff-Pflanz, who resigned in disgust at the handling of this dispute. In the wake of all of these crises the coalition quickly ran into further serious trouble. A dispute over a funding project for a reactor that had been initiated under the previous government and yet more rancour with squatters saw, in autumn 1990, the AL finally throw in the towel. They tabled a vote of no confidence in Mayor Walter Momper shortly before the first all-German election in December 1990. The AL thus effectively dissolved an increasingly fractious coalition experiment in the city, with Momper declaring in disgust that red-green was a 'failed model'.

While the Greens had been in almost constant conflict with the SPD in Berlin, in Lower Saxony the two parties put a coalition government in place in the summer of 1990 that would last for a full legislative term and would serve (at least to some extent) as a model for the later federal red-green coalition. Although the SPD in Lower Saxony was initially relatively suspicious of the Greens, in the run up to the 1990 state election it refused to rule out the possibility of co-operation with them. It certainly helped here that the Greens in Lower Saxony had a much more heterogeneous social base than the AL in Berlin, and they were generally regarded as being much more pragmatic.[16] Unlike the AL in Berlin, the Lower Saxony Greens viewed a possible coalition with the SPD not merely as the only way to end the long run of power by the conservatives but as an historical opportunity to prove that the Greens could be a reliable, stable coalition partner.

Unlike in Hamburg in 1982, Hesse in 1983 and Berlin in 1989, the Lower Saxon SPD had *three* coalition alternatives from which to choose: Grand Coalition, red-green or red-yellow, given that the FDP had managed to secure a respectable 6 per cent of the vote. However, during the campaign state FDP leader Hildebrandt had ruled out a coalition with the SPD, and he reaffirmed this position after the election. The SPD was left with a by-now familiar choice of red-green or red-black. The CDU and Greens were the big losers in the 1990 election, with the former down 2.2 per cent against the previous election, and the latter down 1.6 per cent. The SPD, on the other hand, had done very well, registering 44.2 per cent of the vote. It was this position of strength that undoubtedly helped the SPD in coalition negotiations. The Greens' desire for the Environmental Ministry was, for example, rebuffed by the SPD and the Greens ultimately had to settle for just two cabinet posts in the new government (the Women's Ministry and a Ministry for Federal and European Affairs headed by Jürgen Trittin, future Environmental Minister in the federal government).[17]

The new government enjoyed a relatively long honeymoon, with opinion polls in October 1990 giving the coalition a 46 per cent approval rating.[18] But trouble soon developed on account of several disagreements over economic and transport questions (both of which had been skirted around during the coalition negotiations) as well as the disastrous state of the *Land's* budget.[19] Much as was the case for SPD-Left Party governments in Mecklenburg-Western Pomerania in 1998 and particularly Berlin in 2001, the red-green government in Lower Saxony found itself confronted with a substantial budget deficit and therefore had to initiate a broad programme of spending cuts. Budget constraints severely limited the ability of the new government to initiate new programmes and, unsurprisingly, the Greens' client groups were not slow in voicing their disquiet. One of the hardest hit areas was education. Although the coalition agreement had committed the parties to increased state spending on education, including the creation of 600 new teaching posts, the new government did not believe it was in a position to fulfil this pledge. Teachers were infuriated. Thus the Greens in government found themselves once again squeezed between the demands of their coalition partner and the demands of their client groups.

Along with a dispute over a trade exposition (Expo 2000), three environmental issues – the first regarding a poisonous waste incinerator, the second involving the laying of a gas pipeline through a wetlands area and the third a refusal by the SPD to shut down a nuclear power station – led to friction between the coalition partners and to friction within the Greens themselves. Going into the election of 1994 each party had thus grown increasingly irritated with the other. While the Greens did better in the election than many had predicated, receiving 7.4 per cent of the vote (an increase from 1990), the SPD performed exceptionally well gaining 44.3 per cent of the vote and 80 seats, enough to secure it a slim one-seat majority in the legislature. It could therefore govern without the Greens. Perhaps surprisingly, while the enthusiasm for the coalition in Lower Saxony had dampened on both sides, and while the learning curve for the Greens in moving from an opposition party to a party of government had been high, government participation had clearly been beneficial to the party. One analyst even dubbed the Greens' experience there as a 'professionalisation through regime participation'.[20] Moreover, Gerhard Schröder continued to view red-green as a possible and desirable option for the future – this was certainly not the 'failed model' that Momper had talked of in Berlin.

In contrast to Lower Saxony red-green returned to office in Hesse in 1991 and was re-elected for a second term in 1995. By 1991, the Greens had undergone a remarkable transformation. Already dominated by the *Realo* faction, the Hesse Greens were emboldened by the Greens' poor result in the 1990 federal election. *Realos* within the Hesse party made the argument that the problem with the coalition in Hesse from 1985–87 was not the existence of the coalition itself, but rather the Greens' political immaturity. The SPD agreed. Asked why the chances for a successful red-green coalition in Hesse in 1991 were better than those of the previous red-green coalition, Hans Eichel, the SPD's Minister-President designate, stated that 'both sides have learnt a lot in the meantime'.[21] In particular, Eichel argued that while the SPD had realised that economic growth and environmental protection were not incompatible, the Greens had learned that certain policies (here nuclear power) were the prerogative of the federal government, not the state government, and that therefore policy 'wishes' could not simply be written into a coalition agreement without real authority to affect those policies. Moreover, by the time of the election, almost the entire leadership of the Hesse Greens from 1987 had been replaced. Although this left the party with few leaders with governing experience (save for Joschka Fischer), it did enable the party to speak clearly with one voice, rather than the more fractious situation of 1987.[22] In the event, the SPD and Greens found ample points of policy agreement, and the final coalition agreement promised 'predictable politics' rather than the 'alliance characterised by conflict' of the 1980s.[23]

The SPD–Greens government in Hesse was the first red-green coalition to be re-elected. In comparison with the previous red-green coalition, it was unmistakably more professional and much less conflict-ridden than its previous incarnation. This is not to say, however, that red-green from 1991–99 was without its problems.[24] First, there was the inevitable disappointment of the party's voters over the extent to which the Greens could substantially 'change politics'. Second, Fischer's decision to serve in the *Bundestag* left the Hesse Greens without the services of a talented strategist and media-friendly face. Third, the Greens had received one of their desired ministries (Environment) as well as a 'classic' ministry (Justice). But this came with a price: the Environmental Ministry was combined into a 'Super Ministry' that encompassed not only environmental affairs, but youth, family, health and energy. This super ministry was extremely difficult to administer and the lines of authority between it and lower administrative units (most often headed by SPD appointees) were often unclear. Fourth, while Rudolf von Plottnitz of the Greens was made justice minister, the SPD retained the Interior Ministry, setting up conflicts with the Greens over the policy agenda. Moreover, von Plottnitz was accused of being a purely 'reactive' minister rather than one who took the initiative and directed policies that would satisfy Green voters and activists. Finally, a political scandal involving Fischer's successor at the Environmental Ministry, Iris Blaul, and a dubious appointment that she made deflated the party and turned away some of its voters. This was the first such scandal involving a Green minister in any state government.

On balance, however, the second red-green coalition was indeed more dependable – and the relationship between the coalition partners more harmonious – than was the case first time round. Despite its share of disappointments, many Greens (and many in the SPD, too, for that matter) had got used to the idea of red-green and had more confidence in the model working; perhaps not just at the *Land* level but also in the federal arena too.

Understanding the political development of the Greens

What common threads emerge after this outline of the Greens' development of *Politik-* and *Koalitionsfähigkeit* in the *Länder* and how might this help us to understand the experiences of the Left Party in both the opposition and in government? Initially, the dominant view within the Greens (articulated by Petra Kelly, among others) was that the Greens were an 'anti-system' party or an 'anti-party' party.[25] In their early years, inner-party struggle within the Greens over the understanding of this 'anti-party' role largely centred on participating in coalition governments; proponents argued that '… participation in government would at best change very little; at worst, it might merely serve to legitimise the continuation of the Old Politics of growth, militarism, exploitation of the third world and pollution'.[26] This stubborn, rejectionist stance clearly weakened over time.

As we have seen, as early as 1984, in Hesse some within the Greens had begun to seriously challenge this view. These changes nonetheless happened slowly and varied in scope and speed across the Greens' various *Land* organisations. Bitter battles within the national leadership also took place and, even at the end of the 1980s, the consensus position still remained one of having 'one leg in parliament and another outside in the extra-parliamentary protest movement'.[27] In other words, vote maximising and policy-seeking party goals were clearly more important than office-seeking.

However, by 1990–91 these positions were changing again. In looking at the history of red-green coalitions at the state level then, one could broadly talk of two phases, the first dating from 1980–90 and the second from 1990–present. The dating of these two phases is not arbitrary: although the 'normalisation' of red-green coalition governments was underway by 1990 (illustrated by the second red-green coalition at the state level, in Berlin), unification and electoral disaster for the Greens brought profound changes within the party – and thus to attitudes to red-green coalitions. Among other things, losing their national parliamentary presence in western Germany[28] precipitated a final showdown between the realist and fundamentalist wings of the party, which had as one of its consequences the departure of the last of the *Fundis* in early 1991. Furthermore, at the Neumünster party conference in 1991 the Greens jettisoned many of the 'anti-party' organisational features that characterised their early years by eliminating term limits for party leaders, streamlining the federal executive committee, and creating a new *Länderrat* to help coordinate the party at the state level.[29] Moreover, in terms of policies the Greens moved significantly to the political centre, significantly modifying many of their previous positions. As Paul Tiefenbach has shown, the Greens' positions on nuclear energy, the party's relationship to the military and NATO and the relationship between economic growth and the environment appear to have changed significantly since the party's founding.[30] Thus, gradually through the 1990s, the Greens evolved into a party whose primary goals also now included office-seeking ones, dropping almost all of their early anti-establishment rhetoric and reforming so that its internal structure did not differ significantly from those of the CDU, SPD or FDP.

Why the Greens set off down this road can be explained by looking at the literature on party change. As discussed in Chapter 3, party change can be traced to a number of endogenous and exogenous factors, including external shocks (such as election disappointments). Furthermore, a strong link exists between a party's primary goals, on the one hand, and the specific organisational and leadership tasks required to achieve these goals, on the other.[31] A party that is unable, or unwilling, to adjust its organisational structure to meet shifting primary goals (say, from vote maximisation to office-seeking) will face extreme difficulties. The internal organisation of the Greens in the 1980s consciously attempted to replicate their 'anti-party' image. The Greens' policies of rotation and separation of party and state offices, for example, was meant to illustrate their notion of *Basisdemokratie*, something that they believed set them apart from all other parties.

As discussed above, the most significant of external shocks for the Greens was the 1990 federal election. Its result was the departure of the last of the high-profile *Fundis* and a resulting shift towards the political centre. The election also prompted the Greens to successfully undertake the aforementioned organisational reforms that 'professionalised' the party, making it more fit to govern. Meanwhile at the *Land* level, both electoral failure and unsatisfying coalition experiences prompted the Greens into undertaking significant organisational and ideological change. In Hesse in the 1980s and Berlin in 1989–90 elections brought the Greens into government. Yet the party organisations in these states (most especially Berlin) were not prepared to assume power: their organisations were not particularly professionalised, they had no experience in directing ministries (and met resistance within these ministries from SPD bureaucrats), they continued to be paralysed by inner-party conflict over the very question of governmental participation, and they found no viable ways to manage or contain conflict with their coalition partners. After these coalitions had come to an end, however, supporters of governmental participation were able to eventually convince the party base that the negative experiences in red-green coalitions were not the result *of participation itself* but rather the Greens' ill-preparedness. In order to better serve their interests, *Realos* argued, organisational and ideological change simply had to be undertaken.

The emergence of a 'red-green' model of government

Even though shifts in Green Party goals were undoubtedly occurring, red-green coalitions were certainly anything other than automatic at the state level after 1990. Moreover, less-than-successful red-green coalitions in the 1980s did not presage the more successful coalitions in the 1990s that, in turn, became models for the post-1998 federal government. What conditions, then, have had to be in place in order for red-green coalitions to both come about *and* be successful? Answering this question will offer us some clear indicators of what sort of processes the Left Party is likely to have to undergo if (and it still is an 'if') the party wants to be taken seriously as a party of government.

In his book *The Red-Green Coalition in Germany*, Charles Lees developed a model of red-green co-operation by analysing the literature on coalition-building that we touched on in Chapter 3 of this book. He supplemented these points pulled from the concrete experiences of red-green at the state level in the 1980s and 1990s.[32] As far as coalition formation goes, Lees suggests that for the Greens to enter into coalitions with the SPD, at least one of three conditions has to be met. First, the ideological range and selected policy domains between the SPD and Greens has to be less than the distance between the SPD and other possible partners. With regard to red-green government, the SPD has always had the option of emphasising its more 'materialist' policies, which would make coalitions with the CDU or FDP attractive, or its more 'post-materialist' face, which would permit a coalition with the Greens. Thus the SPD often occupies the 'median' position in the party spectrum, allowing it to form coalitions in either direction. Second, Lees argues, for the Greens to enter government the SPD has to calculate that its office-seeking payoff (both quantitatively and qualitatively) within a red-green coalition would be greater than its payoff in any other kind of coalition. Third, even if neither of these two conditions is met satisfactorily, red-green is still a possibility if other possible partners of the SPD either refuse outright to enter a coalition government with the SPD or make the price of their participation too high for the SPD to bear.

Furthermore, Lees argues that the formation and successful maintenance of red-green coalitions is conditioned by three factors. First, the ability to form a coalition and to have that coalition be successful (defined, at the minimum, as the willingness of each party to continue the coalition for another term of office) is conditioned by the degree of intra-party conflict within the SPD and Greens concerning the desirability of the red-green option. Second, Lees argues that the degree of inter-party conflict also conditions the formation and successful maintenance of red-green coalitions.[33] Third, Lees suggests that it has been crucial for the Greens' perception of the 'success' of any particular red-green coalition that their policy goals have been effectively translated into effective policy for their client groups. Finally, Lees suggests that the maintenance of red-green governments has depended upon the successful resolution of three sets of issues. The first concerns the ideological positions and policy goals of the two parties. As noted above, a precondition of red-green is the SPD's decision to emphasise its post-materialist, rather than materialist, dimension. However, red-green success also depends upon the Greens playing down issue areas potentially disruptive of a coalition, such as defence/foreign affairs, the state's monopoly on violence and economic growth/consumer capitalism projects. The second set of issues needing resolution for successful red-green co-operation concerns the division of cabinet seats and portfolios in coalition government. While the SPD's goals here have been consistently focused on both maintaining numerical dominance and retaining the powerful Ministries of Finance, Economics, and Labour, the Greens have deemed the Environmental Ministry to be their most important cabinet position. They have also wanted to acquire another valued ministry (such as Justice), have shown a high degree of interest in a ministry dealing with women and have wanted to avoid a dilution of their goals and power through the creation of 'super ministries'.[34] The third set of issues concern the staffing and structure of the civil service. Here Lees argues that while the SPD has been consistently 'expertise rich', and thus willing and able to staff the ministries and translate goals into concrete policy effectively, the Greens in contrast were 'expertise-poor' 'with very few in-house resources to call upon when taking over a ministry and precious little experience within the party networks'.[35]

Although Lees's model of red-green co-operation has three different components (with three sub-components for each of these), at base it reflects two of the three different aspects of coalition theory – coalition formation and coalition maintenance – discussed above. In essence, this means that we have two 'models' of red-green co-operation, the first of which outlines the factors essential to the successful *formation* of red-green governments, the second which outlines the factors essential to the successful *maintenance* of red-green. With regard to the former, Lees's model includes five factors – ideological distance/policy divergence, office-seeking payoff for the SPD, the SPD's relationship with possible coalition partners other than the Greens, inter-party conflict within the SPD and Greens, and intra-party conflict between the two parties. In terms of coalition maintenance, Lees's model includes policy divergence between the two parties, cabinet satisfaction for both parties, effective policy making for the Greens' client groups, effective staffing of the civil service for the Greens, inter-party conflict within the SPD and Greens and finally intra-party conflict between the two parties (both of these last two factors, it should be noted, can hamper substantive policy-making as well as public image of the coalition).

As we note below, Lees's model of red-green co-operation can, at least in theory, be adapted to red-red coalitions as well. Be that as it may, Lees provides a solid framework for understanding the nature and evolution of red-green coalitions, as well as the conditions under which the Greens have been able to successfully navigate their way from an anti-establishment, 'opposition' party to a responsible party of government. For example, Lees argues that the successful maintenance of red-green depends upon cabinet satisfaction for both the SPD and Greens, with the latter focusing on obtaining the Environmental Ministry, another high-value ministry, the women's issues portfolio and an avoidance of cumbersome 'super ministries'. The first goal (obtaining the Environmental Ministry) was not met in Berlin in 1989–90 nor in Lower Saxony from 1990–94 – thus contributing to tensions and some problems between the coalition partners. Meanwhile the third and fourth goals (a Ministry for Women and an avoidance of 'super ministries') were not met in the second Hesse coalition, a situation which some observers believe led to paralysis within the party and a subsequent loss of confidence among the Greens in Hesse.

Comparing the experiences of the Greens and Left Party: Some initial observations

The evolution of the Left Party's capacity for *Politik-* and *Koalitionsfähigkeit* shows some remarkable similarities to that of the Greens, even if their paths are not precisely parallel. To us, there appear to be four clear lessons that can be learnt from the SPD/Greens' experience. First and most generally, a clear chronological pattern emerges in looking at the Greens' development from an oppositional party with non-office-seeking goals to a more established one which also pursued pronounced office-seeking goals. At first, the Greens were a self-styled 'anti-party'. Regime participation opponents defined this anti-party role as one which completely eschewed coalitions with the SPD. However, as the Social Democrats softened their line towards the Greens in the mid-1980s, proponents of governmental participation within the Greens gained strength, thus paving the way for early co-operation/toleration agreements with the Social Democrats.[36] This first phase of red-green co-operation was all about the triumph of the realists, a triumph which ended with formal coalition governments at the state level. However, proponents of governmental participation in both parties were soon on the defensive due to the inevitable disillusionment of the rank and file of the party with the coalition's outcomes. Proponents of coalitions within the Greens were often accused of sacrificing not merely ideology, but concrete policy, on the altar of government participation.[37] Yet the return of a 'fundamental opposition' was limited, to be dealt a fatal blow by the election shock of 1990. Indeed, in many respects the very process of participation itself seemed to take the wind out of the more dogmatic opponents and extreme left-wing elements within the Greens. Eventually opposition to governmental participation was limited to criticising the manner, timing and concrete policies of participation, rather than the issue of participation itself.

While the decision to refuse government participation was initially made for the Left Party (i.e. no other party countenanced any co-operation, formal or informal, with the Left Party until 1994), leading figures within the party (as with the Greens) in some states were nonetheless looking at the possibilities of toleration and/or coalition as early as the mid-1990s. Not long after, the Left Party reached a 'toleration' agreement with the SPD and Greens in Saxony-Anhalt, and then in 1998, a coalition government with the SPD in 1998 in Mecklenburg-Western Pomerania. However, proponents of regime participation were soon on the defensive, both in Mecklenburg-Western Pomerania (and, later, in Berlin) and in other state organisations, such as Saxony. The backlash against government participation reached something of a crescendo in the initial weeks following the 2002 election. Yet as with the Greens, governmental participation eventually came to take the wind out of the sails of some of the strongest opponents of this participation. In Saxony, for example, the state party organisation, under the leadership of Peter Porsch, retreated from its position of fundamental opposition by late 2002. The Saxon branch of the Left Party has eventually come to believe that the question for the *Land* party was not whether or not it should participate in government but how and under what circumstances it should look to govern.[38] This is not to say, however, that the issue of governmental participation has been settled in some definitive way for the Left Party. Indeed, the creation of the Left Party will ensure that, for some, the question will remain as salient as ever (see Chapter 8). Thus, despite a significant evolution in this direction, the new Left Party is not quite in the same position that the Greens were in 1991; there is a consensus in favour of governing where possible, but the creation of the Left Party means that it is not as wide or deep as it might be.

Second, neither the Greens (especially during the 1980s) nor the Left Party today are monolithic party organisations. Any characterisation of the Greens or the Left Party as primarily pursuing a particular set of primary party goals must take account of both the parties' dominant national strategy and strategies at the state level. Needless to say, considerable heterogeneity exists both horizontally (between state organisations) and vertically (between the national centre and the states), something which proved problematic for the Greens of the 1980s and for the Left Party today. Vertically, the diversity of the Greens in the 1980s is illustrated by the fact that at the national level the party had exclusively vote maximising and policy-seeking party goals, while at the state level different state party organisations could be characterised by more office-seeking goals (Hesse) or vote-seeking and office-seeking aims (Hamburg). Moreover, this diversity is further illustrated by the fact that in states where red-green became mathematically possible, SPD-Green toleration or formal coalition governments did not always come to fruition or, if they did, had various degrees of intra-party and inner-party conflict during their tenure that helped determine, *pace* Lees, the length of a coalition's time in office and its relative success. Similarly, we will see in the following chapters that the Left Party has considerable diversity at the state level as well as a divergence between the primary party goal pursued at the national level (clearly opposition politics) versus the goals pursued in different states (sometimes vote maximisation, sometimes office-seeking, sometimes policy-seeking). *Despite* the similar trajectories between the two parties, however, there is clearly one major difference: while the Greens have evolved into a more centrally directed party (with a resulting loss of heterogeneity at the state level), the Left Party has not (yet) centralised to this degree. This is undoubtedly due to continued factional struggles within the party. In this respect, the Left Party today has strong similarities to the Greens of the late 1980s and retains a great deal of heterogeneity between *Länder* party organisations.

One reason for this is the effect of external shocks upon each party. The third interesting point to note here, then, is the nature of these shocks as well as the lessons that each party has drawn from them. As we have seen, the biggest external shock for the Greens was the 1990 federal election. This precipitated a final showdown between the realist and fundamentalist wings of the party which had as one of its consequences the departure of the last of the *Fundis* in early 1991. As a result, the Greens moved significantly to the political centre after 1990–91, transforming their positions on, among other things, nuclear energy, the German military and NATO, and the party's position towards economic growth. Just as significantly, the Greens jettisoned many of their 'anti-party' organisational features. In contrast, the biggest external shock for the Left Party was its failure to gain full representation in the *Bundestag* in the 2002 federal election. Yet there was no real 'Neumünster' for the Left Party after this setback. There was no comprehensive reorganisation of the party apparatus, no dramatic changes in policies, and no mass exodus of the extreme left wing of the party. The lesson the Left Party drew from its poor electoral performance appears to be that the party must intensify the expansion of its electoral base, a strategy that has been in place, more or less, since the mid-1990s. In other words, unlike the Greens post-Neumünster it is not office-seeking goals that drive the Left Party at the national level but rather vote maximisation.

Finally, within coalition government both the Greens and Left Party have found themselves in decidedly inferior power relationships. This has to do with these parties' limited strategic coalition options. Thus, while the SPD, as the 'median' party in most coalition calculations, has coalition options – it can make coalitions with more or less anybody – neither the Left Party nor the Greens has up to this point had any other options besides the SPD. Why does the SPD sometimes choose the Left Party, and sometimes not? In the previous chapter we speculated as to the factors conditioning a 'red-red' model of government and offered some preliminary hypotheses: where 'red-red' coalitions have emerged, they have done so when other potential coalition partners are unavailable and/or unacceptable; where the SPD thinks it can maximise its office-seeking payoff through a coalition with the Left Party; where the ideological range between SPD and the Left Party is relatively narrow and where the party organisations of each party are not bitterly divided or hostile to each other. We will return to the question of a 'red-red' model of government in the following chapters, detailing and analysing these conditions more closely. Of course, it would still be precipitate to speak of a 'red-red' model of government as having relevance at the national level: the Left Party is in no position at the present time to build on state level formal coalitions in order to enter government at the national level. In this respect as well, the Left Party today resembles much more the Greens of the late 1980s than the Greens in 2007.

5
The Left Party in Mecklenburg-Western Pomerania

Introduction

If the Left Party was indeed to set out on its own long march through the institutions, much as the Greens had done a decade ago, then base camp was always likely to be in the flatlands of northern Germany, in Mecklenburg-Western Pomerania. To Left Party watchers in the late 1990s it was therefore not a particularly great surprise that the first ever red-red coalition came into being in 1998 in the otherwise innocuous city of Schwerin. Even if the 'successes' and 'failures' of the coalition remain contested, the Left Party's eight-year tenure in government (it left following the September 2006 *Landtagswahl*) undoubtedly taught *Die Linke* politicians some invaluable lessons about the challenges and pitfalls of actually shaping political outcomes. This chapter therefore analyses what effect the Left Party's first experience in *Land* govern-ments has had on both *Die Linke* in Mecklenburg-Western Pomerania and the party as a whole. More specifically, is there evidence of a de-radicalising effect on the Left Party's programmatic agenda? Has the Left Party successfully maintained its anti-political establishment stance and avoided the institutionalisation processes that have characterised Green Party development? If the party has undergone a process of change, what specific factors have been driving it and what evidence do we have of a 'normalisation' of the Left Party? The Left Party in Mecklenburg-Western Pomerania concentrates on developing and implementing specific policies that might help to solve the (many) socio-economic problems that exist in one of Germany's poorest states. This is in (at times sharp) contrast to the Left Party in other eastern German states, where policy-seeking goals play a much less obvious role and office-seeking/vote max-imisation remain more significant.

We structure the next three chapters in the following way. We begin by analysing inner-party relations within the individual *Land* parties since 1990. We argue that processes of leadership change, adaptation to political and strategic challenges and interaction with the rank and file can have fundamental effects on a party's aims, strategies and policies. The changes that have taken place in relationships both between Left Party politicians in each state branch and also between politicians across the various levels are highly significant for two reasons; firstly, they help explain why the Left Party has adopted particular goals and campaigned in particular ways in individual states and, secondly, they offer important pointers in explaining why the federal party struggled to make any impact on German politics post-2002. They also offer strong indicators of where the new Left Party is likely to seek to go in future years. Secondly, we look at the programmes and policies of the different *Landesverbände* with the aim of assessing how government participation has changed (or not changed, as the case may be) the behaviour of both the *Landesverbände* themselves and the federal party. This will offer some indication of how the demands of government participation are affecting the party's programmatic agenda and strategic aims. We then conclude each of the chapters by analysing what the Left Party's behaviour in each particular state/group of states can tell us about the hypotheses that we introduced at the end of Chapter 3.

Of people and personalities: Inner-party relations within the Left Party

Inner-party relations within the Left Party in Mecklenburg-Western Pomerania have been shaped by three particular *Land*-specific features. Firstly, both the state party leadership and the rank and file wish to develop specific policies that will help alleviate some of Mecklenburg-Western Pomerania's (many) socio-economic problems.[1] While every *Land* party in every *Land* is likely to claim such a thing, Mecklenburg-Western Pomerania's economic, geographical and social situation is clearly unique; Mecklenburg-Western Pomerania is rural and the majority of its economic indicators are worrying and this undoubtedly helps explain the more pragmatic approach of all the parties (but especially the Left Party) in that region. There is therefore a consensus that the party should pursue clear policy-orientated goals, and entering any coalition government with the SPD is only a worthwhile exercise if the Left Party is clearly and unambiguously able to change things in Mecklenburg-Western Pomerania for the better. The second characteristic of inner-party relations in

Mecklenburg-Western Pomerania fosters a much lower level of consensus than does the first; the *Basis* is keen to have its say, regularly articulating dissatisfaction with the behaviour of members of the parliamentary party as well as Left Party ministers (in the period 1998–2006). There has therefore always been a tension on the vertical level within the party and the longer the Left Party stayed in power in Schwerin, the more acute these tensions became. The third characteristic of the party became apparent from mid-2004 onwards when a significant number of Left Party MdL (normally a minority, but very occasionally a majority) became disillusioned with the work of the SPD–Left Party coalition and began to advocate a return to the opposition benches post-2006. For some, the dissatisfaction with their own government had deep (pre-2004) roots, but for most the policy failures of the second SPD–Left Party administration highlighted the inability of the Left Party to deliver on its programmatic agenda.

Despite varying levels of internal dissatisfaction with the leadership of the state branch over time, the pragmatic reformers around heavy-weight ministers Helmut Holter and Wolfgang Methling, current party leader Peter Ritter and leader of the parliamentary party Angelika Gramkow have controlled the direction of *Die Linke* in Germany's north-east for the last decade.[2] Wolfgang Leuchter, the leader of the Left Party in Rostock, also enjoys considerable behind-the-scenes influence on the party's affairs, while the Schwerin party branch has traditionally been the most politically significant.[3] The Mecklenburg-Western Pomerania state branch is nonetheless not particularly ideological and groups within the *Landesverband* tend to have relatively fluid member-ships depending on the issues at stake.[4] Despite the return to opposition in 2006, the pragmatists still remain at the forefront of affairs. One important reason for their historical dominance is the fact that there have traditionally only been three parties in the Schwerin parliament – the SPD, the CDU and the Left Party – and of them none have been dominant.[5] The Left Party was therefore tempted by the prospect of actually shaping policy earlier than was the case elsewhere. Co-operation with the SPD became a realistic possibility as early as 1994 when SPD mayors in many constituencies relied on Left Party help to remain in office after local elections.[6] Furthermore, Helmut Holter and SPD leader Harald Ringstorff enjoyed good personal relations and this led to informal talks between their parties about possible coalitions in both 1994 (after the *Landtagswahl* of that year) and in 1996 (after a crisis in the Grand Coalition between SPD and CDU). Few, if any, Left Party politicians expected either set of talks to lead to the Left Party taking up office, but the first moves had been made.[7] Indeed, on both occasions these talks came to nothing, largely as the SPD central office black-balled all attempts to bring the Left Party into the coalition equation – the Left Party nevertheless knew that, under the correct conditions, the opportunity to shape political outputs could come their way sooner rather than later.[8] Even though there was significant opposition within the Party Executive, the parliamentary party and the rank and file to Holter's apparent keenness to govern,[9] this carrot of governmental involvement nonetheless helped the pragmatists to maintain control of the party through the mid-1990s.[10]

Yet, as indicated above, the pragmatists within the Mecklenburg-Western Pomerania Left Party have not had everything their own way and a significant degree of internal discord has always been evident within the *Landesverband*. This is even truer when one compares the Left Party in Mecklenburg-Western Pomerania with the much more docile party in Berlin (see Chapter 6). The leadership is able neither to impose its own policy preferences on other members of the parliamentary party, nor is the rank and file prepared to sit back and let the leadership do more or less as it pleases (as frequently happens in Berlin). Many of long-time figurehead Helmut Holter's comments can also appear positively un-Left-Party-like in nature, further aggravating tensions. For example, Holter shocked many of his colleagues with his claim that Germany should review its decision to gradually close down its nuclear power industry[11], and observations that the Left Party should transform itself from a party looking to redistribute wealth to one that gives extra added value also raised eyebrows. He has subsequently had to put in a great deal of work in convincing, frequently in one-to-one discussions, members of the Left Party that the Social Democrats in Mecklenburg-Western Pomerania were a party with which the Left Party could do business.[12]

Although the parliamentary party traditionally supported (if sometime through clenched teeth) Holter in his attempt carry the party closer to the corridors of power, his relationship with other MdL (Member of a German *Land* Parliament) and the rank and file has not always been an easy one.[13] This was most apparent when Catherina Muth defeated him to become the party's *Spitzenkandidatin* for the *Land* election in 1998 on a ticket espousing a much more reticent attitude to government participation. Indeed, until that point Muth continued to talk of 'toleration' as being a much more attractive proposition for *Die Linke* than outright government.[14] Even Muth's successor[15], Angelika Gramkow, quickly found herself in disagreement with Holter – Gramkow tending to be much less conciliatory (as was the parliamentary party in general) with the Left Party's social democratic coalition partner than Holter wanted to be.[16] Significantly, Holter had to pass his leadership position more and more to Methling whose more consensual, integrative and wonkish leadership style did not cause as much resentment as Holter's.

Despite frequently vociferous objections by the rank and file to the behaviour of their elected representatives, the party leadership still only had to make cosmetic changes to policy on account of members' input. That they have even attempted to listen and act (even if only in a small way) on the sentiments of the membership is nevertheless something that differentiates them from most other Left Party state branches and certainly that of Berlin. Sometimes the inputs from the *Basis* have simply been awkward rather than genuinely problematic; at a party conference following the 1998 *Land* election, for example, delegates refused to grant the leadership independence in negotiating with the SPD over a proposed coalition. On the contrary, the party leadership had to make do with a vague communiqué that expressly stated that negotiations to enter any prospective coalitions had to be open and would not automatically lead to the creation of a red-red government.[17] Following subsequent agreement between the prospective coalition partners, a specially convened party conference supported the decision to enter government but nonetheless exercised its right to vote on the leadership team that Left Party MdLs had put forward for ministerial portfolios.[18] The same scenario was repeated in 2002 – although this time every single ministerial position was discussed and voted upon, something that made life particularly difficult for Holter who has never enjoyed a close relationship with the rank and file.[19] Again, these hurdles are not major hindrances, but they are evidence that the awkward squad can make life much more difficult for Left Party politicians in Mecklenburg-Western Pomerania than elsewhere. What can be said is that government participation has certainly not had a detrimental effect on inner-party democracy; on the contrary, there appears to be mounting evidence that the Left Party's *Streitkultur* is still flourishing.

The Left Party *Basis* has not just articulated its thoughts about the party's performance in government at party conferences. The rank and file have taken a critical interest in the success (or otherwise) of the coalition in achieving particular policy goals. As early as 2000 – so a mere 18 months after the election – the so-called *AG Bilanz* (a working group assessing the successes/failures of the Left Party in government) within the party published a largely positive report on the coalition's achievements thus far. The report also reminded the membership that they had a responsibility to critically assess their government's progress (something not called for so explicitly within the Berlin Left Party) and put it to the party leadership that ministers should give up party offices as and when they entered government.[20] Even though this last recommendation was not passed by the next party conference, it is noticeable that Holter was aware of the sensitivity of the issue and relinquished the leadership of the party by passing it on to Peter Ritter.[21] And, furthermore, it is distinctly plausible that without Ritter's skilful speech praising the work of the coalition, and his tactically astute linking of a vote of confidence in the government with the acceptance that the coalition should be extended beyond 2002, the rank and file may have demanded that the Left Party expressly seek *not* to extend its stay in government any further. As it was, Ritter nipped any such opposition in the bud.[22] Finally, in 2004, an 'extra-parliamentary party commission' also took a positive view of the work of the coalition and went so far as to recommend that the Left Party seek to extend the alliance with the Social Democrats until 2006 and possibly beyond.[23] The critical stance frequently taken up by the Left Party membership is even more surprising when one considers that the usual opponents of governmental participation – the restorative ideologues around the KPF and/or Marxist Forum – were (and are) next to non-existent in Mecklenburg-Western Pomerania. The KPF has never played a significant role in the Left Party in the north-east, with no more than a handful of members, so much so that it was actually dissolved in 2003 while the emancipatory left is also a non-existent force.[24]

There is little doubt that a significant number of Left Party *parliamentarians* in the Schwerin *Landtag* remain disappointed with the coalition's achievements. Some, such as the business manager of the parliamentary party Arnold Schoenenburg, saw government participation as an experiment that, by 2002, had clearly failed and so should be abandoned.[25] Others, estimated at around 20 per cent of the party, were so dismayed by the prevailing societal conditions within which the SPD–Left Party had to operate, that they also favoured leaving the coalition after the 2002 election.[26] By the time of the 2006 election levels of dissent within the parliamentary group had increased further and there was a split into two roughly equal groups, one of which remained sceptical about the Left Party's ability to get enough of its agenda onto the statute book and subsequently doubted the wisdom of remaining in government, while the other thought that despite the difficulties incurred in government the Left Party should seek to carry on shaping politics from the inside rather than from the opposition benches.

Displeasure with the Left Party's position in the coalition concentrated around the '*antikapitalistische Linke*' (anti-capitalist left) and became more prominent within the *Landesverband* from mid-2004, so much so that the SPD became much less enthusiastic about continuing the governmental alliance as polling day in 2006 approached. MdLs who sympathised with the aims of the anti-capitalist left were extremely unhappy with the compromises that had to be made with the Social Democrats and also with the loss of vision that they perceived the Left Party to be suffering as a result.[27] Yet this does not mean that the Left Party has written off government participation in Mecklenburg-Western Pomerania for good. At the time of the 2006 *Land* election a consensus still existed within the party that, if possible, the coalition with the SPD should be continued. The aims have been scaled down (see below), but the goal of improving the lot of citizens of the state is as clear as ever. Electoral support for political parties naturally ebbs and flows and there is certainly no reason to believe that the losses in real terms that *Die Linke* suffered in both 2002 and 2006 cannot be made good in 2010. The Left Party will have time to analyse its time in government, re-think its aims and programmatic ideals and re-assess its electoral strategy. And all of this without the threat of being forced out of the *Landtag* by institutional barriers (i.e. the 5 per cent clause in the electoral system), such as that which always hangs over the federal party.

Of policies and programmes: Local answers to local problems?

The most vociferous critics of the Left Party's performance in government in Mecklenburg-Western Pomerania are unanimous in chastising the party for not fulfilling the programmatic aims that it set itself in 1998. These sentiments have been most forcefully made by a group of left-wing academics around the former Greifswald Law Professor and former parliamentary aide in Schwerin, Edeltraut Felfe.[28] Felfe and colleagues are quick to point out that the Left Party has been unable to fulfil most of the promises that it has made both in its party programme and in the various manifestos that have been produced for elections to the Mecklenburg-Western Pomerania state parliament.[29] Felfe sees the prevailing 'neo-liberal hegemony' as a force that fundamentally constrains *Land* governments, and the Left Party should be well aware that much as it might try it is very difficult (although not necessarily impossible[30]) to hold back the forces of globalisation, capitalism and imperialism from within *Land* administrations.[31] Given that, theoretically at least, *Land* governments can mobilise against these forces Felfe claims that the performance of the Left Party in government should be measured against two specific sets of criteria:[32]

- Has the governing coalition been able to qualitatively improve the daily existences of the majority of citizens in the state?
- Has the SPD–Left Party government began to curtail Germany's (alleged) militarisation, to prevent welfare state cuts from taking place, to counteract (again alleged) increases in the acceptance of neo-fascist political thought and, finally, to break down the institutions of capitalism?

The second of these two points gives Felfe and co's game away. It is very hard to imagine a scenario where a *Land* government (of any colour) might be able to prevent German troops from being sent abroad if this is what the federal government decides to do. *Land* governments also have a constitutional obligation to carry out policies (such as the controversial Agenda 2010 reforms) that are passed in the federal arena and to claim that Left Party government participation is successful if it *refuses* to fulfil such an obligation is unfair at best and downright disingenuous at worst. *Land* governments certainly can try to educate citizens on the dangers of holding right-wing extremist political views, but it is completely impractical to expect quantifiable short-term successes in this area. Finally, breaking down the institutions of capitalism sounds like rhetoric from a Marx or Engels text, and with good reason, as many of the supporters of Felfe's dismissal of government participation hold political opinions that are not too far removed from such thinkers. While keen to stress that they do not wish to dismiss the idea of participating in *Land* governments on principle, other influential politicians on the left of the party such as Hans Modrow are very quick to point out that prevailing societal conditions should almost always deter the Left Party from actually taking up the reins of power.[33]

Another earlier study of the Left Party's performance in Mecklenburg-Western Pomerania, by the social scientists Frank Berg and Thomas Koch, is much more balanced in its initial analysis of the coalition's successes and failures, concentrating primarily on analysing the changes that have taken place in specific policy fields.[34] While claiming that government participation has clearly not brought about the much hoped-for radical changes of policy, Left Party government participation has also not been an unmitigated disaster. Berg and Koch argue that the party has gained valuable new experience of trying to shape policy and of dealing with the SPD, as well as beginning the slow process of gaining a reputation as a party that can actually change political circumstances for the better.[35] Hard and fast successes are therefore only small in nature, but wholesale failures have also largely been avoided.[36]

Leaving detailed academic studies of the Left Party's achievements to one side, it is clear that once in power the Mecklenburg-Western Pomerania Left Party quickly exhibited a style and set of aims that continued to set it apart from other Left Party *Landesverbände*. As touched on above, the Left Party began preparing for government in earnest at the end of 1997 when working groups were created to analyse what could and should be done in various policy areas.[37] Despite an awareness that raising expectations unduly could be counter-productive if the Left Party were to enter government in Schwerin, in 1998 the Left Party could not help but make rather expansive demands. The slogan of the 1998 campaign was 'With the Left Party for Social Justice and Humanity in Mecklenburg-Western Pomerania'. What 'social justice' meant (and means) for the Left Party was, as ever, difficult to pin down, but most supporters of the party identified this with an emphasis on cutting unemployment rates dramatically, reducing income inequalities and financing public spending projects; all in Germany's poorest state and in a federal system where little of the taxes collected actually end up in *Land* governments' hands. The Left Party election manifesto nevertheless explicitly identified several projects that the party would actively pursue in government: a guarantee of short-term employment for those who had just completed apprenticeships, increased state aid to financially strapped local governments, hiring of new public sector workers, reform of the educational system at primary school level and the creation of a non-profit jobs sector.[38]

The Left Party therefore went into the coalition negotiations with a clear set of demands that had been developed in the weeks and months prior to election day.[39] At the end of the two-week coalition negotiations the Left Party had, perhaps understandably, compromised considerably on what a special commission report (published in March 1998) claimed were the minimum requirements that the coalition agreement would need to meet if the Left Party were to agree to take part.[40] The key original aim of the party was to create a publicly funded job-creation scheme (the so-called *Öffentlich geförderter Beschäftigungssektor* – ÖBS) through which the Left Party initially hoped to create around 25,000 new jobs and then, once *Die Linke* had actually entered government, a scaled back figure of around 8000.[41] Unsurprisingly, implementing these ideas in practice proved highly problematic. The numbers of people involved kept coming down as the Left Party was faced with the prospect of actually fulfilling these promises, and by 1999 Holter was stressing that 3500 ÖBS jobs would be created in the (again fuzzily defined) medium term.[42]

The SPD was also not prepared to buckle to the Left Party's demand that all apprentices were to be guaranteed employment when their training finished. Eventually, the Left Party agreed with the SPD proposal to simply 'attempt to find' positions for graduates of apprenticeship programmes. Similarly, the two parties agreed to try the ÖBS on a 'pilot programme' basis and agreed that new spending and public debt would be the first priority of the new government, with the goal being the reduction of the DM 400 million debt over the four-year term of the coalition.

By 2002, the Left Party was nevertheless able to offer a number of concrete achievements to its supporters. A 25 million Euro multi-media initiative had been launched in schools and the coalition had successfully implemented a '12-Jahres-Abitur' (essentially meaning that pupils stayed in schools for a 12 rather than 13-year period). A (not uncontroversial) reform of the state's administrative structures had been undertaken and around 800 school social worker jobs had been created. The coalition passed a law proposed by the Left Party to lower the voting age in local elections to 16, put through a change in the regulations concerning background checks of parliamentarians by the Gauck Commission and, most controversially, agreed on yearly budgets that sharply curtailed government spending. Especially contentious were cuts affecting retirement homes and families (*Erziehungsgeld*) and a freeze on spending increases for the visually impaired and handicapped. The determination of Left Party legislative leaders to adhere to strict budget discipline despite criticism from the party rank and file was especially noteworthy.[43] That having been said, it was still the party *Basis* that appreciated the small policy steps that had been taken; whether the wider population of Mecklenburg-Western Pomerania noticed too much in the way of change is a much more moot point.[44]

Tensions within the coalition were nonetheless never far from the surface. These first public spats occurred over a Left Party proposal concerning the introduction of an 'orientation phase' in primary school that would allow parents and teachers additional time in which to decide on which school track students would follow after the sixth year of schooling. Indeed, isolated calls for the Left Party to leave the coalition unless the SPD backed down from its opposition to the new law were not unheard of within party ranks. Nevertheless, a compromise on the issue was reached. More serious to the coalition's stability was the dispute that erupted between the two parties over Germany's participation in military action during the Kosovo War. While the Mecklenburg-Western Pomerania SPD firmly backed Chancellor Schröder's position on the war, various Left Party legislators and party activists denounced NATO military involvement. Indeed, the rhetoric was often heated from the Left Party, with one parliamentarian, Monty Schädel, denouncing NATO's action as a 'crime against humanity' while accusing Minister-President Ringstorff of being a 'war-monger'.[45] Although this crisis too was eventually defused, both sides were left with some bruised feelings. Finally, tensions between the two parties reached something of a crescendo in 2001 when Harald Ringstorff, representing the state in the *Bundesrat* during a discussion and vote on a new law on pensions, cast a vote for the new law despite opposition from his coalition partner and in violation of the 1998 Coalition Agreement guaranteeing Mecklenburg-Western Pomerania's abstention when the two coalition partners could not agree. The Left Party was furious, and calls to leave the coalition were frequent and shrill. In a special party congress called to debate this development, however, Holter and other party leaders argued that leaving the coalition would ultimately hurt, rather than help, the Left Party. After Ringstorff offered an apology for his actions and promised not to take such a step again, Left Party leaders were able to secure their party's consent to continue in the coalition. Nevertheless, relations between the SPD and Left Party had been damaged and, perhaps more importantly, many supporters of the Left Party clearly lost faith in the party to exert its will within the coalition.

The 1998–2002 government had therefore not changed Mecklenburg-Western Pomerania's world, but small reforms had certainly taken place. The Left Party was much more successful in getting its policy aims incorporated into the post-2002 coalition agreement than it had been in 1998, largely as it was much better prepared for the negotiations and could subsequently argue its corner much more effectively.[46] This was in spite of a poorer performance at the polls in 2002 when the Left Party's share of the vote dropped by 8 per cent (down to 16.4 per cent). Meanwhile, the SPD was able to increase its share of the vote from 6.3 per cent to 40.6 per cent, a figure that, while clearly linked to the last-minute upsurge in the fortunes of the Schröder government (which won a federal election on the same day), was nevertheless surprising given the growing disenchantment with the lack of achievements by both the national coalition and the coalition in Mecklenburg-Western Pomerania. Indeed, in an *Infratest Dimap* poll on party competence in solving particular political problems the Left Party scored in single digits in every category (behind, in some cases, the FDP, Greens and even the Schill party) except for education policy and 'achieving Social Justice'.[47] Not surprisingly then, although the Left Party clearly lost voters to the SPD (some 45,000), it also suffered disproportionately from a drop in voter support (down 8.3 per cent), much of which could be traced to disappointed former *Die Linke* voters who decided to stay home on election day (some 23,000).[48]

Thus the Left Party returned to the coalition negotiating table as a chastened party. The Left Party realised that if the party were to bounce back at the next state election (scheduled for 2006) then it would have to be able to argue that the work of the coalition had had a much clearer Left Party input. Put another way, the Left Party knew that it would have to have clear and concrete achievements to show off. *Die Linke* negotiators therefore went into the 2002 negotiations with a clear set of aims (*'Hauptziele'*) that had been discussed in working groups and the Executive before the *Landtagswahl* had even taken place.[49] The main aims included

- The introduction of a freedom of information act
- An equal opportunities law that was specifically aimed at improving employment opportunities for the disabled and those with serious illnesses
- The retention of all local medical services[50]
- The introduction of a framework to facilitate the integration of migrants
- To maintain levels of support to the state's visually impaired citizens
- The development of a concerted programme – crossing all ministries – to counteract the spread of right-wing extremist political sentiment.

The influence of the *Basis*, through working groups and various organisational fora, in shaping these aims is noticeable. These aims were not just drawn up by politicians in ivory towers in the hope that they somehow hit the right note. The federal executive of the party, the *Landesparteirat*, the heads of the various working groups and the leaders of Left Party local organisations (*Kreisvorsitzende*) met four times a year to discuss progress on achieving these objectives.[51] An 'extra-parliamentary supervisory body' (*'Außerparlamentarische Begleitgruppe'*) was also created in September 2002 to analyse the work of the coalition. This group was composed of Left Party members who were not MdL and who did not have direct links to any of the Left Party's team within the state government. The working group was supposed to follow the work of the coalition critically from a distance and to report to party conferences on the effectiveness of the Left Party's behaviour within government.[52] The Left Party's willingness to assess its own performance in government self-critically is something that is easy to overlook and the reports of this body have, unsurprisingly, frequently caused consternation between the *Basis* and leadership. Be that as it may, it is hard to argue against leader of the state party Peter Ritter's assessment that 'we have certainly tried to create discussion fora that include a wide variety of people so as to oversee and evaluate what we do'.[53]

The pragmatic attitude of politicians such as Ritter and Methling is only one side of the story though. The organisational framework may exist in theory to keep Left Party ministers (and with them their pragmatic orientations) in check, but not an insubstantial part of the rank and file and elements from within the parliamentary party soon became very disenchanted with the work of the 2002–6 administration. Consultation was seen as being all well and good, but too little appeared to change as a result and the '*Aufbruchstimmung*' of the late 1990s was soon replaced by decidedly idealistic calls for more overt rank and file participation in the process of governing. Such claims naturally irritated some Left Party ministers as they revealed a slightly unrealistic understanding, even among members of the parliamentary party, of how shaping policy and governing with another party actually worked in practice.[54] Calls for increased interaction between the levels did not come immediately after the Left Party took office in 1998 and it was only really with the Left Party's support for a federal tax reform in the *Bundesrat* in the summer of 2000 that dissent burst out into the open. For many in the party the reform was simply too neo-liberal and the Left Party should, under no circumstances, be supporting it and grumblings of dissatisfaction grew from there on in. In 2002 Peter Ritter only secured support permitting him to enter into negotiations to extend the coalition as he attached the proposal to a vote of confidence.[55] Birgit Schwebs, an influential member of the parliamentary party since 1998 and currently deputy chairperson of the *Land* party, claims that increased levels of dissatisfaction within the party have arisen as the Left Party no longer appears to be the representative of the socially weak in the state and that its political programme has become diffuse and less clear-cut. 'In 1998' Schwebs claims 'we entered government to fundamentally change the political environment in Mecklenburg-Western Pomerania'. The decision to maintain the coalition in 2002, on the other hand, had – in spite of chastening losses at the polls and in spite of an alleged unwillingness to genuinely assess the work of the previous administration – 'much more to do with simply maintaining power'.[56] Gerd Walther, a young former MdL from rural Ücker-Randow near the Polish border who sat in parliament from 2002–6, was, like Schwebs, always sceptical about the decision to enter government and feared that the Left Party would soon lose its 'differentness' and ability to contribute to the changing society.[57] Schwebs and Walther, as well as a significant number of other MdLs, did not wish to see a further continuation of the SPD–Left Party government post-2006 and hoped that a return to opposition will enable the Left Party to return to its roots and fundamentally re-assess its position towards future alliances with the SPD.

Feelings such as these are illustrative of the divide that came to exist within the parliamentary party. The critical juncture that spawned such internal animosity came at a conference in 2004 when two key decisions were taken; a majority of delegates, among them 7 of the Left Party's 13 MdLs, voted against two of the key tenets of the coalition agreement (a reform of Mecklenburg-Western Pomerania's local government struc-tures and the state's bi-annual budget). MdLs from rural regions – long since unhappy with the apparent neglect of rural interests within the party[58] – were particularly dissatisfied with the financial implications of the organisational reforms and were therefore reluctant to support 'their' government. However, internal spats such as these did not prevent a majority within the party from arguing that the Left Party should nonetheless seek to continue governing with the SPD post-2006. Indeed, Harald Ringstorff would also have liked to continue working with the Left Party but a wafer-thin prospective majority of a mere one seat and a Left Party with a number of clearly ambivalent MdL scared both him and his party off.[59] Dissident groups within the Left Party contributed to the air of uncertainty within the SPD by forming a government-participation critical group (a Mecklenburg-Western Pomeranian branch of the 'Anti-Capitalist Left') just two days before polling day in September 2006, not exactly the type of behaviour of a reliable coalition partner in a tight spot. Shortly after the election a frustrated Peter Ritter openly attacked the movers and shakers behind this movement by claiming that they had damaged the public image of the party by making it look as if the party was divided.[60] He had a point.

Conclusion

The decentralised nature of the German federal system clearly affects party relationships in the *Länder*. Quite what this means in practice will also depend on the ideological make-up of parties themselves and what national pressures are exerted. In this case, the federal leadership of the Left Party clearly gave the Mecklenburg-Western Pomerania branch a lot of leeway to experiment. They wanted to be in a governmental coalition with the SPD, and Mecklenburg-Western Pomerania was a pretty safe place to start thinking about it. The leaders of the Mecklenburg-Western Pomerania branch of the Left Party can, furthermore, do just this more or less regardless of what the party in other parts of the country thinks. The *Landesverband* is dominated by pragmatic modernisers around a group of politicians based predominantly (although not exclusively) in Schwerin. In contrast, modernising socialists, looking to the bigger picture of establishing the Left Party as a serious and trustworthy socialist party with genuinely national ambitions, are few and far between. On the other hand, restorative ideologues and members of the emancipatory left are also small in number and enjoy little influence within the party; Mecklenburg-Western Pomerania thus remains a bastion of pragmatic reformism with party leaders and the rank and file concerned much more with concrete policy outcomes than larger, abstract political gestures.

The pragmatic reformers are nonetheless much more downbeat than they were when entering government back in 1998. The Left Party's eight years in power have illustrated to them that governing is difficult and complicated, and radically changing the structural environment within which politics is forced to function is much harder than many perhaps envisaged. The *Basis* has not shirked from articulating dissent at the government's work and rarely have Left Party leaders been allowed a free rein in the way that has become normal in Berlin (see Chapter 6). The overwhelming preference of the party leadership towards policy-seeking that initially led to office-seeking alliances with the SPD has therefore shifted more towards policy-seeking through renewal in opposition. The 2010 election is again likely to see the Left Party attempt to work (no matter what the rhetoric with the campaign) with the SPD in government. There is therefore plenty of evidence to suggest that the loose-coupled organisational structures of the Left Party, particularly in the period 2002–5, enabled the pragmatic reformers to pursue whichever goals they happened to see fit at the time. These findings also fit in with much of the party organisation literature that stresses that the more frequently and fundamentally leadership hierarchies are changed, the more likely we are to see changes in party goals. Changes in Mecklenburg-Western Pomerania have been (mostly) slow and (mostly) organised; party goals have therefore remained remarkably constant over time.

6
The Left Party in Berlin

Introduction

The Left Party in Berlin is an altogether different beast not just to the branch in Mecklenburg-Western Pomerania but also to all other Left Party *Landesverbände*. If the Left Party has gone down the Green path towards institutionalisation anywhere, then it is here that it has done so most obviously; this is in terms of de-radicalising its ideology, risking the wrath of the part of its electorate that is 'hard left', warming to ideas of shaping rather than opposing policy and also in attempting to appeal to a broader electoral constituency that would (coincidentally) normally have some sympathies with the Greens in cities such as Berlin. The Left Party remains a domain of modern socialism and the other three streams within the party play, at best, a marginal role. The Berlin Left Party has always understood itself, largely as it is rooted in the capital city, as a visionary force within the party, paving the way for the Left Party to embed itself in Germany's party system and, eventually, to shape policy from inside the corridors of power. It is well aware that this strategy will move it away from its radical past and will force it to deal with complex problems that are unlikely to have popular solutions even within its own clientele. Furthermore, Berlin's unique position as an east-west city ensures that politics there simply functions a little differently to that of other German cities as well as other, less urban, *Bundesländer*. There is therefore ample evidence that, in terms of attitudes to taking part in government, the Berlin Left Party is going down the Green path, even if the reasons for this are very different to those in Mecklenburg-Western Pomerania.

The Left Party in Berlin is decidedly more pragmatic than its sister parties in the other *Länder* as well as being broader in programmatic terms. This is so for three reasons; firstly, the Left Party had little choice but to broaden its electoral and programmatic appeal in Berlin more than elsewhere given that it was trying to accrue votes not just in what was once the GDR (i.e. east Berlin) but also in areas that were once in West Germany (i.e. west Berlin). Berlin is therefore a microcosm of the Left Party's strategic dilemma across the whole of the country. The Berlin Left Party attempted to win over many traditional Green voters in central Berlin[1] by stressing its liberalism and libertarianism. *Die Linke* sought to stress diversity, open-mindedness and creativeness alongside an ability to turn around Berlin's moribund economy.[2] Secondly, the Berlin rank and file are more willing to accept the 'avant-garde' leadership claims of their party leaders than is the case elsewhere. Grumbling from below is not something that tends to cause the Berlin leadership too much difficulty,[3] mainly as Left Party members in eastern Berlin have always been more likely – largely because of their conditioning as the most loyal of all GDR citizens – to behave loyally to their leaders than is the case elsewhere in the country.[4] Thirdly, the leadership of the Left Party in Berlin was simply more versatile and visionary than was the case elsewhere, ensuring that they were open to transforming the party into a modern socialist actor to the left of the SPD, stressing serious policy-making and hard-headed strategic calculation. Members of the Left Party in Berlin stress the importance of establishing the party in the *Land* parliaments of western Germany and of working with the SPD and Greens to create constructive majorities. It therefore understands itself, more than any other, as the pathfinder in terms of expanding into western Germany.[5]

Of people and personalities: We're all reformers now ...

The parameters of Berlin's post-*Wende* politics have been ideal in assisting the modern socialists in gaining control of the party branch. They did not, however, do this immediately. Through the period 1990–94 both the parliamentary party and the *Landesverband* appeared disjointed, ensuring that ideological and programmatic development was both diffuse and haphazard. The heterogeneity of the *Landesverband's* membership did not prevent it from engaging in serious debates on whether *Die Linke* should, at some undefined point, look to take over political responsibility in the FRG as early as 1991–92. The primary reason for this was the administrative structure in the city where political offices were distributed evenly, ensuring that some Left Party candidates in eastern Berlin were more or less immediately appointed deputy mayors.

Following controversial debates these positions were taken on by Left Party politicians from 1992 onwards and many of the most stringent opponents of all office-taking left the *Landesverband* there and then.[6] As was indicated in Chapter 3, authors such as Robert Michels would have been anything but surprised at such developments; decentralised organisation structures appeared to be a very ineffective tool in holding back the processes of office accumulation and the centralisation of power in the party in public office. Michels would have wearily viewed the apparently flourishing internal democracy culture of the Left Party as nothing more than a cosmetic side issue as party leaders manipulated party life to suit their own (ultimately office-seeking) interests.[7]

Again as elite theorists are likely to have predicted, a clear divide characterised most inner-party discourse through this period, with one group of Left Party members and activists (mainly in the upper echelons of the party) essentially preferring to stress the importance of shaping political outcomes (*Gestaltungsansatz*) opposing another group, made up mostly of those with a much more ideological view of the world, who wanted the Left Party to be a party of outright opposition (*Oppositionsansatz*).[8] The rank and file were split pretty evenly between the two. Furthermore, approximately 40 per cent of politicians representing the Left Party in the Berlin parliament were not actually members of the party and the parliamentary party was subsequently exceptionally heterogeneous.[9] Added to this that few politicians had time to genuinely engage in strategic thinking, mainly as the overarching aim of survival dominated much of the Left Party's activity at this time, it is clear that the Berlin branch was anything but a coherent ideological unit. This changed noticeably between 1994 and 1997 when a stronger concentration on the Left Party's opposition role took place (largely under the slogan 'change begins with opposition') and it was only towards the end of the decade that more attention was paid to the question of when and under what conditions the Left Party should think about joining any prospective governments with the SPD.

Through the early 1990s the then powerful *AG Junge GenossInnen* exerted not inconsiderable influence within the party. The first generation of younger Left Party activists grew out of the FDJ (Free German Youth – the youth organisation of the SED in the GDR), but their radical ideology quickly became too much for a party fighting to make itself look like a moderate actor in the new Berlin party system. Their representatives were therefore sidelined early on, as were other young latecomers (i.e. young but not old enough to have been active in the GDR) who were just as fundamentalist in their political outlook. It was the next generation of young politicians who made a real impact on the Berlin *Die Linke*. Post-1995 Benjamin Hoff, Stefan Liebich, Gernot Klemm, Stefan Zillich and Petra Pau all raised their profile within the party and began to give it a young (all were barely 30 years old at the time) and more dynamic face.[10] The current deputy leader of the party, Halina Wawrzyniak (born in 1973), and the party's business manager, Carsten Schatz (born 1970), are also relatively young, as are a significant number of local council leaders. If you were forward thinking and undogmatic then the Berlin Left Party was, and still is, a very good place to make a political career.

For a significant number in the federal Left Party – and above all party talisman Gregor Gysi – the rise of this enthusiastic and careerist group of politicians was not inopportune. The modern socialism that they saw themselves as representing fitted in well with the party's long-term strategic vision of becoming a national force to the left of the SPD. Processes of institutionalisation at the federal level could be pushed on by *Land* politicians behaving 'sensibly' and strategically in city states such as Berlin. Among other things, Gysi and the modern socialists also saw the German capital as a test bed for persuading western Germans (in the shape of West Berliners) that the Left Party was not the eastern German demon frequently portrayed in the media. Effective, non-dramatic performance in government was of critical importance in doing this. As early as a December 1996 party conference, Gysi proclaimed – to loud applause from the assembled delegates – that Berlin offered the opportunity to make significant progress in the western states. According to Gysi, the Berlin Left Party needed to play a vanguard role in overcoming the East-West divide in the city by shaping and moulding policy outputs for the benefit of all.[11] The other parties did not, perhaps unsurprisingly, see it this way and it was only with the vote of no confidence that was passed against the CDU in 2001 that the Left Party was really accepted as a serious and constructive actor at the *Land* level.[12] Before then the Left Party's pariah status was, despite its 'structural social democratisation' particularly obvious in Berlin, mainly on account of the city's divided history.[13] Participating in government with the aim of establishing – however slowly – the Left Party in western Germany nonetheless appeared to be the overriding long-term vision of *Die Linke* leadership in Berlin and such thoughts prevailed within the state branch as a whole. The long-time party and parliamentary leader and prototypical political pragmatist, Stefan Liebich, argued, for example, that by taking part in sub-state governments in Berlin and Mecklenburg-Western Pomerania and perhaps also, in the future, in

Saxony-Anhalt the Left Party was undoubtedly facilitating its aim of becoming a nation-wide socialist party[14]. The former minister for Health, Social Affairs and Consumer Protection, Heidi Knake-Werner, has also made similar observations.[15] Berlin *Die Linke* MdA Elke Breitenbach and current economics senator Harald Wolf's assistant, Katina Schubert, have also attempted to increase the Left Party's profile in the West by elaborating on what the future of the whole welfare system might be – another consistent line in the modern socialists' ideological armoury.[16] Visions and long-term aims were clearly not lacking.

It was, however, only post-1998 that the modern socialists within the Berlin branch really began to rise through the party and genuinely exert their influence. Even then, the Berlin Left Party is still by no means the homogeneous entity that it is sometimes portrayed in the press. There are controversies, including over government participation, and groups and sub-groups jockey for positions of influence within the party. The branch soon came to be dominated by Harald Wolf – a western German who was previously a prominent member of the Greens/Alternative List in West Berlin – and the group of young parliamentarians within the parliamentary party mentioned above along with former leader of the *Fraktion* Stefan Liebich, current leader Klaus Lederer and Carola Bluhm (Freundl, until 2005). Wolf cleverly set the tone for the party's programmatic and strategic development and conveyed a vision of left-wing city politics to his supporters before allowing and encouraging them to develop their own ideas and thoughts within the paradigm that had been set. Wolf therefore leads without dictating and his supporters remain loyal, well-organised and extremely influential.[17] They see themselves as strategic visionaries with a view of Berlin as an important stepping stone to maintaining a Left Party presence in the *Bundestag* and also in portraying itself as a serious reforming force. They lead a parliamentary party that is still quite diverse; a significant minority are specialists in specific policy areas (reflecting a clear strategy of Left Party politicians to 'fly in' *Sachkompetenz*) who arrived in the *Abgeordnetenhaus* in the mid/late 1990s. They tend to leave the rough and tumble of party politics mainly to the leadership and much prefer to concentrate their attention on their own fields of interest.[18] Many subsequently play less overtly significant roles in the *Fraktion*. There is also a small 'alternative' wing, reflecting the complicated left-wing heritage of Germany's capital city (see Chapter 4), of 25–40 year olds who tend to stem mainly from western Germany. Although there are tensions, federal MdBs Petra Pau and Gesine Lötzsch also remain close to (if sometimes critical of) Wolf's leadership circle, even if Lötzsch in particular is (highly) sceptical of the Berlin Left Party's pro-government participation stance. These tensions are much more significant than any that may arise between the parliamentary party and the *Landesverband*, which plays a largely insignificant role in Berlin politics.

Following the Gera party conference of 2002, two further factions of significance were created within the Berlin branch's reforming leadership. They have similar aims and similar methods, and both exist nationwide; both began, and have their bases, in Berlin. First, the so-called *Reformlinke* (Reforming Left) – the main instigators of which are Gernot Klemm and Elke Breitenbach and members of the *Landesvorstand* – and second, the '*Forum Zweite Erneuerung*' (Forum of the Second Renewal) around Benjamin Hoff and Stefan Liebich that has a slightly more significant presence in the parliamentary party.[19] The Forum was founded by 70–80 delegates at the Gera conference and sees itself primarily as a discussion platform while the Reforming Left was formed two months later in Prenzlauer Berg and wants to become an institutionalised base in the party for reformers (much as the KPF does for Communist sympathisers).[20] Their aims are therefore very similar and their membership frequently overlapping.

The presence of such a strong set of reforming politicians, frequently with experience in Berlin's local government structures, helped push the Left Party towards participating in governments from the middle of the 1990s, and a group of *Die Linke* politicians were having secret discussions with SPD politicians as early as 2000 (i.e. before the banking scandal erupted – see below) about hard and fast decisions on future coalitions.[21] It was younger members of both the Left Party and the SPD who were the motor of the capital's first red-red coalition and it was clear that for these Social Democrats the idea of ignoring the Left Party because of its past seemed anachronistic. Pau, Freundl and Wolf were all seen as viable ministerial options and the *Landesverband* in general was perceived by the SPD as being an actor with which they could do business. Gregor Gysi's leap back on to the stage of Berlin politics in 2001 did not, curiously, do much for the Left Party's image within the SPD as a party of serious political intentions, mainly as his campaigning style led him to make promises that many knew were simply unworkable in practice. For some, Gysi's campaigning was actually counter-productive for the party as a whole as expectations were raised that could never seriously be fulfilled. Protests from within *Die Linke* were nonetheless barely audible; the prospect of adversely affecting their electoral performance by criticising Gysi was clearly a step too far.[22]

A further factor in prompting the Berlin Left Party to adopt increasingly practical positions is the uniquely difficult financial position that the state finds itself in. Although the extent and scale of the crisis only became evident in 2001, the structural weaknesses of Berlin's economy and ever-increasing levels of post-unification debt offered clear pointers to economic difficulties well before the full scale of the crisis was known. *Die Linke* in Berlin confronted its own membership with an unpopular policy agenda for coming to terms with these structural problems as early as 1997. The *reformpolitisches Sofortprogramm* (political emergency programme) that the leadership presented to party members at the 1997 *Landesparteitag* (*Land* party conference) shocked many delegates, with its demands for a reduction in weekly working hours in the public services *and* a commensurate drop in wages.[23] The rank and file articulated considerable horror at the thought of a socialist party adopting such capitalist policies. They nonetheless supported the leadership at the conference, and the Communist Platform ultimately remained isolated in its (unambiguous) rejection of the policy programme. This dynamic appears to be the typical pattern of events within the Berlin Left Party, permitting the leadership a not inconsiderable degree of practical autonomy in setting the party's agenda and reacting to external shocks.[24]

Following this initial high-profile spat in 1997, steps towards government participation became larger and ever more frequent: in the run-up to the 1999 election to the *Abgeordnetenhaus* (Berlin's state parliament) the rank and file accepted a suggestion from the party leadership that – should it be necessary – the Left Party would tolerate an SPD–Green minority government.[25] A further contribution towards dismantling the isolation of the Left Party came with the publication in (the predominantly western German) *Tagesspiegel* of a discussion between Gregor Gysi and Klaus Landowsky, the then leader of the CDU's parliamentary party, which lent the Left Party increased status as a 'normal' political actor.[26] Even more important for the formation of the first SPD–Left Party coalition was the official apology by the then federal leader, Gabriele Zimmer, for the forced unification of the SPD and KPD in the Soviet Zone of Occupation in 1946, placating many dissenting SPD members and illustrating the Left Party's willingness to make compromises to achieve its long-term goals.[27] The fact that Zimmer was seconded by one of the Left Party's two federal MPs and former leader of the Berlin party branch, Petra Pau, was also significant. Shortly before this the Berlin Left Party stated in an internal strategy paper ('*Vor der Kür kommt die Pflicht*') that entry into a coalition with the SPD should be the party's aim at the time of the next election, then scheduled for 2004, and that the Left Party needed to begin preparing for this sooner rather than later.[28] At the same time, the party leadership again called for clarity and consistency in the Left Party's own political agenda. The aim of this was clear – it would make the process of governing more practicable as and when the need to implement policy arose.[29]

Of policies and programmes: The devil is in the detail

As the full extent of the banking scandal unfolded in 2001, the Berlin Left Party continued to raise the stakes in terms of its own position on entering government. It stressed the importance of taking any opportunities that may arise and the very candidature of Gregor Gysi made the party's intention to seek governmental responsibility crystal clear. If the arithmetic worked out correctly, the Left Party would take the plunge. The charismatic Gysi had the ability to appeal to both younger voters and voters in the western districts of the city, and his contribution to his party's success (47 per cent of the vote in the eastern districts, 7 per cent in the western districts) would be hard to underestimate.[30] The preamble of the election manifesto – written and co-ordinated by the parliamentary party – made a number of specific aims that seemed crafted more for their prospective coalition partner than their own clientele. Not only was there the categorical statement that the Left Party sought to govern in Berlin, but also (perhaps surprising) claims that the Left Party would seek to reduce Berlin's debt to zero within a decade. Reducing debt and consolidating budgets can hardly be considered traditional socialist aims and is further emphasis of the pragmatic orientation that the Left Party leadership in Berlin placed on practical politics.[31]

The Left Party's tenure in office in Berlin thus far has been characterised by a number of distinct phases. Until the federal election of September 2002, the Left Party simply 'learnt by doing' and was unable to really register any notable policy successes. It had to learn how to govern the hard way, mainly as it was not as well prepared as Mecklenburg Western Pomerania's Left Party was pre-1998.[32] Despite possessing politicians with considerable experience of local government, everyone connected with the party was on a steep learning curve. This naturally meant that mistakes were made and the Left Party had to feel its way slowly into government. The Left Party also lacked a genuine project that could guide its behaviour in making policy in specific areas, and the party soon began reacting to events rather than actively shaping outcomes.[33]

This was particularly so given the horror stories that periodically came out of the Finance Ministry about the city's financial plight. Making expansive policy gestures to the Left Party's electoral constituency was therefore never on the cards and an inevitable de-radicalisation of the Left Party's policy package soon began to take place. Left-wing critics within the party in particular were unhappy with the party's inability to stamp its authority on the government and were not slow to articulate their discontent.[34] These usual suspects were, however, frequently dismissive of the Left Party's move into government from the very start and it is unlikely that they would have been satisfied with anything short of radical changes to the structure of Berlin's society. An unfeasible aim and an unfair way of measuring the Left Party's success. In Berlin, as in Mecklenburg-Western Pomerania, the most vocal of these critics (Rouzbeh Taheri and Michael Prütz) soon saw their future elsewhere and moved to form the WASG in the city (see Chapter 8 for more details).

Between September 2002 and the beginning/middle of 2004 the Left Party began to stabilise its position within the red-red coalition. Left Party senators understood a little more about the parameters of the possible, about their coalition partner and they also began to profile themselves in certain policy areas (most noticeably social policy). Since 2004 *Die Linke* has suffered from two divergent trends; on the one hand they can claim a number of (relatively small) policy successes such as the introduction of a 'social ticket' on public transport, maintaining subsidised kindergarten places and making the first moves in stabilising the city's financial situation. For some, there are also noticeable achievements in other areas such as construction where the corruption that existed before has been much reduced, and in the liberalisation of some areas of *Innenpolitik*.[35] The problem is that such things are not particularly easy to sell to the public as, in the words of Rolf Reißig (an academic with close links to the Left Party who has analysed the party's behaviour in the Berlin government in some detail (see below)), 'the need to change things is great, the ability to do so is, however, limited'.[36]

As and when there are disagreements about policy proposals and the outputs of the red-red coalition, they tend to stem neither from conflicts between particular factions nor from objections from the rank and file. The fact that politicians in Berlin who hold seats on local councils (*Bezirksversammlungen*) are not allowed to take up seats in the *Abgeordnetenhaus* (and vice versa) ensures that tensions are also less likely to stem from divergent interests of Left Party representatives across the levels. The highly charged debates about the then education minister Thomas Flierl's student account model for Berlin's university students (a back door way of introducing tuition fees) in 2004, for example, was led largely by student protests and strikes, and not by any particular grouping within the Left Party. The party, it seems, was aware of the difficulties of governing and was willing to go along with Flierl's controversial proposals; whether it would have done so had it been in opposition and others had put the idea forward remains, of course, a much more moot point. The movement that forced Flierl to radically modify his plans did not come from the Left Party *Basis*, but centred around influential parliamentary party members such as the enigmatic Benjamin Hoff – and Hoff rapidly distanced himself from the methods of the protestors on the streets once Flierl moved to shelve his controversial ideas.[37] A similar pattern emerged in debates over Flierl and Liebich's intentions to halve subsidies to a children's theatre with the *Fraktion* prompting the government to alter its plans while the rank and file remained largely distant from the process.[38] These two cases remain the most important examples of the government changing policies once the ideas had entered the public domain. Other controversial topics such as increasing day-care centre charges or the reduction of welfare payments to the blind did lead to grumbling within the party but were nonetheless implemented by the governing coalition. According to Liebich, reducing Berlin's mountain of debt can now be considered to be a genuine left-wing form of politics as ever-increasing debt simply means that ever-higher interest payments have to be made to banks.[39] A minority of others claim that Berlin's social infrastructure is actually very good (in terms of places available in Kindergarten, for example), and a Left Party government should not shirk from making the case for actually *cutting* subsidies in some of these areas.[40] Given this, Berlin can in no sense be seen as a Waterloo for modern socialists.

When negotiating the coalition agreement with the SPD in 2001, the Left Party managed to avoid being forced into any major consensus-threatening compromises.[41] This was not so much because the Left Party in Berlin had learnt anything from the experiences of the party in Mecklenburg-Western Pomerania – Berliners (of all persuasions) have never been particularly inclined to look north to Schwerin for inspiration[42] – but more because both the Left Party and SPD really wanted the negotiations to succeed.[43] The Left Party was well aware of specific demands that were likely to prove untenable to the social democratic rank and file and the party also had a small number of MdAs who had learnt harsh lessons about expecting too much of governments when they were members of the 1989 Alternative List that had governed alongside the SPD.[44] The Left Party managed to secure the relatively uncontroversial (and deliberately imprecise) agreement that savings would be made in a way that did not endanger the social fabric of Berlin society and that no savings would be made in the areas of culture, science and education.[45] The party basis accepted and supported the rigid savings course that the government planned without so much as a murmur of discontent as the party leadership reaped the benefits of having crafted a degree of autonomy that would appear specific to office-seeking parties.[46] This remained the case 12 months after the Left Party entered the coalition when the lead motion – written by Stefan Liebich – at a 2003 *Landesparteitag* gained over 80 per cent support even though it comprised little of genuinely socialist substance. It is also noticeable how the younger generation of Left Party politicians were 'remarkably aggressive' in attacking the critics of government participation, many of whom came from the western part of the city.[47] It would appear that the critics tended to come from representatives of the radical alternative scene within the party – a faction that moved increasingly towards the renegade Berlin WASG from 2005 onwards.

Left Party insiders see one of the principal successes of the party's time in government as being the clear break with what went before. Martina Michels, deputy president of the *Abgeordnetenhaus*, claims that 'we were able to bring about a change in mentality in Berlin politics' while former MdL Michail Nelken simply argues that there is now 'more honesty, more openness and more transparency' in the work of the government.[48] The parliamentary party's finance spokesperson, Carl Wechselberg, also observed that the red-red coalition signifies 'a political, cultural and above all financial turnaround' in the city's fortunes.[49] Given the culture of corruption (*Filz*) that had pervaded the city's politics up until 2001 this is a claim that clearly has some mileage; Berlin has (significant) problems, but it is at least now trying to do something about them. The Left Party has, however, always shied away from claiming that they have a socialist manifesto for Berlin that will heal all of the city's ills. In fact, the lack of a coherent socialist programmatic profile was abundantly evident both to Left Party insiders[50] as well as to those (both critical and sympathetic) looking in from the outside.[51] Eventually, after three years in government, this vacuum did, however, prompt Harald Wolf to stress that the Left Party should move away from just doing what it could to stabilise Berlin's finances and to start finding ways of facilitating the 'strategic aim' of westward expansion of the party's voter base. His preferred approach to doing this was nonetheless likely to sit uneasily among many of the classical Left Party clientele in eastern Germany – Wolf claimed that the Left Party needed to stress its liberal credentials with the aim of winning over previous Green voters in the inner-city areas of central-western Berlin. Internationalism, heterogeneity and creativity were to be the key terms while the party should stress its competence in economic management. Somewhat less surprising than these ambitious goals was Wolf's desire to continue working in coalition with the SPD after the next election of 2006.[52] The Left Party is evidently willing and capable of articulating goals and aims that go well beyond those of its rank and file, and also arguably beyond those of its most loyal electorate.[53]

Other policy compromises abound Left Party ministers abstained in the vote on whether Berlin should accept or reject the European Union's proposed constitution, permitting Berlin's Mayor, Klaus Wowereit, to vote for the constitution when the issue was discussed in Germany's upper chamber, the *Bundesrat*. The fact that the rest of the Left Party – at federal and sub-state levels – had more or less unanimously rejected the constitution appeared to play no role in the Berlin Left Party's discussions on the matter.[54] The issue of vote maximisation was clearly pushed into the background as the Left Party took a chance that Berlin's voters would not punish it for this apparent internal inconsistency. Harald Wolf even speculated that the Left Party could win *too many* votes in forthcoming sub-state elections if it were not careful, observing that 'it really would not be good if the Left Party ended up with more votes than the SPD as this would mean that the SPD is likely to be much more reluctant to enter into a coalition with us'.[55]

As in Mecklenburg-Western Pomerania the Left Party sought academic analysis of the successes and failures of its time in the Berlin coalition. Also as in Mecklenburg-Western Pomerania, the main study, by Rolf Reißig, that had been carried out had not been uncontroversial. Reißig's detailed account of the Berlin Left Party's first three years in office appears for many to paint their achievements in too rosy a fashion.[56] Indeed, it almost looks as if the study exists to offer supporters of government participation ammunition with which to argue their case. Although Reißig is careful to point out that the prevailing structural conditions of Germany's market economy make the task for any socialist government exceptionally difficult, he nonetheless argues that the Left Party can be proud of a number of specific achievements. Social policy has, for example, clearly returned to the forefront of the policy agenda in the city and although the steps forward are small (publishing a yearly 'poverty report', the creation of a 'social structure atlas',[57] the creation of a parliamentary committee solely for the purposes of looking at the city's social policy questions and so forth), they are nonetheless steps in the right direction. The 'neo-liberal privatisation euphoria' as well as any further erosions of civil rights have also been halted. Vivantes, the largest public hospital complex in Europe, the *Berliner Verkehrsbetriebe* (BVG) and the *Berliner Stadtreinigung* (BSR) all remain under public control, as does Berlin's exhibition centre. Important structural reforms, he argues, have also been implemented in some of Berlin's most forward-looking sectors (such as higher education and high culture) and the Berlin government has resisted calls to shut down (at least) one of the city's three opera houses or any of its theatres.[58] Reißig claims that the Left Party has made a noticeable contribution in bringing Berlin's politics back into the real world and the delusions of grandeur that Berlin suffered through the 1990s have been banished, much as has the subsidy culture that dominated Berlin's thinking not just pre-1989 but also through the last decade of the 20th century.[59] However, even the eternal optimist Reißig found himself forced to admit that the Berlin Left Party does not possess a genuine *Leitidee* with which it can hope to shape and transform the city's outlook.[60]

Over and above arguments about policy successes and failures, the Left Party in Berlin clearly possesses considerably more room for manoeuvre than the party does in Mecklenburg-Western Pomerania and the other *Landesverbände*. Despite the fact that a number of modern socialists are active in the federal arena, most criticism of the *Landesverband's* behaviour tends to come from the federal level – and, more noticeably, from WASG members and, even more specifically, from its most prominent member, Oskar Lafontaine. Lafontaine has not shied away from describing the policies of the Berlin Left Party as 'an aberration' while Klaus Ernst, the leader of WASG and deputy leader of the federal parliamentary party, stated that the Berlin *Die Linke* was 'losing the plot' in agreeing to continue their coalition with the SPD in late 2006.[61] It is here where tensions and frictions are most likely to develop post-2007 when the Left Party really attempts to find its feet as a national party organisation (see Chapter 8).

Even the most vocal proponent of government participation in Berlin would have to concede that the list of policy successes with which the party was forced to go to the polls in 2006 was not earth-shattering. If it had not done so before, the Left Party had clearly entered the world of hard and complex decision-making and, interestingly, this had not put off its leaders in Berlin from attempting to return to office. The relative inability of the Berlin Left Party to change the policy environment around it was, as was also the case in Mecklenburg-Western Pomerania, put down to three specific factors; first, a mass of federal regulations existed that severely limited the party's ability to shape policy in a number of areas where it had clear and concrete plans (such as social policy). Second, the multiplicity of organisations and lobby groups who sought to influence policy was larger and more difficult to deal with than many within the Left Party expected and, third, expectations were simply so high that the small steps forward that were made were overlooked.[62]

The Left Party's electoral performance in 2006 was below expectations (which were officially to gain more than 17 per cent of the vote). The candidature of WASG in Berlin (see Chapter 8) did not help (they polled 2.9 per cent of the vote) but it was the large number of previous Left Party voters who either stayed at home or voted SPD who worried the party leadership more. It is worth putting the Left Party's performance in some context though; the Left Party did indeed lose 17 percentage points in eastern Berlin compared to its 2001 result, but this figure was actually only 1 percentage point lower than that which it achieved in the 2005 federal election and all this without the candidature of Gregor Gysi to hoover up votes for the party. The Left Party was, despite the concerted efforts of the Green Party, therefore able to maintain its governmental alliance with the SPD – mainly on account of the very reasonable (some would argue far too reasonable) claims that it made on its prospective coalition partner. The core of these claims was that public utilities would not be privatised, the ÖBS would be further tested out and *'gemeinsames Lernen'* (children of all abilities being taught together) would be trialled in Berlin's schools.[63] Even following the disastrous (for Berliners) judgement by the federal constitutional court on Berlin's claim for external assistance in paying off its mountain of debt, the coalition was still able to promise some extra spending on account of the higher than expected tax revenues that were announced at the same time.[64] Kindergarten charges were, for example, to be abolished (something that the SPD actually pushed rather more than the Left Party).

Conclusion

The Left Party's development in the German capital is one of pragmatism and institutionalisation. After an initial period of confusion the modern socialists firmly grabbed control of the party branch and successfully manoeuvred it down a very similar path to that which the Green Party took in the 1980s and early 1990s. The Left Party has proven itself to be a reliable and eminently sensible coalition partner and although the SPD did briefly consider other coalition options it was perhaps no real surprise when the SPD opted to continue governing with the more dependable Left Party (rather than the more volatile Berlin Greens) in the aftermath of the 2006 election. The fixation on office-seeking may indeed have cost the Left Party votes in the 2006 poll but its leaders feel that this is a price worth paying if it ensures that the modern socialists' project of being taken seriously as a party that shapes policy outcomes moves forward. Furthermore, as Harald Wolf observed, a worse performance than 2001 was always on the cards and polling more than one vote in four in eastern Berlin is not the electoral disaster that some more excitable analysts have claimed it to be.

When leadership changes occur in the Berlin Left Party then they do so very much along the line that classic political science would expect. As authors such as Angelo Panebianco are more likely to expect, politicians such as Klaus Lederer (the current leader) and Elke Breitenbach (MdA since 2003) have been co-opted into the leadership circle, ensuring rejuvenation and change within the leadership while largely leaving other structures intact.[65] The balance of power between personalities and wings within the Berlin Left Party has, much as is the case in Mecklenburg-Western Pomerania, remained stable and constant, ensuring that the modern socialist ethos of government participation with a view to long-term stabilisation in the national party system has remained unchanged. The restorative ideologues and the emancipatory left have been, again as was the case in Mecklenburg-Western Pomerania, effectively and efficiently sidelined – much as were the more fundamentalist groups within the Green Party in its early years. They grumble from the sidelines, their representatives are permitted a fiery speech or two at party conferences, and then they are more or less completely ignored. The rank and file may well sympathise with some of this more critical rhetoric, but there is scant evidence of such discourse filtering up into the party's leadership circles. The Left Party in Berlin is anything but populist, as a whole array of policy decisions ranging from supporting the draft EU constitution to (quietly and efficiently) implementing Gerhard Schröder's Agenda 2010 package of welfare cuts illustrates. Even the Left Party's own policy initiatives have specific answers to specific problems and if any evidence of populist politics is to be found, it would be in the dogmatic fight to save Berlin's high culture infrastructure. If, however, this is all that critics of the Left Party who claim it is unfit to govern can come up with, then they are skating on thin ice at best.

The analysis of the Left Party in Mecklenburg-Western Pomerania and Berlin illustrates that although they govern for different reasons and they pursue different policies on account of the qualitatively different challenges that they face, it is nonetheless clear that the Left Party is a party of government at the sub-state level like any other. Its performance has been positively undramatic in both states, and the hard-line critics on the far left remain as far removed from positions of influence as they have ever been. But what of the Left Party in states where it does not, and never has, governed? Is the radical streak in its ideology still present in its programmes there? Or has the Left Party in other eastern German *Länder* gone down the same route towards de-radicalisation that we have seen in northern Germany? It is to these questions that we move next.

7
The Left Party in Opposition

Introduction

There is plenty of evidence to indicate that the Left Party in government has developed into a reliable, ideologically pragmatic and eminently 'normal' political party. This, of itself, should not be altogether surprising. But what of the Left Party's branches elsewhere? Is there evidence that the other eastern German *Landesverbände* are watching, learning and emulating the pioneers in Mecklenburg-Western Pomerania and Berlin?[1] Are they perhaps, on the contrary, scowling and scolding from a distance, becoming ever more resolute in their wish *not* to lose that radical touch and become part of the political establishment? Or are *Land* political arenas small, more or less independent, worlds that force Left Party politicians to forge their own individual paths, no matter whether they are keen to do so or not? Put another way, although Left Party branches in other parts of the country are not compelled to do so, can we see evidence of 'Green-like processes' elsewhere even though the branches have not (yet) been in government? This chapter tracks the behaviour, in terms of both programmatic development and political strategy, of the Left Party in two states where it is, and always has been, a party of opposition.[2] Most of the analysis stems from detailed case studies of Saxony and Brandenburg. We concentrate on these states for a number of specific reasons. Saxony is the largest of the Left Party's *Landesverbände* in terms of membership numbers and has traditionally had an ambivalent attitude towards the policy shaping instincts of its more northerly sister branches. If we can see evidence of institutionalisation here, then it is likely that there will be similar processes at work in most places. Brandenburg's politicians (of all persuasions), on the other hand, have always kept a close eye on what has gone on in the German capital. The state's geographical location, if nothing else, has always ensured that. We can therefore be pretty sure that if the Brandenburg Left Party takes little or no notice of what the Berlin Left Party does or, at the least, feels no inclination to act upon the party's actions in government then we will know that other state branches will also have the option of acting more or less independently of what the Left Party does in government elsewhere.

Of people and personalities: The (not quite so) 'Bunte Truppe'?

The Left Party's branches in Mecklenburg-Western Pomerania and Berlin are in many ways straightforward bodies to make sense of. They have their quirks and their idiosyncrasies, but one group (the modern socialists in Berlin and the pragmatic reformers in Mecklenburg-Western Pomerania) dominates their strategic thinking and practical politics and this has led to (relatively) clear and consistent patterns of behaviour. Where leaderships successfully shape and direct personnel development and policy debates, we would expect to find strong elements of continuity in the political messages that *Landesverbände* espouse. This is clearly the case within the first two Left Party branches that we have analysed. This is not quite so obviously the case in the Left Party's other branches across eastern Germany, and the branches in Saxony and Brandenburg have not been so good at co-opting (to use Panebianco's term) new members into existing leadership circles. The balance of power within each of these *Landesverbände* has subsequently been much more precarious. Internal conflicts, normally based around clashes of strong personalities, have affected the (often delicate) equilibriums within these branches and change – albeit reasonably well-controlled and relatively stable – has frequently occurred. Indeed, the Brandenburg and Saxon branches are emblematic of this.

The Left Party branch in Brandenburg is characterised by a number of distinct paradoxes. The most immediately apparent of these is that as the Left Party has done ever better at the polls, it has slipped further and further away from power and towards political isolation. The Brandenburg Left Party is, like its counterpart in Berlin, dominated by the parliamentary party and it is disputes within the *Fraktion* which have tended to shape the party's work. Within the *Fraktion*, there are plenty of pragmatic politicians with experience not just of *Land* and national politics, but also of local government.[3] Many of the Left Party's biggest beasts are active within the Brandenburg party – Lothar

Bisky, for example, is chairman of the federal party, Rolf Kutzmutz is his business manager and Dagmar Enkelmann is one of the deputy leaders – and personal rivalries have always simmered just below the surface. The leadership of the party has changed no less than six times since 1990 and even in late 2006 the strategic aims of the Left Party in Brandenburg remain anything but clear, largely as yet another round of leadership changes is currently taking place. This uncertainty has led the Left Party to sway between stressing a *Realpolitik* agenda that inevitably pushes it towards government participation and articulating – frequently in an overtly populist fashion – periods of anti-establishment protest.

Until 1994 the Left Party was granted – by virtue of the so-called Brandenburg Way – a considerable consultative voice in policy areas ranging from school reform to creating the *Land* constitution.[4] Even after the SPD gained an overall majority post-1994, informal contacts between the Social Democrats and the Left Party remained plentiful – largely through the activities of the Left Party's most influential behind-the-scenes wheeler-dealer, parliamentary business manager Heinz Vietze.[5] The creation of a Grand Coalition between the SPD and CDU in 1999 altered this situation. Some within the Left Party used this change in Brandenburg's government to articulate their unhappiness with the *Landtagsfraktion's* domination of internal party life. A significant proportion of the rank and file felt that the likes of chief strategist Michael Schumann, national party leader Lothar Bisky and Vietze paid little heed to the wishes of the grass roots – and the *Basis* subsequently felt that this was a good time to reassert its position within the party. This push by the rank and file for greater recognition was one of the reasons that in the 1999 leadership contest Anita Tack's opponent from within the KPF performed as well as he did.[6]

The Left Party was now proclaiming that it was not a governmental partner in waiting. It claimed that if it took on this role it would simply be used by the SPD as a blackmail tool with which to influence the CDU.[7] The loss of influence that the Brandenburg Left Party suffered went hand in hand with a further increase in tensions within the party and a difficult tenure in office of then party leader Anita Tack.[8] Tack's job, much has been the case for other Brandenburg Left Party leaders before and after her, was not made easier by the nascent generational conflict that periodically leads to internal discord. The younger members of the parliamentary party, grouped principally around Dagmar Enkelmann, favoured a strictly oppositional course. This clashed significantly with the much more conciliatory course proposed by Bisky and Vietze, who continued to seek contacts with the SPD.[9] Tack remained unable to genuinely 'fit' into either category and so became – through 2001 – ever more isolated, prompting Ralf Christoffers, a close friend of Bisky's and Vietze's, to take over her position. Christoffers tipped the balance of this particular conflict by arguing strongly for a pro-government-participation course, even choosing to risk the wrath of the *Basis* by speculating over long-term possible coalitions with the CDU.[10] Inner-party communication nonetheless remained as problematic as ever; the older generation around Vietze is locked in a culture where decisions are made and then implemented without too much in the way of discussion. The younger generation much prefer a discussion culture that is more open, perhaps more conflictual and certainly less disciplined. Battles between these politicians from different political worlds were pre-programmed from an early point in time.

On replacing Tack as leader, Ralf Christoffers subsequently attempted (reasonably successfully) to pull the party away from its self-preoccupation and to cajole it into channelling its efforts into attempting to gain power in 2004 – so much so that in 2002 there was even speculation as to who would be allocated which ministerial portfolio.[11] However, the circle around Christoffers made a conscious effort to avoid taking clear programmatic positions in order not to ignite old internal feuds. In spite of (or maybe even because of) its increasing isolation and internal heterogeneity, the Left Party stumbled from one election victory to the next, culminating in its most successful electoral performance to date when it polled 28 per cent of the vote in the 2004 *Land* election.

Many of the divides and controversies that are evident in the Brandenburg Left Party are also evident in Saxony. The leadership in Saxony is split into a number of competing (and antagonistic) factions while the *Basis* appears to be more traditional and conservative in outlook than is the case elsewhere. There are, however, three important differences between the Brandenburg and Saxon Left Party; firstly, the Saxon Left Party lacks a behind-the-scenes wheeler and dealer like Vietze, meaning that internal conflicts have much greater potential to spiral out of control. Secondly, given the electoral and political weakness of the Social Democrats (the SPD polled less than 10 per cent of the vote in the 2004 *Land* election in Saxony) and the Saxon SPD's traditionally distanced relationship with the democratic socialists, the Left Party cannot seriously expect to govern in the near future – and this made the option of adopting outright confrontational and oppositional positions much more attractive than they might otherwise have been.

Thirdly, in strategic terms, the Brandenburg Left Party appears to periodically have fallen back on brazenly populist rhetoric and anti stances, while the Saxon Left Party – somewhat curiously – has developed a more pragmatic, practical – even office-seeking – style.

The Left Party in Saxony has, for most of its existence, shown little interest in either modern socialism or pragmatism of any sort, concentrating instead on rhetorical warfare with the CDU. The reasons for the adoption of such tactics were twofold – rank and file members were, despite the occasional flirtation with *Realpolitik*, inherently suspicious of instrumental attempts to try and gain power and, secondly, internal fighting within the leadership prevented any sort of pro-government-participation consensus from developing. Under the leadership of Reinhard Lauter (1995–97) the Left Party almost became unleadable, and at a number of points appeared to be on the brink of implosion.[12] Lauter tried to develop and emphasise what he termed 'eco-socialism', but with little success, remaining – for the most part – isolated within leadership circles. The fact that Lauter was elected leader of the Saxon Left Party in the first place had much more to do with the inherent unelectability of his then opponent, Ronald Weckesser, who wanted to work towards achieving 'left-wing majorities' with a view to taking the Left Party into power in Dresden. This approach was roundly rejected by the party's rank and file and Lauter gained support precisely as he *was not* Weckesser.[13] Under Lauter's leadership the conflicts within the *Landesverband* escalated, centring principally (although not exclusively) around fundamental ideological disagreements between pragmatic members from Dresden and a much more orthodox Leipzig faction. This dismal period only ended in 1997 when the influential former Leipzig University professor Peter Porsch (once again) took over the leadership of the party. Porsch established himself quickly and, although he was never likely to be able to unite the party around one coherent message, he did at least have enough authority to stop the various factions waging war on each other. Porsch stressed that a divided and antagonistic party was in no one's interest and although he was not as successful at integrating the different factions as Bisky is at the national level, he did nonetheless ensure that some sense of unity and purpose was restored. Porsch remained in this position until 2001, when Cornelia Ernst took over, but – even now, and despite the loss of authority that went with his very public fight to clear his name after being accused of working with the Stasi – he remains an influential figure within the Saxon Left Party.[14]

Of pragmatic populism and internal rancour

As the Brandenburg and Saxon Left Party approached *Land* elections in 1999 they both had to deal with the question of what, if only theoretically in the Saxon case, they would do if government participation became a viable option. The Brandenburg Left Party originally adopted a highly pragmatic position. Positive vibes were made towards the SPD as early as 1997 when a conference resolution was passed recommending that the Left Party seek to join a coalition government with the Social Democrats or, at the very least, tolerate an SPD minority administration.[15] Even prior to this the Left Party leadership published an open letter to the SPD stating its intention of working closely with the SPD to form such a coalition.[16] 1997 was in many ways the highpoint of Left Party pragmatism in Brandenburg, as schisms slowly developed between the membership, the parliamentary party and other party employees, largely centring on (at times high octane) personality clashes rather than any sort of major disagreement over policy content. Rather than concentrate on entering government, the Left Party began more and more to concentrate on vote-maximisation strategies and this led to the government-participation-orientated leader, Wolfgang Thiel, being deposed in 1998.[17] The party *Basis* also appeared to think very little of the pragmatic-reform course that most members of the *Landespartei* were originally enthusiastic about. In the run-up to the 1999 *Land* election the Left Party in Brandenburg therefore presented a rather incoherent public face: Vietze supported participation in future governments with the SPD, Tack was firmly against such ideas. Tack might well have been rather isolated in the parliamentary party, but she received not inconsiderable support from the rank and file who remained sceptical of the pragmatic positions of the likes of Vietze and Lothar Bisky.

Debates on this issue in Saxony were progressing rather differently. In spite of Porsch's unity drive, the Saxon Left Party nonetheless remained distinctly heterogeneous. The scope of the positions taken ranged from outright opposition to government participation (mostly from restorative ideologues) to an emphasis on pragmatic policy-orientated positions. Weckesser and the leader of the Dresden Left Party, Ingrid Mattern, continued, for example, to campaign relentlessly for a more pragmatic, problem-solving approach within the party.[18] In view of the internal disagreements that continued to take place it is perhaps even more surprising that in the run-up to the 1998 election the Left Party actually moved away from articulating populist, anti sentiments towards a more pragmatic line. It is likely that this had much to do with the fact the Left Party had taken the role – initially in the public eye and later, post-1999, in the Dresden *Landtag* itself – of the main opposition party away from the SPD.

Despite the pragmatic exterior, the Left Party in Saxony nonetheless remained internally true to its more radical roots. Shortly after Cornelia Ernst took over the leadership of the party she wrote an open letter to the Saxon SPD offering to create a political alliance with it. The letter proved controversial. The left wing of the Left Party's parliamentary party was decidedly displeased, as was a large proportion of the rank and file. The Saxon SPD – never keen on working with the Left Party anyway – also went on to reject the offer out of hand. The SPD leader, Constanze Krehl, observed curtly that there was no point even discussing such ideas.[19] At the same time Porsch was trying to push through a cross-party vote-of-no-confidence in Kurt Biedenkopf – to no avail.[20] Even after his departure from office in 2001 Porsch never tired of stressing that the Saxon Left Party was open to co-operation with the Social Democrats and was making a conscious effort to stress its office-seeking credentials.[21] Yet, the party still managed to show its other face when discussing the reasons for the lost federal election of 2002. The loss of support that *Die Linke* suffered in Saxony was attributed to the performance of the Left Party in northern German governments in Mecklenburg-Western Pomerania and Berlin. Ernst complained to her party friends in Berlin that 'all the experiences that we have had ... (since the Left Party came into existence in 1989–90) ... have been as a radical, oppositional force. That is also the way that it is going to stay'.[22] When addressing the Left Party in Mecklenburg-Western Pomerania she added that 'your loss of support in the ... (2002) ... *Landtagswahl* must logically lead you to consider seriously where your coalition with the SPD is heading'.[23]

The move to embrace a more populist agenda had rather different motives in Brandenburg. The '*Brandenburger Weg*' had always been a pet project of the party leadership and, more specifically, Michael Schumann, the influential Vietze and Bisky. Unlike in Mecklenburg-Western Pomerania, however, the leadership was never able to genuinely convince the rank and file of the necessity of such a pragmatic approach. Brandenburg's politicians (perhaps sub-consciously) expected the rank and file to simply follow their lead, much as they had done in a different context pre-1989. This was something that the *Basis* was simply not prepared to countenance any more and the rank and file became ever more vocal in articulating its unhappiness. When Michael

Schumann died tragically in a car accident in 2000 a conceptual vacuum came to exist within the party. Ralf Christoffers was particularly keen on filling this void, but some of his unconventional policy preferences[24] prevented him from moving the *Landesverband's* centre of gravity back towards more pragmatic territory. The leading lights of the Brandenburg *Die Linke* were by now well aware of the internal tensions within the party and systematically avoided taking up clearly definable policy positions, relying instead on 'anti' campaigns to mobilise support: no to *Hartz IV*, no to Berlin-Brandenburg's proposed new airport and no to a fusion of the two *Bundesländer*.

By the time of the 2004 *Land* election, the old lines of conflict – particularly within the parliamentary party – began to reappear. Dagmar Enkelmann, having returned from the federal political arena to the Brandenburg stage, publicly criticised Christoffers and went on record wishing that 'the Left Party would gain more of an oppositional profile.'[25] Christoffers, on the other hand, speculated as to how much financial room for manoeuvre any future SPD–Left Party government might have and what they might choose to do with it.[26] Given such divergent positions, the socialist daily newspaper *Neues Deutschland* – a generally sympathetic observer of Left Party affairs – conveyed surprise that the *Landesvorstand* actually managed to find any sort of consensus in the run-up to the election.[27] The decision to put forward Enkelmann as the party's *Spitzenkandidatin* nonetheless had a considerable impact on the basic orientation of the election campaign – as did the national feeling of dissatisfaction with the *Hartz IV* labour market reform laws. The party realised that it could conduct a vociferous election campaign against a clear set of statewide policies without having to present anything too concrete in return. In this context Enkelmann was a clear compromise candidate who did not (yet) challenge the positions of power eked out by the likes of Bisky, Vietze and Christoffers. Enkelmann illustrated her less-than-overflowing enthusiasm for government participation by observing 'the fact that we are the strongest party in the opinion polls, in no way compels us to form the next government'.[28]

Vietze subsequently led a populist election campaign based on criticising the package of welfare reforms recently proposed by the federal government. Campaign slogans such as '*Hartz IV – Armut per Gesetz!*' (Hartz IV – Poverty by Decree) struck a chord with the Brandenburg electorate and the Left Party registered a thoroughly respectable election result, giving the party enough confidence to walk away from coalition negotiations with the SPD when they did not progress as the Left Party wished. For many in the rank and file this was precisely what they wanted; otherwise the poisoned chalice of government participation may have seen them suffer in the way that the Left Party was perceived to have done in Mecklenburg-Western Pomerania and Berlin.[29] In the negotiations the Left Party demanded that the Brandenburg SPD support a catalogue of demands for changes to welfare reforms recently introduced by the federal government.[30] Such an attitude was a logical consequence of the Left Party's election campaign – but it was also clearly going to be impossible for the Brandenburg SPD to do (even if it had wanted to) anything of the sort given that such sentiments would have been tantamount to a rebellion against the federal party. The failure of the coalition negotiations was all the more surprising given that within the SPD there was genuine interest in working with the democratic socialists in what would have been a third red-red government. The federal Left Party was, however, worried that entry into another *Land* government might endanger its prospects of re-entering the *Bundestag* in the forthcoming federal election.[31] The Left Party in Brandenburg therefore currently finds itself in a period of upheaval: given that the likes of Enkelmann and Bisky left for the *Bundestag* in 2005, Kerstin Kaiser has risen to be leader of the parliamentary party, although she does not possess a particularly large power base in the party[32]. Christoffers – for reasons of personal ill-health but also disenchantment with the failed coalition negotiations – has passed on the party leadership to the much lower profile Thomas Nord.[33]

Upheaval might be on the cards in Potsdam, but traditional – and highly personal – disputes and controversies still set the agenda in Saxony. Alongside long-standing ideological (see below) and territorial (between the three most significant city branches of Chemnitz, Dresden and Leipzig) disagreements, the Saxon *Die Linke* also has to deal with a generational clash.[34] On the one side there is the rather pejoratively named '*Jugendbrigade*' (the 'Young Brigade') that is allegedly composed of a younger, post-unification, generation of career-orientated Left Party activists.[35] On the other there is a group of pragmatic reformers led mainly by Cornelia Ernst, the former leader of the Saxon Left Party, and influential Dresden politicians Ingrid Mattern and Ronald Weckesser. While the Young Brigade is not as homogeneous as it is frequently portrayed in the media,[36] they do certainly have strong links with the (now very influential) emancipatory left, a faction that differs in just about every way (political style, communication methods, policy content and longer term aims and objectives) to the pragmatists. Put another way, the Young Brigade tends to put emphasis on the importance of a vibrant extra-parliamentary milieu around the party; the pragmatists seek to forge majorities in parliaments. The Young Brigade has a culture of dialogue, discussion and '*Selbstbestimmung*',[37] whereas the pragmatists have respect for those in office as well as for decisions made at conferences. The Young Brigade wants to challenge overarching societal structures; the pragmatists seek to shape everyday practical politics. Given these differences in cultural heritage, it is no wonder that members of the two groups disagree on so much.

Disputes between these two factions became so heated in the run-up to the 2004 election that issues of who should get which list place almost prevented Porsch from finding any sort of consensual position at all.[38] The significance of this last point should not be underestimated. Delegates at the 2004 conference were simply presented with a list that they were expected to approve. It had taken time, and a considerable degree of diplomatic negotiations, before the key placings were – behind closed doors – agreed upon. The relevant factions within the Left Party actively sought to push their own members as high up the list as possible with the aim of strengthening their own positions within the party. Once the party leadership had finally managed to negotiate acceptable compromises it fully expected conference delegates to support their decisions – and the fact that a majority of delegates were required to vote for any changes was undoubtedly meant to prevent critical voices from genuinely affecting the list's substance.[39] The *Basis*, naturally somewhat irritated that it was expected to have little say in who represented it in the Dresden *Landtag*, subsequently used the conference to articulate its not inconsiderable discontent with such procedures. These apparently undemocratic methods prompted two Left Party politicians to challenge them in the courts – and with this indirectly the whole election itself (it would have had to have been repeated had they been successful).[40] They lost, but the lesson was clear for all to see – ignore the rank and file and it will cause you difficulties. The internal conflicts that were so apparent in the late 1990s therefore clearly still exist. The course that the party has followed also remains flexible and enigmatic; in the 2004 election campaign the Left Party pressed the protest button, stressing its opposition to federal chancellor Gerhard Schröder's welfare reforms and running an even more overtly populist campaign than was evident in Brandenburg (where voters went to the polls two weeks earlier).[41] After the 2004 election Ernst nonetheless stressed that the Left Party was not simply a party creating expensive shopping lists and she once again offered the SPD her support in 'getting the very best out of the coalition negotiations with the CDU'.[42]

Of policies and programmes: From populism to pragmatism ... and back again?

Given that both of the *Landesverbände* have yet to experience life inside government it is not surprising to see that their policy preferences remain more expansive, more adventurous and less detailed than is the case in Mecklenburg-Western Pomerania and Berlin. Policy prescriptions in both states remain vague and general, Left Party politicians being safe in the knowledge that they can be 'hardened up' at an undefined later date. The most obvious example of this came at the Brandenburg *Landesparteitag* of 2003 when Heinz Vietze claimed that in spite of Brandenburg's financial plight, there was no need for the Left Party to start developing a savings plan for when it entered government. Such plans were only ever going to be developed under the pressure of actually having to craft political outcomes. Vietze, on the other hand, observed that for the time being the Left Party should do precisely the opposite of this, illustrating exactly where cuts *would not* be made. Vietze paid little attention to the Left Party's money-saving drive in Berlin or to its much more specific practical orientation in Mecklenburg-Western Pomerania and continued to display a genuine flare for the populist. Such strategies are permissible in opposition, no matter more or less what a sister branch of the same party is doing elsewhere.

For most of its history the Brandenburg Left Party has subsequently stressed vote-maximisation goals over and above office-seeking and policy-seeking ones. The only real exception to this was a short period after the election of Ralf Christoffers to the leadership of the party in 2001. Such an emphasis on vote-seeking assists the party, and particularly parts of its younger and more dynamic leadership, in overcoming some of the (at times quite nasty) internal disputes alluded to above and to appeal to diverse voter coalitions. They do this by stressing a variety of vague issue-packages. Given the personality clashes evident in the Brandenburg Left Party it is perhaps a good job that policy issues are less controversial than elsewhere; the Brandenburg *Die Linke* does not have a controversial administrative reform to push through (Mecklenburg-Western Pomerania), nor does it have to make extraordinarily difficult financial decisions (Berlin).[43] Such a vote-seeking approach is also appealing to a Brandenburg *Basis* that remains inherently suspicious of the idea of crossing the floor and entering government. Concerning the party list in the run-up to the 2004 *Land* election the Brandenburg Left Party displayed a penchant for campaigning on what it did *not* stand for stressing its opposition to the Agenda 2010 package (and particularly the *Hartz IV* labour market reforms) as well as two of its traditional objects of derision, the construction of a new *Großflughafen* in Berlin and the fusion of Berlin and Brandenburg. However, this is not to say that a particular group of nay-sayers is dominating proceedings. On the contrary, the disputes between strong characters within the party make it virtually impossible for it to agree on positive policy prescriptions that are supported by all of the parliamentary party, the rank and file and party workers. The policy disputes are not deep; they are the proxies through which groups have sought to out-manoeuvre each other. This naturally leads to negative campaigns and an acceptance that minimal positions of agreement are the best that the party can manage. Indeed, Lothar Bisky hit the nail on the head when he wryly observed that his party is '*zwar regierungsfähig, aber nicht regierungswillig*' ('able to govern, but not willing to do so').[44]

The fact that almost half of all current Left Party MdL in Brandenburg entered parliament for the first time in 2004, have plenty of experience in local politics and are significantly more orientated towards specific areas of policy is also likely to affect the strategic direction that the party takes in future.[45] Some of the new MdL quickly became frustrated with their inability to change a great deal from the solitude of the opposition benches. As Torsten Krause, the 25-year-old spokesman on youth politics in the parliamentary party has put it 'now, of course, we do lots of work and see little end product'. Krause claimed that in the 2005 debate on the budget the Left Party suggested 100 amendments and not one of them was accepted. For practical 'doers' such as Krause this is all the more galling when 'members of other *Fraktionen* come up to you and say "yes, Herr Krause, you're actually right, but we can't act on that suggestion for political reasons"'.[46]

In 2006 a pivotal external development appears to have further accelerated moves towards much more pragmatic stances. The CDU in Brandenburg descended into chaos when a former general secretary, Sven Petke, was forced to resign and squabbles broke out over who should succeed long-time leader, Jörg Schönbohm. The Left Party realised that the CDU was losing support among not just the Brandenburg electorate at large but also from the SPD; the prospect of a red-red coalition was becoming ever more likely. While the CDU was struggling with these internal problems the Left Party *Landtagsfraktion* published a surprisingly detailed document outlining how it saw Brandenburg developing in the short and medium term – a document that many understood as a conciliatory move towards the Social Democrats.[47] Alongside the wide and varied criticisms of the 'neoliberal' hegemony that is allegedly gripping Germany, the Left Party was also prepared to move (in policy terms) towards the SPD in a way that it certainly was not in the aftermath of the 2004 *Land* election; it was now prepared to accept a fusion of Brandenburg and Berlin as long as it took place '*auf Augenhöhe*' (as a marriage of equals); it was prepared to think about a thorough administrative reform in the state (something that the Grand Coalition had not yet had the courage to put on the political agenda); it was also prepared to support the building of a new, and still controversial, airport at Schönefeld and, perhaps most surprising of all, the party was prepared to concentrate financial support for initiatives to reinvigorate the economy in a small number of specific areas (and these were to be fewer in number than even the CDU-led government of the time was suggesting).[48] With this in mind it would almost appear that the future aims and strategy of the Left Party in Brandenburg has as much to do with the fate of the CDU as it does with anything else. If the Brandenburg CDU continues to slip from one internal scandal to the next then the pragmatic and modern socialist forces within the Left Party will gain in strength and future participation in government will begin to look like a genuine prospect. Such a point in time may come sooner than people think as the Brandenburg SPD is already having to refute claims that it is trying to sideline the CDU in order to bring *Die Linke* into the coalition equation.[49]

The Left Party's position in Saxony is more complicated, yet it too is slowly moving (if at a decidedly pedestrian, and occasionally erratic, pace) towards a more pragmatic position. This was particularly evident around 2002 and 2003 and although the old personality conflicts raised their heads again in 2004 and 2005 there is still evidence that when the backstabbing stops thoughts return to how the Left Party might shape a future Saxony. Pre-2000 the Left Party was much less prepared to engage in programmatic discussions, even within the privacy of its own four walls. The populist tactics that the Left Party invoked in the late 1990s prompted it to almost completely disown itself from all detailed programmatic positions as it continued to try and hammer away at the CDU. The SPD, struggling with its own myriad of problems, looked on meekly from a distance. Although such tactics are used intermittently by the Left Party across all levels, the national Left Party nonetheless thought that in the run-up to the 1998 federal election the Saxon *Die Linke* went too far in its negative, anti-politics rhetoric and warned the Saxon Left Party that its policy documents were so devoid of concrete proposals that the party risked being labelled merely as a left-wing-conservative populist grouping.[50]

Even though Porsch always rejected (often in public) the criticisms made by the federal Left Party that Saxon politicians were too populist, even he criticised his own *Landesverband* for entering the 1999 Saxon election campaign with no clearly definable economic agenda. He subsequently demanded that future policies be clear and properly costed.[51] For the increasingly influential members of the emancipatory left this meant distancing themselves from the 'full employment myth', lowering expectations of what the state can actually achieve and ending the 'fixation on demographic issues'. Politicians such as the increasingly prominent Katja Kipping argue for a fundamental reorganisation of Germany's welfare state and the introduction of a minimum wage from which everyone could theoretically live.[52] The SPD's 1999 electoral implosion (it polled a meagre 10.7 per cent of the vote and the Left Party replaced it as the second force in the state) also prompted further moves towards practical policy suggestions. Visible evidence of this new pragmatism was first evident in 2000 when the Left Party published an alternative budget to that of the governing CDU, with Weckesser's demands for a 'debt-free socialism' sounding positively Berlin-like in tone. Such modern socialist proposals were not completely new within the party; as early as 1996, for example, the Left Party-friendly employers' association around Dresden MdL Barbara Lässig, the '*Offener Wirtschaftsverband von klein- und mittelständischen Unternehmen, Freiberuflern und Selbständigen im Freistaat Sachsen*' (The Association of Small and Medium-sized Businesses and the Self-Employed in Saxony – OWUS), campaigned for a two-day buffer period in cases of illness when employees would continue receiving full pay in return for a reduction in the number of job creation schemes – a thoroughly pragmatic approach to welfare policy, the likes of which the more ideological Leipzigers would never dream of proposing.[53] This type of proposal was, however, only made with some sort of coherence and consistency from around 2000 onwards.

By 2004 the Left Party was publishing an 'Alternative State Development Plan' ('*Alternatives Landesentwicklungskonzept*' – *Aleksa*) that set out, in quite some detail, where the Left Party planned to take Saxony in the future.[54] Aleksa soon drifted away from the centre of the Saxon Left Party's thoughts, but it is likely that a reinvigorated version of this will appear in the run-up to the 2009 *Land* election.[55] Nine *Die Linke* members of the Dresden city council also emphasised their pragmatism and realism shortly after the 2005 federal election when they supported the sale of a significant number of publicly owned housing associations.[56] Sections of the Left Party in Saxony (primarily in

Dresden) were displaying few of the populist tub-thumper traits that had traditionally been the staple diet of Saxon Left Party politics and were beginning to look and sound ever more like the modern socialists that many within the party (primarily the restorative ideologues and a considerable section of the rank and file) detested so much. The sale of the housing associations was also met by consternation within sections of the federal parliamentary party and co-leader Oskar Lafontaine could not resist claiming that these Left Party politicians should consider nothing less than leaving the party and going elsewhere.[57]

A further trait of the Saxon *Die Linke* is the emancipatory left's tendency to occasionally let its libertarian instincts run free – to the consternation of the (much) more conservative, older generation of both office-seekers and virtually all of the rank and file. Reactions to the much publicised 'right to possess drugs' ('*Recht auf Rausch*') and 'right to be lazy' ('*Recht auf Faulheit*') initiatives of MdL such as Julia Bonk are symptomatic of the different worlds that these factions live in.[58] 'We argue' claims Bonk 'that everyone should have the right to make their own decision on whether they take drugs or not'.[59] Few people in the Left Party either over 40 and/or outside of the emancipatory left are likely to even vaguely sympathise. Despite loud noises of discontent from within the party, Bonk and like-minded colleagues further claimed, in their '2004 youth election manifesto', that 'getting high on drugs is an important part of many people's lives'. They did not stop there. 'Alcohol and tobacco, sex, consumption and illegal drugs; the right to indulge must exist for everyone' before finishing by claiming that 'we don't want anyone to tell us which drugs we are and aren't allowed to take. We want to be able to live our lives independently, with or without drugs'.[60] This rather serial episode came to a head shortly before the 2005 federal election when the party's youth wing, led by the Saxon Left Party's youth spokesperson Juliane Nagel, planned a publicity campaign to discuss such issues. This idea was quickly nipped in the bud with Cornelia Ernst moving to prevent it from taking place. Even then, the outcome was a rather peculiar compromise allowing (perhaps in classical dialectical fashion) the four events that were planned to nonetheless take place.[61] Drugs policy has subsequently been something that Left Party grandees have been trying to keep well and truly off the political agenda.

Controversial debates such as these did naturally not prevent debates on government participation from rumbling on. Moves, however patchy, towards office-seeking in both Brandenburg and Saxony were not prompted by any particular sources of inspiration from either Mecklenburg-Western Pomerania or Berlin. The Left Party's experience in government was noted and observed from afar but there was certainly no template for direct emulation. The Brandenburg Left Party did nonetheless consult with both *Landesverbände* before it set out on coalition negotiations in 2004. It did so primarily to make sure that it wasn't taken for a ride by a much more experienced (in terms of coalition negotiations) SPD.[62] There is also little doubt that sections of the Berlin Left Party, in particular, firmly wished to see the Left Party in Brandenburg enter government, if mainly as this fitted in nicely with their modern socialist ideology and, given their geographical location, the two states inevitably have closer links than most.[63] There is, however, little evidence to suggest that overt policy learning or policy transfer has taken place across *Land* boundaries.[64] With the loss of the federal parliamentary party in 2002 various institutional bodies were created to co-ordinate politics at the horizontal level across the *Länder*; the most prominent of these being the *Fraktionsvorsitzendenkonferenz* (regular meetings of *Land* parliamentary leaders) and meetings between MdLs with similar portfolios. These meetings happen surprisingly frequently, roughly every six weeks according to some estimates.[65] Once or twice a year entire parliamentary parties also meet with their representatives from other states.[66] Useful though such fora are for co-ordination purposes, there is little concrete evidence to suggest that they act as transmission belts for specific policies to be imported and exported across *Land* borders. What these institutions certainly do facilitate is discussion, co-operation and co-ordination between the Left Party's key representatives at the *Land* level – and this in turn has led to a much higher profile for the *Länder* as a unit. Even though this very rarely comes through in specific policy terms it certainly does help the eastern German branches to talk with one (stronger) voice within the party as a whole. This was significant when no national parliamentary party existed (2002–5) as the Left Party's leaders in the *Länder* were effectively leading the party.[67] It is also likely to remain significant in the (much wider and diverse) post-2006 Left Party where the eastern German states as a whole are likely to have interests that unite them rather more than divide them (see below).

Sachpolitiker (MdLs who have a specific and long-standing interest in a particular policy area) do certainly maintain regular contact with each other, exchanging experiences and discussing problems and solutions, but the uniqueness of each *Land* environment does still prevent this from getting beyond anything but the most superficial of levels. Exceptions do exist though. Despite commenting that he knew virtually no one in most of the other Left Party *Landesverbände*, Brandenburg

MdL Torsten Krause claimed that in the high profile area of employment policy, the 1000 jobs that the Mecklenburg-Western Pomerania government created for youngsters in the ÖBS is a model that could be implemented in Brandenburg. And, should the SPD and Left Party ever enter coalition negotiations again, then Krause has no doubt that a similar commitment (for 500 jobs) will find its way into the coalition agreement. In Krause's words, 'the SPD-Left Party government in Mecklenburg-Western Pomerania has illustrated that it is possible and practical to do this and we would like to follow suit'.[68]

Conclusion

In states where it does not govern, the Left Party's branches have been, for the most part, heterogeneous bodies. They have been plagued by personality clashes, possessed little more than vague and decidedly general policy packages, developed a taste for populist rhetoric and suffered persistent internal and external communication problems. Clashes between 'old school' politicians with conservative, more traditional understandings of how internal affairs within the Left Party should be conducted and younger, more *'diskussionsfreudig'* and confrontational groups of activists have been evident everywhere. No one group has managed to dominate proceedings in either of the states analysed in detail here and, for most of the 1990s, the *Landesverbände* subsequently swayed between different aims and strategies as a result.

In recent times, however, there has been an undoubted convergence in both of these things; the pivotal question of whether the Left Party should enter sub-state government has been answered (at least in leadership circles) in the affirmative and the question is now much more under what conditions should the Left Party take the governmental plunge. The vast majority of the Left Party's leading politicians in the *Länder* are now quite pragmatic about this, and differences in political behaviour can normally be accounted for by looking at strategic rather than fundamental differences between territorial units. The Left Party's party strategists are more than aware of this increased convergence and a recent analysis by the 'Forum for Democratic Socialism' explicitly claims that the new Left Party's success will largely depend on whether the party is accepted as a serious and reliable coalition partner in both eastern *and* western German *Landtage*.[69] Given the heterogeneity of the parliamentary party in the *Bundestag* such conclusions seem eminently plausible as it is at the *Land* level where the Left Party is likely to need to demonstrate its ability to shape and craft policy outputs.

The conflicts that do still exist at the *Land* level have either been of a personal nature or have come down to (in theory largely avoidable) communication problems, both with political opponents and also within individual *Landesverbände*. In states where it does not govern, Left Party politicians have shown a startling tendency to talk past each other and to remain hostage to cultural and communication conflicts that reflect the heritage of the Left Party politicians involved. The Left Party in Berlin has been much better at avoiding such conflicts than has the party in, for example, Mecklenburg-Western Pomerania – although it has still done a better job at this than is the case in Saxony and Brandenburg. This means that the more evident the clash in political styles, the less likely that, over time, a coherent set of political aims and programmatic objectives will be agreed upon and systematically pursued. These can, under certain conditions, lead to more populist outbursts and ever-greater stress on what *Die Linke* does not stand for. They are, naturally, also not conducive to the Left Party entering *Land* governments.

In Brandenburg the Left Party has long been in a state of flux. Its future nonetheless appears to be strongly linked to that of the CDU. If the Christian Democrats keep a lid on their own internal problems then the Left Party is likely to be pushed back towards the peripheral position it has occupied for most of the time since 1999. There would be less need for the Left Party to develop hard and fast policy proposals and a move towards more populist campaigns such as that of 2004 would also seem likely. If the CDU continues to struggle to overcome its current factionalism and fails to find a suitable replacement for long-time leader Jörg Schönbohm then the Left Party will naturally become a much more serious coalition option for the SPD.[70] This is unlikely to be lost on *Die Linke* politicians and corresponding changes in both policy and rhetoric, much as began to happen in the early 2000s, is likely to be on the cards. In Saxony, meanwhile, the Left Party continues to try to transform itself into a genuinely relevant actor at *Land* level. The SPD's weakness does not help, but the aim of a parliamentary majority to the left of the CDU is nonetheless likely to tempt the Left Party to develop more plans such as *Aleksa* and to contribute to bringing the ideologically and culturally diverse groups within the state back together. The cultural clashes will not vanish, but the effect that they are likely to have is likely to be shaped by the opportunities that the Left Party sees for entering government.

One factor left largely out of the above analysis is the role that the federal party is likely to play in shaping, persuading and encouraging the party's *Land* politicians. The creation of the Left Party out of the PDS and WASG has ensured that the federal parliamentary party is much more diverse than had been the case for a number of years previously. Widely different opinions exist on questions such as when and where the Left Party should govern, under what conditions and what it should try to do when it gets there. Furthermore, will the far left of the Left Party around the restorative ideologues in the Marxist Forum and what is left of the KPF form an unseemly alliance with the not insignificant number of WASG members who are critical of Left Party government participation at the *Land* level? Given that prominent critics such as MEP Sahra Wagenknecht and MdBs Wolfgang Gerhcke, Diether Dehm and Oskar Lafontaine have little directly to do with *Land* politics in the East, is this the next conflict line that the Left Party will need to overcome? It is to the development of the Left Party at the federal – and more specifically its metamorphosis into a new party in the spring of 2007 – that we turn in the next chapter.

8
From the PDS to the Left Party

Introduction

Pre-2002 the PDS survived in the *Bundestag* without ever really setting down roots in western Germany. The 1.2 per cent of the vote that it won in the western states in 1998 were, of course, certainly vital in helping it achieve *Fraktionsstatus* (full rights as a parliamentary party) for the first time, but the party still looked (and for many within the party no doubt felt) like a fish out of water in western Germany. As Florian Weis wryly noted in 2005 'if you want to measure the extent of the PDS's steps forward in western Germany through the years, then you're going to need extremely sensitive instruments to be able to do so'.[1] In the minds of the vast majority of western Germans, the PDS remained very much an eastern actor talking an eastern language, and prospects of this ever changing appeared, even for the most optimistic PDS activist, to be pretty dim.

There are a number of reasons why the PDS failed to expand westwards through the 1990s and early 2000s. Some (more conservative) observers claimed that the PDS simply did not possess any vital interests in western Germany and could therefore never speak for any particular group of western Germans other than perhaps those on the extremist fringes.[2] Although clearly not completely wide of the mark, this did not prevent members of the PDS – more or less unanimously – from seeking to expand their membership and voter base westwards.[3] Others argue that the judgement of the federal constitutional court in September 1990, stipulating that parties could enter the national parliament by polling 5 per cent of the popular vote in *either* eastern or western Germany prompted the PDS to concentrate too much of its efforts on obtaining eastern German votes at the expense of creating viable and rigorous structures in western Germany.[4]

Be that as it may, the PDS's membership and activist base in western Germany has traditionally been altogether different from that in eastern Germany. Although the PDS's membership in the West has been wide and diverse, three particular groups quickly manifested themselves within the 'new' party; firstly, a group of hard-left political activists who had previously been active in the *Bund Westdeutscher Kommunisten* (Association of West German Communists – BWK). These new PDS members frequently had Maoist sympathies and, most noticeably in Hamburg, attempted to infiltrate the party in classic Communist style, transforming it into a bigger version of the BWK.[5] Secondly, another significant group of Communists joined the party, but this time from the German Communist Party (DKP). These members were ideologically close to the eastern German KPF and most of these members held traditional, orthodox Communist positions. Finally, a group of young and politically very inexperienced individuals found their way to the PDS who lacked any sort of grounding in party politics.[6] Most of these members were male, many of them held opinions bordering on the extremist and few had any genuine experience of being a part of a large and complex political party. By the end of 1990 it became crystal clear that these people were not going to lead to the PDS establishing itself as a mass membership party in western Germany any time soon.

Given the background of the PDS's fledgling membership in western Germany and the general lack of consensus on strategies for expanding the party's political base, it should not come as too much of a surprise that PDS membership numbers remained very low and electoral support minimal. Gregor Gysi's 1994 'Ingolstadt Manifesto' – a clear attempt at appealing to the more libertarian instincts of some left-of-centre western German voters – fell, for example, on completely deaf ears.[7] The federal party and the eastern *Landesverbände* were also at a loss about what to do with the western branches, and the first of a number of fiery disputes between these factions took place in 1995 at a party conference in Schwerin.[8] The federal party either could not and/or would not invest considerable time and resources into training members of the western branches in the art of political communication and it is no coincidence that the PDS did a little better at local level (when the occasional semi-respected politician stood on a PDS ticket) and national level (when the image of the federal party came into play) than it did in western *Land* elections (when the PDS appeared, to many people, to be nothing short of mad).

The situation did not even improve after the federal election success of 1998. The resignation of Oskar Lafontaine as finance minister in the spring of 1999 prompted talk of the PDS manoeuvring itself into the vacuum that was now perceived to exist to the left of the SPD as the Social Democrats moved off in search of the centre ground.[9] High-profile PDS politicians again went looking for western votes; the call to pressure the red-green government from the left (*'Druck von links'*) was largely directed at disgruntled western voters, as were Gregor Gysi's '12 theses for modern socialism'.[10] Yet such strategies could not deflect attention from the extremism of some of the western *Landesverbände* and with this the awful impression that they continued to make on western voters. Throw in the PDS's continued reputation as an eastern party and, perhaps most significantly, structural anticommunism and it is no wonder that the PDS continued to find life in western Germany extremely challenging.[11] The PDS's political and electoral insignificance should nonetheless not deflect from a number of important factors that could, at least theoretically, help a left-wing party accrue support. Roughly 15 per cent of western Germans claim to possess broadly left-wing political beliefs; a significant number of western Germans were also becoming ever less satisfied with the alleged move rightwards of German politics in general. Western Germany might therefore not be a place where the PDS could win support, but another left-wing party with a different cultural background might just be able to.

The origins of the WASG and early relations with the PDS[12]

The emergence of such a party nonetheless came about much to the surprise of many. The Electoral Alternative for Work and Social Justice (*Wahlalternative: Arbeit und Soziale Gerechtigkeit* – WASG) was established as a direct result of the so-called Hartz reforms announced by Chancellor Schröder after the 2002 federal election. As part of his attempt to revive the economy in the face of continuing economic problems and stubborn unemployment figures, Schröder commissioned a study group under then VW Chairman Peter Hartz to suggest changes to Germany's labour market laws and welfare system. Although the Hartz Commission ultimately made a number of concrete proposals such as the restructuring of unemployment offices and the loosening of restrictions governing part-time work, it was the fourth bundle of proposals – what came to be known in shorthand as Hartz IV – that were the most far-ranging and by far the most controversial. In Hartz IV the VW chief suggested, among other things, shortening the period in which the unemployed could receive full benefits as well as cutting the gross amount that claimants would actually receive.

Schröder's announcement that he intended to implement these suggestions provoked a storm of protest, most especially (and not unsurprisingly) from the trade union movement. Going beyond the initial public demonstrations, a number of Hartz opponents – based mainly in northern Germany and including Axel Troost (an economist and leader of the working group 'Alternative Economic Policy'), Joachim Bischoff (editor of the journal *Socialism* and a former member of the PDS Executive committee) and Ralf Krämer (secretary of the public service union 'Ver.di') – met on 5 March 2004 in Berlin to plan a concerted strategy of defiance. The group put out a call to action for all interested opponents of *Hartz IV* and created a website with the name *Wahlalternative* (Electoral Alternative). Independently of this another group of Hartz IV opponents from southern Germany (and principally Bavaria) convened, this time representing many local and regional representatives of the powerful trade union IG Metall (traditionally very close to the SPD). This group, naming itself the 'Initiative for Labour and Social Justice' (ASG), was led by union leaders (and SPD members) Thomas Händel and Klaus Ernst. In early summer 2004 the two opposition groups gathered together for the first time and some two months later merged their organisations into the WASG. Thus, from the beginning, the WASG was a relatively heterogeneous group made up primarily of disillusioned SPD members, trade union functionaries and left-wing intellectuals.

The SPD reacted swiftly to this challenge, expelling the founders of the WASG from the party. Yet the membership of the new WASG – until January 2005 still an interest group rather than a political party – continued to grow, with some 5000 people signing on as members by the end of autumn 2004. Emboldened by its success, the membership voted to found a new party and to compete in the state election in North Rhine-Westphalia in May 2005. Initial reaction from the PDS to the new WASG was decidedly cool. Although Lothar Bisky suggested that the emergence of the WASG was to be welcomed (not the least because it would 'shake up' the PDS in both western and eastern Germany[13]) and former campaign chief André Brie proposed that the PDS and WASG band together for the 2006 federal election, more typical was the reaction of Bodo Ramelow, parliamentary leader in Thuringia (and future campaign manager for the 2005 federal election); he suggested in the spring of 2004 that co-operation with the WASG was out of the question, as the latter party was 'prisoner to a style of thinking that has nothing to do with finding all-German, real-world solutions'.[14]

This initial reaction to the WASG was perhaps somewhat surprising: given the WASG's resonance in western Germany (especially strong in former industrial areas of the western states, but almost completely absent in eastern Germany) and the PDS's notorious failure to establish itself there, the WASG would seem to have presented an ideal partner for the PDS. It was 'anti-neo-liberal' (whatever that meant), it was anti-Hartz IV and it had the potential to mobilise a trade union-inspired western German left wing in a way that the PDS never could hope to. Yet the PDS's instinctive defensiveness stemmed from a number of simple calculations; the thought of a rival to the left of the SPD in western Germany posed a real threat to the (albeit very small) inroads that the PDS itself had made over the previous decade and a half – and with this the chances of the PDS polling 5 per cent of the vote nationwide in federal elections. The difficult experiences that the PDS had had with some of its own western German members was also firmly in the forefront of some eastern members' minds as was the WASG's clear hostility to the PDS's participation in regional governments in Mecklenburg-Western Pomerania (MV) and Berlin.

Be that as it may, for its part the WASG was also initially quite hostile to the PDS. As the first mass email communication of the ASG argued, the PDS 'has stayed an eastern party ... and has further disqualified itself [as a partner] through its participation in government in Berlin and Rostock'.[15] In addition, the growth of the WASG in Berlin (discussed further below) could in large part be traced to its explicit opposition to the SPD–PDS coalition government in that state. Prospects for co-operation between the PDS and WASG in the early spring of 2005 thus looked slim. And yet there were two wild cards in the relationship between the parties – Oskar Lafontaine and Gregor Gysi. Lafontaine, the former chancellor candidate of the SPD and long-time Minister-President of the Saarland, was the doyen of the SPD's left wing and therefore ideologically close to many in the WASG. He was also on very good terms with the PDS leadership (and especially Gysi) and as early as 2003 rumours surfaced that Lafontaine and Gysi were hatching plans for co-operation between anti-Schröder, SPD-rebels and the PDS – and even, perhaps, the founding of a new left-wing party.[16] The catalyst that precipitated eventual co-operation between the WASG and PDS, and a subsequent drive for merger, was the fallout from the North Rhine-Westphalia state election of May 2005 – namely, an unexpected new federal election in the September of that year – and Lafontaine and Gysi's push for a new electoral alliance to compete in this contest.

The rush to the Bundestagswahl

The North Rhine-Westphalia (NRW) state election proved to be a decisive event shaping the relationship between the WASG and PDS. Going into the state election, there were four possible electoral outcomes for the two parties. First, the WASG could enter the state parliament while the PDS failed. This would put wind in the sails of the WASG and encourage it to run on its own in the next federal election while the PDS would be left to ponder whether the WASG could rob it of its own chances of achieving national representation. Second, the PDS could overcome the 5 per cent hurdle while the WASG failed. In this case, the PDS would have no reason to co-operate with the WASG. Given the PDS's dismal electoral performances in western German state elections this outcome appeared highly unlikely. Third, both could poll 5 per cent of the vote. In this case, each party would feel emboldened but also threatened. Party competition, not co-operation, would undoubtedly be the order of the day. Finally, both could fail to gain seats in the new state parliament. Depending on how well each party performed relative to the other, this would be the only scenario in which each party would believe there would be a substantial political and electoral advantage in working together.[17] In the event, the WASG received 2.2 per cent of the vote, enough to encourage the leadership of the WASG that the party had some clout in western German politics while falling well short of the 5 per cent barrier – and below even what many in the WASG had expected. Meanwhile, the PDS scored a mere 0.9 per cent of the vote, even managing to lose vote share compared to the last state election in NRW five years previously. Party strategists on both sides thus had to reconsider their stances. This rethinking of the relationship between the two parties was further accelerated by an even more significant consequence of the NRW election – Chancellor Schröder's call for a new federal election a full year ahead of schedule following the SPD's own disastrous performance in NRW and the (allegedly) untenable situation for the SPD in the *Bundesrat*.

At this point, the actions of Lafontaine and Gysi drove events forward. In an interview with *Bild*, Lafontaine argued that 'Social Democrats, union members, PDS, and WASG must coalesce in a new party that will stand in contrast to the policies of social dismantling that the establishment parties in Berlin are pursuing'.[18] Furthermore, Lafontaine stated that he would be ready to serve as a candidate for such a left-wing grouping. Lafontaine's announcement galvanised the leadership of the PDS and WASG and arrangements for the first preliminary discussions between the two groups were hastily made.[19] Meanwhile, Gregor Gysi announced in early June of 2005 that he would be willing to serve as a direct candidate in the – distinctly winnable – Treptow-Köpenick (Berlin) constituency in the upcoming federal election. This was a district that the PDS had only just lost to the SPD in the 2002 election, with the effect that the party failed to register three constituency seats in the *Bundestag* – thus ensuring the loss of its much prized *Fraktion* status. Gysi's return to active political life signalled a claim to reassert his influence and authority within the PDS, influence and authority which would be used to create a more viable left-wing political force with his friend Lafontaine.

At their initial meetings, the leadership of the two parties were faced with having to sort out not only ideological and policy disagreements, but also legal and technical questions about what was (and was not) permissible if the two were to run together in the forthcoming federal election – and all of this in an extremely abbreviated time period. In essence, co-operation in the election could assume three forms: the founding of a new party (and a disbanding of the two existing parties), a quick merger of the two parties or the placement of WASG candidates on a PDS 'open list'. The first option was simply unthinkable, while the second was completely impractical. Only after the federal election could discussions on a party merger seriously take place; this despite the fact that both parties saw a future merger as a realistic (if not uncontroversial) development. This left the third option. The end result of the negotiations was what Gysi termed a 'co-operation agreement with a perspective for a merger' signed on 10 June by Klaus Ernst, representing the WASG, and Lothar Bisky, representing the PDS.[20] According to the new agreement, discussions on a 'new project for the Left in Germany' would proceed further, the PDS executive board would examine the possibility of changing the party's name (which it would later do), neither party would put up candidates against each other, WASG members would submit themselves as candidates on the open lists of the PDS and the PDS would strive to include them (leaving the actual decision-making process on this to the individual PDS state organisations). Although the final agreement and 'roadmap' for the merger met with much criticism (discussed below) from the membership of each party, WASG and PDS party conferences approved the agreement with decisive majorities.

Through the summer of 2005 the new 'Left Party' subsequently became one of the most intriguing stories of the federal election campaign. The party generated enormous interest – despite, or perhaps because of, it's unknown potential – and rode high in the polls (recording as much as 12 per cent in pre-election opinion surveys). Despite legal challenges to the running of WASG candidates on the Left Party's open lists, as well as an increasingly difficult situation developing in the Berlin and Mecklenburg-Western Pomeranian WASG organisations (discussed below), as election day approached the 'new' party continued to gather momentum. And even though enthusiasm for the party dampened somewhat in the early autumn as voters began to more carefully consider their choices, the Left Party nevertheless garnered 8.7 per cent of the vote on election day – far more than the PDS ever received, and undoubtedly far more than the WASG and PDS together would have managed had they run as separate parties.

Trouble in paradise: Conflicts between, and challenges facing, the two parties

A wave of public enthusiasm and intra-party goodwill had carried the new Left Party to a tremendous election result. However, points of conflict between the two parties were not hard to discern beneath the (initial) happy exterior. First of all, the two parties differ enormously in size and in respective voting milieus. While the Left Party could count some 61,000 party members, the WASG numbered around 12,000.[21] Many in the WASG feared that their organisation would be simply swallowed up by the Left Party, much as they thought Alliance 90 had once been effectively taken over by the much larger (western) German Greens in 1993. As one WASG activist put it, the Left Party was 'only seeking useful idiots … we know what they mean by an alliance'.[22] This fear was hardly becalmed by the descriptions of leading Left Party figures of the new party as 'PDS-plus', and recommendations that WASG members simply join it after disbanding their own organisation.[23] Some Left Party pragmatists were decidedly defensive about the whole merger idea, mainly as they feared that greater ideological diversity would lead to a loss of *Politikfähigkeit*. The modern socialists, meanwhile, tended towards a completely different position, believing that an amalgamation with the WASG finally offered them the opportunity to expand westwards and to embed themselves there. For some WASG members, these statements (and others, such as Helmut Holter's remark that the WASG should accommodate itself to the Left Party – not vice versa) were proof that the WASG was being used by (factions within) the Left Party for their own means.[24] The differential regional support for the two parties also posed a problem: while the WASG is overwhelmingly a western-anchored political grouping, with more than four-fifths of its membership in the western states, the renamed PDS – as is well known – is a *de facto* eastern party, with only about 4000 of its members in western Germany. Viewing the glass as half full, one could say that the two parties compliment each other; indeed, the WASG's membership strength (and electoral potential) in western Germany is precisely what the new Left Party found attractive. Viewing the glass as half-empty, on the other hand, one could say that such a sharp divide between an eastern Left Party and western WASG could simply raise the potential for a 'wall in the head' to become embedded in the new party. Indeed, the east-west conflict within the new Left Party was evident early on, with criticisms ranging from the details of the co-operation agreement to an outright rejection of the ideology and policies of one party or the other. In the wake of the initial co-operation agreement in the early summer of 2005, for example, protests in WASG organisations in Hesse, Bavaria and Baden-Württemberg erupted, with some WASG members complaining that the co-operation agreement represented nothing more than a capitulation of the WASG to the PDS. Others within the WASG rejected any co-operation with the Left Party outright, for, as one WASG member belonging to the 'Leverkusen Circle' – a grouplet of anti-Left Party activists within the WASG – complained, 'we want a social party but not a socialist one'.[25] Meanwhile, PDS members in eastern Germany feared that the creation of the new Left Party would mean a change of identity and a subsequent loss of the party's eastern profile, while Left Party members in the west feared the wholesale takeover of their local and state party organisations. These members had always felt their work to be unappreciated and unrewarded, now they felt overrun by events. Criticising both the style and policy ideas of some WASG politicians, Bodo Ramelow of the Left Party (and in charge of the merger process) suggested that the WASG's political strategy was to put forward a list of maximum demands (a strategy Ramelow described as '*größenwahnsinnig*' – megalomaniacal) more suited to radical trade union tactics than the give and take of everyday politics.[26]

Beyond these very real fears, points of conflict could be found in the policies of the two parties. An October 2005 study of their respective programmes by the (Left Party-affiliated) Rosa Luxemburg Foundation highlighted this starkly.[27] Not only was the Left Party programme more expansive and detailed (befitting the party's longer history as well as its experience in actually formulating policy and governing) than that of the WASG (befitting *its* origins as a protest party), the two parties' programmes also reflect their different self-understandings and policy prescriptions. For example, while 'democratic socialism' is a key concept in the current Left Party programme, framing many of its policy prescriptions, 'socialism' is not a term that appears in the WASG document, and is a term that is anathema to many in the WASG. The closest thing to a similar key concept for the WASG is the term 'social justice' – a concept also used by the Left Party but nevertheless not one that frames its self-understanding in quite the same way as democratic socialism does. Opposition to 'neo-liberalism' also figures prominently in both party programmes; however, its definition is very imprecise and seems to be a synonym for all the domestic and global policies with which the two parties disagree. Thus what 'neo-liberal' actually is, is quite open to debate, allowing the WASG in Berlin, for example, to label the red-red government's policies there as being precisely this. There are, of course, agreements too; both parties want more state intervention in the economy, have similar taxation policy goals (i.e. they want the rich to be taxed much more), argue for a reduction in working hours along with a raising of wages and want to continue traditional state involvement in pension and unemployment programmes. Yet some of the two parties' specific policy prescriptions also differ markedly. While the WASG, for instance, seems to have no problem whatsoever with incurring governmental debt in order to pay for their wish list of social programmes, the Left Party acknowledges the problems inherent in massive state debt and argues for 'economically responsible' policies (a position that would in Berlin be the stuff of major conflict between the parties). Moreover, the neo-Keynesian prescriptions found in the party programme of the WASG reflect its fairly narrow orientation towards a clientele of disaffected SPD supporters and union members. There is little mention of non-economic issues, such as feminist issues, environmental concerns, rights for gays and bisexuals or even foreign policy. In contrast, the Left Party is much more than a one-note party. While its economic prescriptions do indeed resemble classic expansionist social democratic, welfare-state policies, the Left Party's social ideas reflect rather more its left-libertarian/green orientation, something not really present in the WASG.

Berlin rears its head

Certainly the thorniest problem the new Left Party was confronted with at the beginning of the merger process concerned two state WASG organisations, those of Berlin and MV. Although the Mecklenburg-Western Pomeranian WASG and its leader, Karsten Dörre, proved as troublesome to its Left Party state counterpart and to the national leadership of the WASG and Left Party as Berlin did, the latter state received much more attention, befitting the city's symbolic nature as the dividing line between east and west and the one place where the Left Party could most visibly demonstrate its capacity for government and reliability as a coalition partner. The WASG in Berlin began as a protest movement against both the policies of the SPD-led national government and against the red-red state government in Berlin. Although, as illustrated in Chapter 6, the Berlin Left Party membership was relatively docile in the face of the red-red government's pragmatic, budget-cutting course, opposition to its policies surfaced soon after it took office among union organisers, displaced workers, various small left-wing groups and some former Left Party activists. Indeed, some leading figures within the WASG Berlin were themselves former Left Party members such as Helge Meves, Michael Prütz and WASG Berlin founder Martin Reeh. Adding to the more radical dimension of the WASG Berlin, its executive board included two members of a Trotskyite organisation (the *Sozialistischen Alternative Voran*, SAV), Lucy Redler and Hakan Doganay, who rarely missed an opportunity to escalate the conflict between the WASG and the Berlin government.[28]

In 2004 the WASG Berlin initiated a campaign demanding the resignation of the Left Party from the Berlin government. The red-red government's budgetary course was labelled a policy of 'social demolition' (*Sozialabbau*) that targeted the most socially vulnerable groups in the city. The WASG in Berlin was supported in its effort by left-wing groups within the Left Party, such as the Communist Platform, which had long accused the Left Party in Berlin of abandoning the true principles of democratic socialism through its 'neo-liberal' course.[29] Expressing the sentiments of many of these left-wing groups, Lucy Redler argued that 'one can't talk about socialism on Sunday and then pursue social demolition on Monday'.[30] For its part, the Berlin Left Party dismissed the Berlin WASG as a collection of radical leftists divorced from political reality, with Stefan Liebich of the Berlin Left Party labelling the WASG Berlin a '*Gurkentruppe*' (band of fools). Meanwhile, Left Party economics senator Harald Wolf described WASG demands for an end to Hartz IV and an immediate employment programme for some 100,000 unemployed workers in Berlin as completely unrealistic.[31]

The conflict in Berlin only really heated up after the 2005 federal election. Pursuing its course of confrontation, the executive board of the WASG in Berlin voted to run its own candidates for the 2006 Berlin state election, a decision confirmed by a special state party congress of the WASG in late January 2006 and, shortly thereafter, by a special poll of the Berlin membership – all this despite appeals from the national leadership of the WASG and Left Party, and the intervention of a special envoy from the Left Party in the *Bundestag*, Hüseyin Aydin, to try and overt this course of action.[32] The WASG in MV soon followed suit, with 76 per cent of its membership voting to field its own candidates in MV's upcoming state election. These developments went beyond mere irritation for the Left Party, or even a challenge to the Left Party in these two states alone. Rather, they threatened the entire merger process of the Left Party and WASG since a party which ran against itself, so to speak, would not pass legal muster. Thus even the Left Party's representation in the *Bundestag* might be challenged (and, indeed, it subsequently was by several constitutional experts) as an electoral sleight-of-hand.[33] The Left Party/WASG's response was swift: the executive boards of the WASG in Berlin and MV were ousted, a more sympathetic leadership was put into place in the two states, and the aforementioned special deputy, Hüseyin Aydin, was put in charge of affairs in Berlin.[34] Meanwhile, the national WASG and Left Party exhorted WASG members to vote for the merger in a national vote of the membership of the WASG in early April 2006. In the event, a majority of the membership voted in favour of what the Left Party termed a 'further development of the party-building process between WASG and Left Party with the participation of social movements', a result confirmed at a special party congress of the WASG a few weeks later.[35] Nevertheless, the result could hardly be termed an overwhelming vote of confidence: while some 78 per cent of those who filled out a ballot came out for the merger, 'yes' votes constituted only a plurality (some 45 per cent) of all members, since turnout for the election was a disappointing 57 per cent. In other words, large numbers of WASG members abstained from voting altogether. Puncturing the balloon even further, the Berlin and Mecklenburg-Western Pomeranian WASG executive boards were reinstated by judicial order and permitted to run their own candidates for the Berlin and Mecklenburg-Western Pomeranian state elections in the autumn of 2006.[36] It appeared there was a chance that the new Left Party would, in the words of *Der Spiegel*, 'sink into merger chaos'.[37] Reportedly, it also began to plan for the future contingency that the merger would fail.[38] At this point 'PDS-plus' began to look like it might in fact become 'PDS-minus'.

'The early euphoria has gone': A more sober Left Party nevertheless moves ahead

In late August 2006 – as tensions with the WASG in Berlin and MV were running high and pre-election polls were indicating huge possible losses for the Left Party in both states – Party Chairman Lothar Bisky was interviewed on a television programme. Asked about the conflicts in Berlin and MV and the intense discussions concerning the merger process, Bisky admitted that, in view of all the challenges the Left Party faced, 'the merger can still fail', for it was obvious that 'the early euphoria [of the merger process] has gone'.[39] Nevertheless, Bisky added, 'there still seems to be enough momentum and, in any case, we have an obligation to our voters'. Things seemed to go from bad to worse in September for the Left Party, as state elections in Berlin and MV brought more bad news (see Chapters 5 and 6).

And yet things were not as bleak for the Left Party after the elections as some made them out to be. Although the party did indeed suffer some dramatic losses in Berlin, some of this could be explained by both the party's extraordinarily good election result of 2001 and by a natural decline in vote share for any party in office. In other words, the Left Party's 2006 Berlin state election result, while hardly encouraging, was far from devastating. Indeed, those looking to trace the Left Party's result in Berlin (or in MV) to angry WASG supporters had to look elsewhere: the Left Party in MV lost only a marginal number of votes to the WASG, and in Berlin it lost only about 16,000 – around 1 per cent – to the renegade party. Clearly, the WASG rebels had failed to mobilise anti-Left Party, anti-government sentiment – or there were simply less of these people than many had thought.

Indeed, the state elections in Berlin and MV seemed to bear out Bisky's words of August of 2006: there was enough 'momentum' for the merger that even election losses could not slow the process down. In late October 2006, the Programme Committee for the merger process – which included Michael Brie, Wolfgang Gehrcke and Dieter Klein of the Left Party; and Joachim Bischoff, Ralf Krämer and Axel Troost of the WASG – released a document entitled 'Programmatic Considerations on the Way to a new Left Party in Germany'.[40] This document, in effect a working draft for a future revised party programme, outlines the programmatic points of agreement between the two parties. Meant to smooth over the policy/ideological differences between their existing programmes, it emphasised the different heritages of the WASG and PDS, while stressing that 'another world is necessary', a world in which the new Left Party could play a key role, not the least in its attempt to 'unite the left' in Germany against 'neo-liberalism'. Although much of the document remained very general, it nevertheless demonstrated that both parties continued to see fundamental points of agreement in their political ideology and policy prescriptions. At the same time, the steering committee for the merger process – comprised of the leadership/executive boards of each party, including Lothar Bisky, Katja Kipping and Bodo Ramelow of the Left Party, and Klaus Ernst, Axel Troost, and Helge Meves of the WASG – released another document meant to outline the future organisational structure of the Left Party.[41] Especially interesting here was section seven which dealt with a 'transitional phase'. Similar to changes put in place by Alliance 90/Greens during their own merger process, during this transition period the new Left Party would make some structural changes meant to ensure that neither WASG nor Left Party members would feel overrun by the other. For example, the document envisions that the representatives to the 2008 party congress of the Left Party will come from three groups: 160 from the 16 state organisations, proportionally based on the size of the state; 170 from the 10 western German state party organisations (in other words, those dominated by the WASG) and 170 from eastern German state party organisations (those where the 'old' PDS dominates). After 2008, representatives from the last two groups will be reduced and those of the first increased. Similarly, the new executive board will consist of equal members of WASG members and old PDS members, while until 2010 the party will be lead by two party leaders, chosen from recommendations made by the Left Party and by the WASG. These structural and programmatic changes will, in turn, be voted on in parallel party conferences by the WASG and Left Party in March 2007, to be followed in April 2007 by a membership vote of the two parties to ratify the merger. Provided that these all pass the 'official merger' conference of the Left Party will then take place in June 2007.

The merger of the Greens and Alliance 90: A parallel to the PDS/WASG merger?

Chapter 4 discussed the development of the Green Party in Germany and Chapters 5–7 presented empirical evidence on the Left Party that we will use to test whether the party is treading a similar path towards de-radicalisation in the conclusion. Here, we concentrate exclusively on the two merger processes that the two sets of parties have undertaken with a view to drawing out possible lessons for the PDS.Left Party/ WASG. The merger of the Greens with Alliance 90 provides some interesting similarities and contrasts. Alliance 90 began its life as an umbrella organisation/electoral alliance of the most important citizen groups – Initiative Democracy Now, Initiative for Peace and Human Rights, and *Neues Forum* – which emerged during 1989.[42] Operating as Alliance 90, the electoral alliance received 2.9 per cent of the vote, and 12 seats, in the first (and last) free parliamentary elections in the GDR. In addition to Alliance 90, the eastern German Green Party/Independent Women's organisation (also an umbrella organisation for several environmental and women's groups) was the other key player in the development of the merger process. Running its own electoral list, it received 1.96 per cent of the vote and 8 seats in the March 1990 *Volkskammer* election.

The eastern German Green Party – most of whose members were decidedly leftist and thus had more commonalities with *Fundis* in western Germany – did not survive long, and most of its members joined the established (western) Greens.[43] The membership of Alliance 90, on the other hand, was initially apprehensive about any possible east-west merger, a development that was, in any case, rejected by the majority of the (western) Greens until late 1991. Yet the two parties intensified discussions concerning electoral co-operation during the summer months of 1990 – making the Greens the last major western party to find a partner in the east for the upcoming federal election. In the event, the Greens and Alliance 90 agreed to run as an electoral alliance (with the future possibility of a full merger), but independently in east and west. Although the Greens failed to clear the 5 per cent barrier in western Germany, Alliance 90 received 6 per cent in the east, thus netting it 8 seats in the new *Bundestag*.

After the 1991 Neumünster conference of the Greens – a party conference which set in place wide-ranging structural reforms as well as clarifying the power relations between the different wings of the party – merger talks between the Greens and Alliance 90 developed apace. Nevertheless, the merger process would last almost two full years.[44] It proceeded in two stages. First, Alliance 90 constituted itself as a fully-fledged party (rather than an electoral alliance) in September 1991, then entered into negotiations with the Greens in the spring of 1992. Formal negotiations ended with the signing of an association treaty in November 1992 which was then ratified by separate congresses of the two parties in January 1993. By the terms of the treaty, the old federal executive of the Greens was to be replaced by a new 'states council' designed to 'increase the role of elected state party leaders and parliamentarians in federal decision-making'.[45] Alliance 90 was to receive a minimum of three seats on the transitional 11-seat federal executive as well as a delaying veto in the new states council. Furthermore, the Greens attempted to soothe anxieties of easterners by giving Alliance 90 members overrepresentation on the executive of the party as well as giving them the right to form intra-party associations. Of course, these measures were only temporary and could be (and were) revised at later party conferences. Nevertheless, they represented significant concessions on the part of the Greens. After the merger was submitted to the memberships (passing with overwhelming majorities in each case) the new party – now known officially as *Bündnis '90/Die Grünen* (the name change signalling another victory for easterners in negotiations) – was formally founded at a special party conference in May 1993.

The initial reluctance of Alliance 90 and the German Greens to merge with one another was indicative of the structural, cultural and ideological differences dividing the two parties. Structurally, the two parties differed vastly in size: whereas the Greens had a membership of over 37,000, Alliance 90 had only about 2700 members. The membership of Alliance 90 thus had real fears of being swallowed up by the larger Greens, something the merger agreement, as mentioned above, tried to allay. More important were differences in political culture, style and ideology. As a citizen movement in an authoritarian dictatorship, Alliance 90 had developed a very different political culture than that of the Greens. Alliance 90 members were more likely to favour a discussion-orientated, consensual style of resolving political disputes (based primarily on their experience of the roundtables of 1989), were more disapproving of constraints on individuals and less likely to slot themselves politically as 'left' or 'right'.[46] Moreover, many Alliance 90 members were horrified at the aggressive nature of western Greens and turned off by the latter's infighting, which they viewed as childish. Indeed, although the Neumünster party conference in 1991 can ultimately be seen as moving the party more towards the political centre, the conference itself was turbulent and Alliance 90 members were put off by what they experienced there. Be that as it may, there was a general feeling among some Alliance 90 members that a new Green Party was likely to be dominated by westerners. As one Alliance 90 activist would later say, a half decade later 'the party as a whole is essentially still a western German party. Even today, [east and west] operate out of totally different political conditions. Our [easterners] concerns are not their concerns'.[47] There were sharp differences in ideology as well. Even after Neumünster, the Greens remained a left-leaning party, if a more pragmatic centre-left one. By contrast, Alliance 90 was ideologically heterogeneous, with more members who could be classified as belonging to the centre-right than was the case with the Greens. Alliance 90 members, for example, had a far more favourable opinion of the capitalist system and market economy than most Greens. In short, there were plenty of conflict points between the two groups. Indeed, even though the merger can be considered a successful one, east-west cultural and ideological differences still mark the German Greens, something of course not altogether surprising and hardly exceptional among German political parties.

Is there a message in all of this for the Left Party and WASG? First of all, like the Greens and Alliance 90, the Left Party and WASG differ greatly in size. This has led to fears and misunderstandings on both sides: while the membership of the smaller party (Alliance 90 and the WASG) fears being taken over and overrun by the larger party (Greens and Left Party), the latter party has felt that its concerns and interests are not, in light of its pre-eminent numerical position, given their due. Second, differences in political culture and style have played a role in both merger processes. While Alliance 90 members were turned off by the more aggressive, conflict-oriented style of the Greens (with some viewing Greens as spoiled rich kids playing at politics), the Greens in turn had little understanding for the more consensual style of their partners. Similarly, WASG members have been turned off by the pure 'easternness' of the old PDS and the importance that its members attach to the notion of democratic socialism. For the WASG, democratic socialism is an alien and historically anachronistic concept that betrays the Communist origins of the Left Party; thus WASG members fail to understand that democratic socialism for the majority of Left Party members has more to do with political identity than with members' political ideology (and even less, of course, with the party's concrete policies). Third, ideological differences also divide the WASG and the old PDS just as they once did Alliance 90 and the Greens. However, it would be a mistake to see these ideological differences as a straightforward representation of different ideological positions. To be sure, there are many within the WASG who believe the Left Party has moved too far towards the political centre, but this sentiment can be found in the Left Party itself. The ideological differences between the two parties is less about abstract, general differences of left versus right but rather about how positively each views regime participation by the new Left Party. The mainstream sentiment within the WASG appears to be that governmental participation is to be eschewed; it would prefer the new Left Party to be a party of fundamental opposition. Thus it pursues a strategy of vote maximisation. The Left Party, on the other hand, sees itself very much as a party that can and should strive for coalitions with the SPD, even though the various players in the party that support this differ as to the conditions under which this should be done. It is thus a party that, in different ways and in different places, pursues strategies of vote maximisation, policy-seeking and office-seeking goals.

On the other hand, the differences over governmental participation between some in the WASG and Left Party have led to problems in Berlin and MV which are completely different from the Greens' experience. While the Greens never faced the problem of rebellious state party organisations (nor, for that matter, the common cause made between currents in one party being supported and encouraged by factions within the other), the Left Party and WASG continue to struggle with their prodigal *Landesverbände* in Berlin and MV. This development, as we have seen, has caused no end of headaches for the new Left Party. The ultimate impact of this on the final merger process is not yet clear. However, at the very least it can be said that it has complicated proceedings in significant and unanticipated ways. Moreover, the combination of size and ideological differences/attitudes towards governmental participation found in the merger experience of the old PDS and WASG is also unlike the experience of Alliance 90 and the Greens. While the larger Greens were a left-wing party that gradually began to moderate its positions and strive for governmental participation as a result of its merger with the smaller, more moderate (and less easy to classify politically) Alliance 90, the larger Left Party is generally considered to be the more moderate and/or more pragmatic partner. Certainly there is the possibility that the Left Party will, under the influence of the WASG – and here the role of Oskar Lafontaine may prove to be crucial – move away from its more pragmatic, centre-left position. Furthermore, unlike Alliance 90, the WASG – the smaller partner in the merger process – has a politician of enormous stature and charisma that provides a powerful counterweight to the Left Party. Although sharply critical of WASG rebels in Berlin and MV, Lafontaine's well-known scepticism and less pragmatic attitude towards governmental participation in the *Länder* gives tremendous support to other WASG critics of governmental participation. Thus, rather than moderating the party, the merger might well have the effect of moving the new Left Party away from more moderate positions. Whether this will indeed be the case is likely to be determined by the future power constellations along the Lafontaine–Gysi axis that develop in the Left Party after the merger.

Conclusion

The history of the transformation of the PDS and WASG into the new Left Party can really be divided into three stages: an initial period of mutual scepticism and wait-and-see attitudes on the part of both party members and leaders; a subsequent period of euphoria and good will, as the new electoral alliance took shape to contest the 2005 federal election; and a (yet unfinished) period of soberly confronting challenges, facing disappointments, and diligently working to bring the merger process to fruition. Along the way, the Left Party has encountered issues not unlike those that faced the Greens and Alliance 90 in their own party merger process, namely issues concerning the relative weight and strength of the two partners, east-west political cultural misunderstandings and ideological and policy divides. Unlike the Greens and Alliance 90, however, the Left Party and WASG have been faced with rebellions in two of their state party organisations. Furthermore, unlike the former partners, the Left Party/WASG's particular combination of size and ideological direction – most specifically, each party's attitude towards governmental participation – has made the merger process a more delicate one. Indeed, this combination may have the effect of pushing the new Left Party towards the left, away from the more pragmatic politics that have characterised it in the last several years, both nationally and, more importantly, in several of the states. Finally, the smaller WASG has a politician of enormous stature, Oskar Lafontaine, who gives the WASG and its policies a powerful counterweight to the strength of the Left Party. Only time will tell, however, whether a move to the left will indeed come to pass, or whether a further process of normalisation – the 'Green Road', as it were – will continue to develop.

9
Conclusion

Introduction

The stabilisation of the Left Party in the German party system has been one of the most unexpected outcomes of the unification process. Perhaps less surprisingly, the Left Party has attracted, as has become evident through the course of this book, an exponentially large amount of academic interest; studying the survival strategies of a party that many thought would simply curl up and die was always likely to be much more appealing than studying the much less controversial parties of the political centre. That the many doomsayers who predicted imminent death were proven wrong can be put down to an eclectic mix of internal factors (skilful leadership, clever election campaigning, loyal support of members during the lowest times, shrewd marketing strategies), external factors (negative fallout from unification, helpful clauses in German election laws, muddled and self-defeating responses of the other parties, Agenda 2010) and luck (the very existence of Gregor Gysi and the appearance of Oskar Lafontaine).

Post-1989 the Left Party successfully introduced democratic structures and shed the worst of its ideological baggage; it managed to programmatically reinvent itself and compete with powerful western German political organisations in the open struggle for votes. The Left Party's leadership and the party's intellectual heavyweights managed to forge (frequently uneasy and often less than convincing) compromises between the positions of members who sought to defend the GDR's attempt to create the first socialist state on German soil with the need to look forward and develop a new image as a democratic party to the left of the SPD. This they did originally by stressing the Left Party's commitment to defending (self-defined) eastern German interests and to articulating subjective feelings of dissatisfaction with the unification process. Thrown in a bedrock of committed SED-loyal support, and the Left Party managed to make slow and steady political and electoral progress. It would be too much to say that it flourished; it survived and moved, at least until 2002, cautiously from one small triumph to the next. Re-entering the *Bundestag* in 2005 signalled a qualitative step forward for the party and, for the first time, it can now look to the future with genuine optimism. It is now a party of social justice, pacifism and political protest with a strong base in eastern Germany. It is beginning, after 15 years of trying, to make electoral inroads into western Germany; thanks mostly to its merger with the WASG and transformation into the new Left Party. It is being taken seriously as a coalition partner in eastern Germany. Given where it started from, all of these achievements are not to be sniffed at.

This book has attempted to analyse the underlying trends as well as the short-term events and personalities that have assisted the Left Party in reaching this point. It has also attempted to use the existing political science literature to throw more light on the Left Party's development thus far. This conclusion assesses the applicability of the Green Party's path towards normality in understanding the route that Left Party politicians across the levels have taken. Is the Left Party 'doing a Green Party' or are there qualitative differences in both style and substance? This conclusion will also analyse the aims that the Left Party is likely to pursue in the future; is it likely to remain primarily a vote-seeker, or are office-seeking and policy preferences likely to be more significant in the long term? Might this differ across the levels and how is this likely to be perceived by the outside word? This final chapter will also analyse in what way the Left Party can perhaps help us to deepen, nuance and develop some of the ideas and theories surrounding an hypothesised de-radicalisation of left-wing parties once they enter government – therefore contributing not just to our knowledge of the Left Party but also to testing some long-held assumptions about what parties do once faced with what Wolfgang Müller and Kaare Strøm call the 'hard choices' inherent in governing.[1] This also enables us to add an international dimension to our analysis by speculating on how the Left Party fits into broader understandings of left-wing parties across continental Europe.

On the Green road to institutionalisation?

The evolution of the Left Party's capacity for *Politik-* and *Koalitionsfähigkeit* does indeed show some remarkable similarities to that of the Greens. Although the parties have different cultural heritages and have traditionally articulated slightly different forms of societal protest, the comparisons nonetheless remain clear. Much like the Greens, the Left Party began its own march through the institutions in the *Länder*. Much as happened with the Greens, there is also little reason not to believe that at some undefined point in the future the Left Party will find itself partnering the SPD in a coalition at the federal level. This is highly unlikely to be in 2009, but for federal elections after this all options remain very much on the table. There are two major obstacles that need to be cleared out of the way; the Left Party will have to moderate, just as the Greens were required to, its foreign policy stances (entering national government with the stated aim of, for example, abolishing NATO is inconceivable) and Oskar Lafontaine will either have to move on to new pastures or, more likely, have to step back from the front ranks of Left Party politics. Given his behaviour in 1999, it is inconceivable that any Social Democrat will be prepared to work with him again.[2]

Four rather more specific points are also of relevance when comparing the trajectories of the two parties. First, and most obviously, the chronological paths that they have taken are similar. The Greens started life as a party that stressed opposition to prevailing societal norms before warming, initially at the sub-state level and then later in the federal arena, to office-seeking goals. The Greens were indeed an out-and-out 'anti-party', yet as the Social Democrats warmed to the idea of working with this new competitor and as the Greens slowly overcame the internal factionalism between *Realos* and *Fundis*, ideas of co-operation became ever-less controversial within both parties and, eventually, within society at large. Proponents of governmental participation in both the Greens and the SPD – much as is the case in the Left Party and the SPD now – were often accused of sacrificing not merely ideology, but concrete policy, on the altar of government participation. The Left Party has long been accused of such things by its own left wing and the merger with the WASG is unlikely to see such criticisms dissipate. Eventually internal opposition to governmental participation in the Green Party became limited to criticising the manner, timing and concrete policies of participation, rather than the issue of participation itself – much as already, left-wing fundamentalists aside, is the case in the Left Party now.

Second, it has become more than clear that neither the Greens nor the Left Party are monolithic organisations. Assessing the aims of the party is made more complex by the institutional space offered to each *Landesverband* within Germany's federal system. Some Green and Left Party branches are genuine office-seekers, while others remain much more sceptical of entering *Land* governments. Needless to say, considerable heterogeneity exists both horizontally (between state organisations) and vertically (between the federal party and the *Länder*), something which proved problematic for the Greens of the 1980s and for the Left Party today. Vertically, the diversity of the Greens in the 1980s is illustrated by the fact that at the national level the party had exclusively vote maximising and policy-seeking party goals, while at the state level different state party organisations could be characterised by more office-seeking goals (Hesse) or vote-seeking and/or policy-seeking goals (Hamburg). Similarly, through the 1990s and early 2000s the Left Party exhibited considerable diversity at the *Land* level as well as a divergence between the primary party goal pursued at the national level (oppositional politics) versus the goals pursued in different states (sometimes vote maximisation, sometimes office-seeking, sometimes policy-seeking). *Despite* the similar trajectories between the two parties, however, there is clearly one major difference: while the Greens have evolved into a more centrally directed party (with a resulting loss of heterogeneity at the state level), the Left Party has not centralised nearly as much, undoubtedly on account of continued factional struggles within the party. In this respect, the Left Party today has strong similarities to the Greens of the late 1980s and retains a great deal of heterogeneity between *Länder* party organisations – and this leads to a greater diversity of strategies being developed by Left Party politicians.

The third point to note here is the nature of external shocks that the Greens and Left Party have experienced and what lessons each party has drawn from them. The biggest external shock for the Greens was the 1990 federal election. This precipitated a final showdown between the realist and fundamentalist wings of the party, which had as one of its consequences the departure of the last of the *Fundis* in early 1991. As a result, the Greens moved significantly to the political centre, transforming their positions on, among other things, nuclear energy, the German military and NATO, as well as its position towards economic growth. Just as significantly, the Greens jettisoned many of the 'anti-party' organisational features of the early days. In contrast, the biggest external shock for the Left Party was its failure to gain full representation in the *Bundestag* in the 2002 federal election. Yet there was no real 'Neumünster' for the Left Party after this election; in other words no comprehensive reorganisation of the party apparatus, no dramatic changes in policies, and no mass exodus of the extreme left wing of the party. This is not to say that *no* organisational changes took place post-2002 – these changes were, however, more for internal rather than external consumption. As was discussed in Chapters 5–7, once Bisky was re-elected chairman he (along with Peter Porsch) set up a substitute for the expertise lost when the federal parliamentary party vanished – the parliamentary leaders' conference (*Fraktionsvorsitzendenkonferenz*). The body's main task was strategic co-ordination, not decision-making. However, within the Left Party the parliamentary leaders' conference clearly reflects a qualitatively new dimension of horizontal integration, at least compared to that which existed immediately prior to 2002. Whereas electoral defeat in 1990 prompted the Greens to reform *both* their vertical structures (i.e. the relationship of the leadership to the rank and file) and their horizontal linkages (between *Landesverbände*), the Left Party only reformed its horizontal relations after 2002. The general lesson that the Left Party drew from its poor electoral performance nevertheless appears to be that the party must intensify the expansion of its electoral base, a strategy that has been in place, more or less, since the mid-1990s. In other words, unlike the Greens post-Neumünster, it is not office-seeking goals that drive the Left Party at the national level but rather purely vote-maximising ones.

Fourth, within coalition government both the Greens and Left Party have found themselves in decidedly inferior power relationships. This has to do with these parties' limited strategic coalition options. Thus while the SPD, as the 'median' party in most coalition calculations, has coalition options – it can make coalitions with the Greens, the Left Party, the FDP, even various flash parties (*Arbeit für Bremen*, the *Statt Party*) or the CDU/CSU – neither the Left Party nor the Greens has up to this point had any other options besides the SPD. This has clear repercussions for future coalition models involving the two parties – something that is discussed in more detail below.

Of programmes and policies

Another of the central aims of this book was to analyse in detail how Left Party politicians – campaigning on programmatic platforms that clearly challenge the mainstream political consensus – behave once elected to government. Are they able (and/or willing) to maintain this radical political streak once they take the plunge and accept governmental responsibility? Or is a process of 'de-radicalisation' inevitable? We also asked, given that some watering down of programmatic positions is inevitable in all systems where coalition governments exist, to what extent can and do particularly radical parties remain true to the political agenda that helped them get elected in the first place? The case of the Left Party is particularly interesting here as we have a set of conditions highly conducive for testing other related sets of hypotheses; how does the participation of a radical party in a *sub-national government* affect the behaviour of politicians of the same party in *other sub-national* units? Is there a divergence in rhetoric and behaviour between parties across sub-national units or is the non-governing branch able to maintain its previous line? Put another way, are the difficult compromises made in government transferred into other political/electoral arenas? Do the results of these hard choices appear to manifest themselves in party programmes across time and space?

As this book has illustrated, there is some evidence of Left Party *Landesverbände* converging on pro-government participation positions. These changes in attitude have only genuinely set in post-2002 and, even then, it is clearly not a simple and linear process. Our interview partners certainly had wide and varied opinions on when and under what conditions the Left Party should seek to govern at the *Land* level and some were much more enthusiastic about the idea than others; hardly any, however, ruled it out on principle. The modern socialists, seeking to stabilise the party as a genuine socialist alternative to the SPD, remain most keen on governing. The social and left-liberal pragmatists – the type of people who have been significant in moving the Left Party into government in Mecklenburg-Western Pomerania – also remain keen on moving the Left Party away from an 'opposition-only' position. And this despite leaving government somewhat chastened in September 2006.[3] This local problem-solving emphasis (still) naturally pushes them closer to the corridors of power even though they are now more than well aware of how difficult it was to change things and how, in the short term at least, this can cost you votes. The third group, restorative ideologues, remain as recalcitrant as ever; for politicians such as Sahra Wagenknecht and Uwe-Jens Heuer governing is not only a waste of time, it is dangerous for the whole anti-capitalist project as it is the Left Party that will change and not the system as a whole. They point to the de-radicalising tendencies and (in their eyes) the failure to stop the dismantling of some of the core pillars of the welfare state of the Berlin and Mecklenburg-Western Pomerania branches as ample evidence supporting their case. They are likely to argue this for many years to come, no matter what the Left Party does. They are also likely to be largely ignored. Finally, the radical-alternative wing remains more open to the idea than do the ideologues, but they are nonetheless sceptical of what governments can actually achieve. Some of the younger members of the Saxon *Landesverband*, in particular, were also quick to realise that emancipatory socialism could also be a very useful vehicle in furthering their own careers. These differing factions can be found across all of the *Landesverbände*, although it is clear that some branches such as Berlin (modern socialists) and Mecklenburg-Western Pomerania (pragmatic reformers) have become relative strongholds of particular groups.

The evidence in this book suggests that Berlin is the easiest of the Left Party's *Land* branches to make sense of. The leadership is very much in control of the party, it has little difficulty keeping the rank and file at bay and it's programmatic and policy lines have been mostly consistent. If anything, there is evidence that the Left Party is becoming ever more centrist and de-radicalised as time goes on. The coalition negotiations in 2006 illustrated this more clearly than ever before and the fact that it was a Left Party senator who agreed to completely liberalise the open-ing times of Berlin's shops, for example, is noticeable indeed.[4] The Mecklenburg-Western Pomerania branch has not, however, sailed the same consistent course towards ever more institutionalised positions. It is not an officer-seeker in the most overt sense and by the time of the 2006 *Land* election there were many within both the parliamentary party and the rank and file who were hoping to return to the opposition benches. Although Left Party politicians were not slow to stress what they thought were their policy achievements (see Chapter 6), a sense of dissatisfaction and despondency with the government's performance prevailed. That is not to say that the Left Party in Mecklenburg-Western Pomerania has given up on the idea of governing, but it certainly needs the opportunity to try and make sense of where and what it would try to do better next time. The general approach to governing (that the party should do it as it has an obligation to improve the lives of the state's citizens) has not changed; quite how the Left Party attempts to do this in the future may do though.

The evidence in states where the Left Party has never governed is any-thing other than crystal clear. Yet even the extremely diverse Saxon branch of the party is making consistent noises in the direction of the SPD, stressing that it is willing to take on government responsibility as and when the time comes. Still, the Left Party in opposition in the *Länder* remains heterogeneous. These branches have been plagued by personality clashes, possessed little more than vague and decidedly general policy packages, developed a taste for populist rhetoric and suffered persistent internal and external communication problems. No one group has managed to dominate proceedings and the *Landesverbände* have subsequently swayed between different aims and strategies as a result.

In recent times, however, there has been an undoubted convergence in both of these things (aims and strategies); Left Party politicians at the *Land* level are now highly pragmatic and differences in political behaviour can normally be accounted for by looking at strategic rather than fundamental differences between territorial units. Given the heterogeneity of the parliamentary party in the *Bundestag* such conclusions seem eminently plausible as it is at the *Land* level where the Left Party is likely to need to demonstrate its ability to shape and craft policy outputs. The conflicts that do still exist at the *Land* level have either been of a personal nature or have come down to (in theory largely avoidable) communication problems; both with political opponents and also within individual *Landesverbände*. In states where it does not govern, Left Party politicians have shown a startling tendency to talk past each other and to remain hostage to cultural and communication conflicts that reflect the heritage of the Left Party politicians involved. The Left Party in Berlin has been much better at avoiding such conflicts than has the party anywhere else (including Mecklenburg-Western Pomerania – although it has still done a better job than is the case in Saxony and Brandenburg) and the more evident the clash in political styles, the less likely that, over time, a coherent set of political aims and programmatic objectives will be agreed upon and systematically pursued. Where leadership change has been gradual and controlled, policy and strategic consistency has been maintained. Where it has been less controlled, lurches in substance and style have been much more frequent. These can, under certain conditions, lead to more populist outbursts and ever greater stress on what the Left Party does not stand for. They are, naturally, also not conducive to the Left Party entering *Land* governments.

The role that the federal party is likely to play in shaping, persuading and encouraging the party's *Land* politicians is also important. The lack of any body co-ordinating the activities of the *Landesverbände* between 2002 and 2005 gave the regional branches an opportunity not just to profile themselves within the party but also to work together as a unit to further their own interests. Furthermore, the creation of the Left Party out of the PDS and WASG has ensured that post-2005 the federal parliamentary party is much more diverse than had been the case for a number of years previously. Within the Left Party's 54 strong team of MdBs widely different opinions exist on questions such as when and where the Left Party should govern, under what conditions and what it should try to do when it gets there. This is something that came out clearly in the analysis in Chapter 8. There is also the possibility that conflicts between federal level politicians and eastern German *Land* ones may be exacerbated by some of the restorative ideologues in the Marxist Forum and what is left of the KPF forming an unseemly alliance with the not insignificant number of WASG members who are critical of Left Party government participation at the *Land* level. Given that prominent critics such as MEP Sahra Wagenknecht and MdBs Wolfgang Gehrcke, Diether Dehm and Oskar Lafontaine have little directly to do with *Land* politics in the East, is this the next conflict line that the Left Party will need to overcome? These politicians have certainly had different political training and are much less enthusiastic about the Left Party's efforts to shape outputs from with *Land* governments. Conflict, it would seem, is pre-programmed.

Of the future

The short history of the relationship between the WASG and the PDS/Left party means that it is probably a little early to make expansive predictions about where the party is likely to end up in the long term. But, one thing is clear. For the first time in the history of the Federal Republic the SPD has a serious and potential durable partner on its left flank with which it has no choice but to deal. The German party system has moved a long way from the classic 'two-and-a-half' parties of the 1960s and 1970s and is now nothing short of a five party system. Throw in systematic processes of partisan dealignment, the lack of sustainable realignments, lower turnout rates and widespread dissatisfaction with politics in general and democratic Germany is clearly in unknown territory. As are, naturally, its political parties.

The malleable nature of the current German party systems appears to give the Left Party, at first glance, a good opportunity to continue making its voice heard. It has an immediately obvious political constituency and appears able and willing to challenge the parties of the centre – particularly on social welfare issues – in ways that they have proved thus far inept at counteracting. It remains, at the federal level, a vote maximiser at heart and the Left Party's experience of leaving the *Bundestag* in 2002 should ensure that the party does not take the 5 per cent hurdle for granted (again). Office is not, publicly at least, on the Left Party's radar and while the party is apt at campaigning on single issues such as that of implementing a minimum wage, policy remains – at present – a tool to be used for greater purposes.

Yet many within the Left Party are abruptly aware that there are also clear challenges for the Left Party – most of which have been sketched out in the course of this book. Unlike the Greens and Alliance 90 – and this is something that became very clear through Chapter 4 – the merger between PDS/Left Party and WASG is not the final chapter. Alliance 90 and Green members may well have held different positions and have had different views of what the new party that they created should look like, but once the deed had been done it was clear to the vast majority that life moved on. For some in the Left Party there remains deep unease with the new party; WASG's political culture and very *raison d'être* are altogether different to that of many Left Party members and activities, and frictions – already evident – within the national parliamentary party may be a sign of things to come. Differences in ideological self-understanding have also facilitated disputes over governmental participation and it is this issue which continues to cause the most inner-party head-scratching. Indeed, the combination of a more traditional left-wing faction within the party (incorporating many WASG members) may contribute – in the public eye at least – to moving the new Left Party towards the left, away from the more pragmatic politics that have characterised it in the eastern states over the last few years. Some sort of collision of powerful forces would appear – at some point – unavoidable. The Left Party must simply hope that it does not come at a politically inopportune moment (such as just before a federal election).

The most difficult thing about predicting the future is that such predictions normally involve people. And some people can be anything other than predictable. The WASG may be much smaller than the PDS/Left Party, but it does possess a politician of enormous stature in Oskar Lafontaine. Yet Lafontaine can be a difficult customer to deal with. He is certainly not a proponent of political correctness and he is always good for a quote or ten. He gives journalists great value, but he can be a real problem for ostensibly like-minded fellow travellers. Quite what influence Lafontaine will have on the party remains to be seen. It is, however, unlikely that he will have none at all – and it is the nature, extent and effect of this influence which may have more of an effect on the party than many in the Left Party perhaps care to imagine.

Of coalitions and governments

As indicated above, the institutional framework of German federalism certainly gives the Left Party's politicians more than enough opportunity to pursue different goals in different arenas – and without open conflict automatically ensuing as a result. The worries of some federal politicians are unlikely to stop eastern *Land* politicians from continuing to consider the possibility of participating in regional governments. Although hard lessons were learnt in Mecklenburg-Western Pomerania and Berlin, there is little evidence to suggest that Left Party politicians have been fundamentally put off the idea. What sort of conditions are most likely to produce coalitions with Left Party participation though? Or, put another way, were Mecklenburg-Western Pomerania and Berlin unique to the time, place and structural conditions that spawned them?

Although the data set (both of red-red governments and cases where red-red governments did not happen even though they were numerically feasible) is small, we can nevertheless make a number of tentative claims based on the evidence accrued thus far. It is clear that SPD–Left Party coalitions only emerge in quite specific environments. Their chances increase when other potential coalition partners are either unavailable or unacceptable to the SPD. This is the most important factor in explaining why the Social Democrats preferred the Left Party in 1998 in Mecklenburg-Western Pomerania, for example, and yet opted for the CDU in Brandenburg in 1999. They are also more likely when the SPD perceives itself as being able to maximise its office-seeking pay-offs. This was evident both in Mecklenburg-Western Pomerania and Berlin, where the Social Democrats benefited from being a much stronger partner than the Left Party, but this was not the case in Brandenburg in 2004 where the Left Party was stronger in electoral terms. The ideological range between the two parties also needs to be relatively narrow. This was the case in Mecklenburg-Western Pomerania and Berlin – the Schwerin coalition being more to the left than the Berlin one. Ideological ranges were, however, much larger in Brandenburg in 2004 and this remains an issue in Saxony, even though the two parties are not (yet) in a position to form such a government even if they wanted to. Finally, personal chemistry needs to be good between the respective leaderships and the *Landesverbände* need to be relatively united in terms of the messages that they espouse (again, both of these apply to Mecklenburg-Western Pomerania and Berlin, but not to Brandenburg and most certainly not to Saxony).

Within coalition government the Left Party has found it difficult to genuinely leave its footprint on proceedings. The various models that purport to explain the behaviour of partys in coalitions (see Chapter 3) would indicate that this in itself should not be too surprising. The Left Party has no other prospective coalition partners and remains relatively new to the world of coalition politics. But in states where the FDP and Greens remain small and relatively ineffectual, the Left Party's position may well become stronger over time. It is no coincidence that some

Left Party politicians occasionally muse in public about the possibility of working (in some form) with the CDU or of stressing that there are not as many issues driving the two parties apart as there once were.[5] Not now, and not in the medium term, but at some undefined point in the future.

These findings challenge, at least in one way, the conclusions of some scholars who infer that placing the behaviour, attitudes and strategies of far-left parties in an overtly comparative context is, in the end, not a particularly fruitful exercise. One has to be careful in making generalisable claims (when does one not?), naturally, but our analysis of the Left Party leads us to believe that the uniqueness of individual far-left parties should not prevent us from attempting, where possible, to use existing frameworks purporting to explain the behaviour of *all* parties in an attempt to understand left-wing actors. This is something that empirical political science has, thus far at least, been remarkably reluctant to do. The way that Left Party politicians at all both *Land* and federal levels trade off vote-seeking, office-seeking and policy goals is, for example, clear evidence of their 'normalness'. We therefore are sceptical of findings such as those by Anna Bosco, for example, who argues that in the cases of the Communist parties of Greece, Portugal and Spain, the individual history of each party is rather more helpful when trying to understand their behaviour towards other parties and towards the issue of when, and if indeed, to enter government than is simple membership of the same ideological family and/or adoption of the same form of party organisation in the same international context.[6] Bosco claims that once far-left parties are recognised as actors with which the established parties can do business, this in itself does not guarantee a rapid route into government since the latter 'depends on the contingencies of the political game; on the capacity of the parties to exploit them; and, possibly, on new phases of party adaptation'.[7] This is an argument we find difficult to sustain so equivocally. We certainly *do not* claim that left parties adopt a uniform approach to the issue of when and under what conditions they should see to enter governments. The experiences (positive and negative) of co-operation with Social Democrats in other political fora, the long-term relationship between democratic socialists and Social Democrats, the views of civil society organisations and particularly personal relationships between politicians will all have an important, place-specific effect on the nature of any governmental co-operation between parties. But the motives, considerations and constraints which impact on that participation are not as heterogeneous as Bosco would appear to infer and they do not appear, to us at least, to be completely unique to left-wing parties. We therefore concur strongly with Tim Bale and Richard Dunphy who argue that in spite of considerable variation in heritage, the leaderships of most left parties in post-industrial democracies can be considered as 'normal' political actors who develop political strategies based on their own particular sets of goals and interests.[8] They are, in other words, thinking and acting just like other parties in the political system – and this is something that analysts of far-left parties perhaps needs to accept a little more readily.

Notes

Introduction

1. Gregor Gysi, speech at the Schlossplatz, Berlin, 18 September 2005, quoted in Gabriele Oertel, 'Dem Trübsinn ein Ende', *Neues Deutschland*, 19 September 2005. Available at http://sozialisten.de/sozialisten/medien-spiegel/index.htm?year=2005&month=09 (viewed on 18 December 2006).
2. Sabine Hoffmann, 'Die Picknick-Politikerinnen', *Der Spiegel*, 20 December 2002. Available at http://www.gesine-loetzsch.de/kat_echo_detail.php?v=45 (viewed on 18 December 2006).
3. A party is entitled to the status of 'parliamentary party' if it polls 5 per cent of the popular vote. If it polls less than 5 per cent of the vote but still manages to secure parliamentary representation by winning three (or more) parliamentary constituencies directly, then it has the status of a 'parliamentary group'. Parliamentary groups are not accorded the same set of rights and privileges that parliamentary parties are. The PDS's MdBs in the 1994–98 *Bundestag* possessed this status as, despite polling 4.4 per cent of the vote, the PDS sent 30 MdBs to parliament as it won four constituency mandates (all of them in eastern Berlin). If a party does not win three mandates (as was the case in 2002, when the PDS won two, Berlin Marzahn-Hellersdorf (Petra Pau) and Berlin Lichtenberg-Hohenschönhausen (Gesine Lötzsch)), then they receive no surplus seats and simply retain the constituency seats that they have won directly. For more information on Germany's electoral system, see Geoffrey Roberts, *German Electoral Politics* (Manchester: Manchester University Press, 2006), pp. 11–26.
4. For an excellent analysis of events surrounding the 2002 federal election see Ian King, 'A Damned Close-Run Thing: The German General Election of 2002', *Debatte*, 10 (2), 2002: 123–139.
5. For more on Gysi's resignation, see 'Up and Away', *The Economist*, 8 August 2002. See also 'Gysi tritt wegen Bonusmeilen zurück', on http://www.tagess-chau.de/aktuell/meldungen/0,1185,OID9741 22_NAV_REF1,00.html viewed on 5 March 2006.
6. Gysi had suffered serious health problems through 2002 and 2003 when he had a brain tumour and two heart attacks, and it was by no means sure that he would be able to work as enthusiastically for the PDS cause as he had in previous years. See Constanze von Bullion, 'Wandlungen eines Dampfplauderers', *Süddeutsche Zeitung*, 3 June 2005. Available on http://www.sueddeutsche. de/,tt1l1/deutschland/artikel/258/54204/ (viewed on 18 December 2006).
7. 'Gregor Gysi zum Dritten', *Der Spiegel*, 1 November 2004. Available on http://sozialisten.de/sozialisten/medienspiegel/view_html/zid24501/bs1/ n54 (viewed on 5 March 2006).
8. Using precise terminology when analysing the development of the PDS and Left Party can be difficult and decidedly cumbersome. This is largely as the party changed its name from the PDS to the Left Party (*Linkspartei*) in the run

up to the 2005 election and then again in June 2007 (to *Die Linke*), technically speaking, merged with another party (WASG) in 2007 – even though it kept precisely the same name it had in the period before then (!). For the purposes of clarity and consistency we use the term PDS throughout Chapters 1 and 2 except when referring to the 2005 election or beyond. We do this for the simple reason that during the period 1990–2004 this is, put simply, what the party was called. In Chapters 3–7 and Chapter 9 we use the term Left Party. There are occasions where we refer to the pre-2005 period and yet still use that name. We feel this simply facilitates readability and ask for a little leeway in terms of terminological precision. We use both PDS and Left Party in Chapter 8 as we discuss the development of one into the other and therefore need to be clear and precise about which party we are talking.

9. For more details on the 'Hartz Reforms' see 'A plan to put Germans back into jobs', *The Economist*, 22 August 2002.

10. The most detailed and sophisticated German-language study of the PDS's development remains, curiously, the (now decidedly dated) analysis produced by Gero Neugebauer and Richard Stöss. See Gero Neugebauer and Richard Stöss, *Die PDS: Geschichte, Organisation, Wähler, Konkurrenten* (Opladen: Leske und Budrich, 1996). For further analysis of the PDS's history see in particular Wilfred Barthel et al., *Forschungsbericht Strukturen, Politische Aktivitäten und Motivationen in der PDS* (Berlin: Trafo Verlag, 1995); Eva Sturm, *Und der Zukunft zugewandt? Eine Untersuchung zur Politikfähigkeit der PDS* (Opladen: Leske und Budrich, 2000).

11. Gero Neugebauer, '1994 im Aufschwung Ost: Die PDS. Eine Bilanz', *Gegenwartskunde*, 43 (4), 1994: 431–444.

12. Jürgen W. Falter and Markus Klein, 'Die Wähler der PDS bei der Bundestagswahl 1994. Zwischen Ideologie, Nostalgie und Protest', *Aus Politik und Zeitgeschichte*, B51-52/94: 24; Hans-Georg Betz and Helga A. Welsh, 'The PDS in the New German Party System', *German Politics*, 4 (3), 1995: 92.

13. Eva Sturm, 2000, p. 315.

14. Günther Minnerup, 'The PDS and the Strategic Dilemma of the German Left', in Peter Barker (ed.), *German Monitor – The Party of Democratic Socialism. Modern Post-Communism or Nostalgic Populism?* (Amsterdam: Rodopi B.V, 42, 1998), p. 214.

15. Jürgen P. Lang, *Ist die PDS eine demokratische Partei? Eine extremismustheoretische Untersuchung* (Baden-Baden: Nomos, 2003); Viola Neu, *Das Janusgesicht der PDS. Wähler und Partei zwischen Demokratie und Extremismus* (Baden-Baden: Nomos, 2004).

16. Jürgen P. Lang, 'Nach den Wahlen 1994: PDS-Strategie im Wandel?', *Deutschland Archiv*, April 1995, p. 380.

17. Viola Neu, 'Party of Government in Waiting', *German Comments*, April 1997, pp. 20–24.

18. The PDS and the Left Party have continued to align themselves with all the fundamental requirements of the constitution, and the parties' programme and policy documents do not seek to overthrow the democratic structures on which the FRG has been built. A number of commentators focus considerable attention on the alleged 'anti-constitutional' activities of the KPF, neglecting the fact that the party has clearly renounced all claim to societal transformation by any other means than through the democratic process.

19. Jens Bastian, 'The *Enfant Terrible* of German Politics: The PDS between GDR Nostalgia and Democratic Socialism', *German Politics*, 4 (2), August 1995: 95–111 and Hans-Georg Betz and Helga A. Welsh, 1995, pp. 92–111.
20. Stefan Hradil, 'Die Modernisierung des Denkens. Zukunftspotentiale und "Altlasten" in Ostdeutschland', *Aus Politik und Zeitgeschichte*, B20/95, p. 7.
21. Michael Vester: 'Milieuwandel und regionaler Strukturwandel in Ostdeutschland', in Michael Vester, Michael Hoffman and Irene Zierke (eds): *Soziale Milieus in Ostdeutschland. Gesellschaftliche Strukturen zwischen Zerfall und Neubildung* (Köln: Bund, 1995), pp. 10–11.
22. Markus Klein and Claudio Caballero, 'Rückwärts in die Zukunft. Die Wähler der PDS bei der Bundestagswahl 1994', *Politische Vierteljahresschrift*, 37 (2), 1996: 229–247.
23. Sigrid Koch-Baumgarten, 'Postkommunisten im Spagat: Zur Funktion der PDS im Parteiensystem', *Deutschland Archiv*, 30 (6), 1997, p. 872; Dan Hough, '"Made in Eastern Germany": The PDS and the Articulation of Eastern German Interests', *German Politics*, 9 (3), 2000: 125–148.
24. Kaare Strøm, 'A Behavioral Theory of Competitive Political Parties', *American Journal of Political Science*, 34 (2), 1990: 566–568.
25. Wolfgang C. Müller and Kaare Strøm, 'Conclusions: Party Behaviour and Representative Democracy', in Wolfgang C. Müller and Kaare Strøm (eds), *Policy, Office, or Votes? How Political Parties in Western Europe Make Hard Decisions*, (Cambridge: Cambridge University Press, 1999), p. 279 and p. 283.

1   Unification and the Fight for Survival

1. See Dan Hough, *The German Bundestag Election of September 2005* (Brighton: University of Sussex, EPERN Election Briefing No.23, 2005), pp. 11–13. Available on http://www.sussex.ac.uk/sei/documents/epern_eb_23_germany2005.pdf (viewed on 28 July 2006).
2. Franz Oswald, *The Party That Came Out of the Cold War: The Party of Democratic Socialism in United Germany* (London: Praeger, 2002), p. 3.
3. Heinrich Bortfeldt, *Von der SED zur PDS: Wandlung zur Demokratie* (Bonn: Bouvier, 1991), p. 155.
4. Franz Oswald, 2002, p. 4.
5. One source has claimed that in 1992 the SPD had assets amounting to DM 276.8 million, while the PDS could register a remarkable DM 438.7 million. *This Week in Germany*, 20 January 1995, p. 5.
6. For a detailed analysis of the PDS's development out of the SED, see Peter Barker, 'From the SED to the PDS: Continuity or Renewal?' in *German Monitor: The Party of Democratic Socialism. Modern Post-Communism or Nostalgic Populism?* (Amsterdam: Rodopi B.V, volume 42, 1998), pp. 1–17.
7. Franz Oswald, 2002, p. 5.
8. See http://sozialisten.de/partei/strukturen/agigs/index.htm (viewed on 24 July 2006).
9. For a particularly critical analysis of the PDS's development see Patrick Moreau, *PDS. Anatomie einer postkommunistischen Partei* (Bonn: Bouvier, 1992); Patrick Moreau and Jürgen Lang, *Was will die PDS?* (Frankfurt am Main: Ullstein, 1994); Patrick Moreau and Viola Neu, *Die PDS zwischen*

Linksextremismus und Linkspopulismus (Sankt Augustin bei Bonn: KAS, Interne Studien 76, 1994); Patrick Moreau and Jürgen Lang, *Linksextremismus. Eine unterschätzte Gefahr* (Bonn: Bouvier, 1996); Patrick Moreau, 'Mit Lenin im Bauch … ? Die PDS auf der Suche nach einer Berliner Republik von Links', *Politische Studien*, 349, September/October 1996: 27–42; Viola Neu, *Die Potentiale der PDS und der Republikaner im Winter 1997–98* (Sankt Augustin bei Bonn: Konrad Adenauer Stiftung, 1998); Patrick Moreau, *Die PDS: Profil einer antidemokratischen Partei* (Munich: Hanns Seidel Stiftung, 1998); Viola Neu, *Die PDS 10 Jahre nach dem Fall der Mauer* (Sankt Augustin bei Bonn: Konrad Adenauer Stiftung, 1999); Jürgen P.; Lang, 2003; Viola Neu, 2004; Florian Hartleb, *Rechts- und Linkspopulismus. Eine Fallstudie anhand von Schill-Partei und PDS* (Wiesbaden: VS, 2004).

10. The PDS does not state that the socialism that existed in central and eastern Europe was fatally flawed *from the beginning*, but it does admit that its failure was necessary in view of its inability to react to the economic demands that competition with capitalism placed upon it. Furthermore, its deficiencies in terms of democracy and the inability of the leaders of the state-socialist countries to implement reforms suitable for counteracting such deficiencies rendered it doomed to eventual failure. See http://sozialisten.de/download/ dokumente/grundsatzdokumente_partei/parteiprogramm1993.pdf (viewed on 24 July 2006). For a broader analysis of the PDS's interpretation of life in the GDR, the reasons for its failure and the SED's role in this see http://www.pds-online.de/geschichte (viewed 24 July 2006). The PDS has, in spite of the production of these documents, still found the path to reconciling itself to its past difficult. At the time of writing a clear and coherent explanation of what went wrong in the GDR, why and what this means both for the PDS and any socialist future world is lacking. But, while it is clear that parts of the PDS membership are never likely to be able to come to terms subjectively with the failings of the SED and the GDR, the reforming leadership of the party has made strides in this direction. The most notable example of this was an open letter by Gregor Gysi to the party in August 1996. In it he expressed his belief that most of the PDS membership were, in some form or other, party to 'real-existing socialism', and were therefore a part of its failure. He stated that admitting this very fact was indeed painful, but there was no way of avoiding it. He claimed that the membership of the SED and the PDS had done too little to change the GDR for the better and that 'we' had defended undemocratic and anti-emancipatory practices for too long, even though these practices were not worth defending. Those people who still have not realised this, according to Gysi, clearly have not grasped the nature of the reform project on which the PDS is built. See Gregor Gysi: 'Zur gegenwärtigen Diskussion in unserer Partei', *PDS Pressedienst*, 34, 1996, pp. 9–12. For the struggle between reformists and the orthodox wing see also Eva Sturm, 2000, pp. 159–228; Michael Gerth, *Die PDS und die ostdeutsche Gesellschaft im Transformationsprozess* (Hamburg: Dr. Kovac, 2003), pp. 116–40 and Michael Koß, 'Durch die Krise zum Erfolg? Die PDS und ihr langer Weg nach Westen', in Tim Spier et al. (eds), *Die Linkspartei: Zeitgemäße Idee oder Bündnis auf Abruf?* (Wiesbaden: VS, 2007).

11. See paragraph 5 on http://sozialisten.de/download/dokumente/grundsatzdokumente_partei/parteiprogramm1993.pdf (viewed on 24 July 2006).

Furthermore, the PDS has also stated that the market is a necessary component of contemporary society. In one document, for example, it has claimed that "we have to accept the market, but we don't want 'Markt pur' (purely the market)". See http://www.pds-online.de/geschichte/9808/weizsaecker-brief.htm (viewed on 24 July 2006).

12. The PDS has explicitly stated this on a number of occasions, of which one of the most prominent came in a letter to ex-President of the FRG, Richard von Weizsäcker in August 1998. See paragraph three on http://sozialisten.de/geschichte/9808/view_html?zid=3359&bs=41&n=40 (viewed on 24 July 2006). The process of *Geschichtsaufarbeitung* does, however, remain an uneven one within the PDS, hence differing groupings and platforms within the party often have different (and on occasion diametrically opposed) opinions on the same events. No issue highlights this more than the building of the Berlin Wall in August 1961. Unequivocal condemnations of the event can be found in statements made by a number of younger PDS members (including Halina Wawczyniak, then a member of the PDS Executive) in 'Geschichtsaufklärung versachlichen! Erklärung junger PDS-Mitglieder zum Politbüro-Prozess', in *PDS Pressedienst*, 36, 1997, p. 11, as well as in statements made by Petra Pau MdB, and Carola Freundl, former leader of the PDS in the Berlin city parliament in *PDS Pressedienst*, 33, 1997, p. 43. A much less unequivocal analysis of the event can be found by referring to Hans Modrow: 'Zum Jahrestag des 13. August 1961. Persönliche Erklärung von Hans Modrow', in *PDS Pressedienst*, 35, 1997, p. 11.

13. See paragraph five on http://sozialisten.de/download/dokumente/grundsatzdokumente_partei/parteiprogramm1993.pdf (viewed on 24 July 2006).

14. For more details on this particular event, as well as Flierl's defence of his behaviour, see http://www.dradio.de/dkultur/sendungen/fazit/482963/ (viewed on 24 July 2006).

15. Michael Brie, 'Das politische Projekt PDS – eine unmögliche Möglichkeit', in Michael Brie, Martin Herzig and Thomas Koch (eds), *Die PDS – empirische Befunde und kontroverse Analysen* (Cologne: Papyrossa, 1995), p. 37.

16. See Michael Koß, 2007.

17. Michael Brie, 1995, p. 28.

18. The late Michael Benjamin, for example, publicly defended the building of the wall as late as 1999. See 'CDU fordert Ausschluß von PDS-Mitglied: Kritik an Benjamin wegen Äußerungen zur Mauerbau', *Berliner Zeitung*, 26 January 1999, p. 22 (also available on http://www.berlinonline.de/berliner-zeitung/archiv/.bin/dump.fcgi/1999/0126/lokales/0125/index.html – viewed on 28 July 2006); 'PDS Vorstandsmitglied verteidigt Mauerbau', in *Schweriner Volkszeitung*, 25 January 1999, p. 1; Michael Benjamin: '7. Oktober - war da nicht was?', in *Junge Welt*, 7 October 1999, p. 2. An ambivalent analysis of the same event can also be found by referring to Hans Modrow, 1997, p. 11.

19. See, for instance, Hans Modrow, *Aufbruch und Ende* (Berlin: Konkret Literatur, 1991); Lothar Bisky, Uwe-Jens Heuer and Michael Schumann, *Rücksichten: Politische und juristische Aspekte der DDR-Geschichte* (Berlin: VSA, 1993); Hans Modrow, *Ich wollte ein neues Deutschland* (Berlin: Dietz, 1998).

20. Michael Brie, 1995, p. 28.

21. Franz Oswald, 2002, p. 9.
22. Franz Oswald, 2002, p. 9
23. Manfred Gerner, *Partei ohne Zukunft? Von der SED zur PDS* (Munich: Tilsner Verlag, 1994), p. 242.
24. For more analysis on the results of this election see Dieter Roth, 'Die Wahlen zur Volkskammer in der DDR. Der Versuch einer Erklärung', *Politische Vierteljahresschrift*, 31, 1990: 369–393.
25. Franz Oswald, 2002, p. 28.
26. Helmut Zessin, Edwin Schwertner and Frank Schumann, *Chronik der PDS: 1989 bis 1997* (Berlin: Dietz, 1998), pp. 59–60.
27. Heinrich Bortfeldt, 1991, p. 233.
28. All three were originally charged, somewhat strangely, of acting against the interests of their employer – the PDS. Whatever else might have been morally and ethically wrong about their behaviour, it is hard to claim that they were guilty of that particular accusation.
29. Franz Oswald, 2002, p. 17.
30. For particularly pessimistic analyses of the PDS's future from this period, see Heinrich Bortfeldt, 1992, p. 295; Patrick Moreau, 1992, p. 459; Manfred Gerner, 1994, p. 59; Heinrich Bortfeldt, 'Die Ostdeutschen und die PDS', *Deutschland Archiv*, 27 (12), 1994: 1283–1287.
31. Otto Hauser: 'PDS stimmt für Höppner – heftige Kritik aus Bonn', *Leipziger Volkszeitung*, 27 May 1998, p. 1.
32. Geoffrey K. Roberts, '"Emigrants in their own Country": German Reunification and its Political Consequences', *Parliamentary Affairs*, 44, 1991: 373–388.
33. Dan Hough, 2000, pp. 125–148.
34. See http://sozialisten.de/download/dokumente/grundsatzdokumente_partei/ parteiprogramm1993.pdf (viewed on 24 July 2006).
35. See http://sozialisten.de/download/dokumente/grundsatzdokumente_partei/ parteiprogramm1993.pdf (viewed on 24 July 2006).
36. Franz Oswald, 2002, p. 81.

2 Policies, Programmes and Personalities: The Post-1998 PDS

1. See footnote 3 in the introduction for further explanation of the different positions that parliamentary groups and parliamentary parties take up in the German *Bundestag*.
2. The Rosa Luxemburg Foundation has a history that predates 1998 although it was only able to expand its activities after this point in time. For more details see http://www.rosalux.de/cms/index.php?id=stiftung (viewed on 28 July 2006).
3. Wagenknecht's failure to be re-elected was important for its symbolic value. She returned to the Executive in 2000 and still remains a member now (late 2006). For more on Wagenknecht's personal history within the party, see http://www.sahrawagenknecht.de/de/html/kurzbiografie.php (viewed on 1 August 2006).
4. PDS Parteivorstand, *Das Rostocker Manifest. Für einen zukunftsfähigen Osten in einer gerechten Republik* (Berlin: Parteivorstand der Partei des Demokratischen Sozialismus, 1998).

5. Harry Nick, *Alternativen '98? Die Wahlprogramme von SPD, PDS und Bündnis 90/Die Grünen im Vergleich* (Berlin: Diskussionsangebot der PDS, Grundsatzkommission der PDS, 1998), p. 35.

6. Dan Hough, *The Fall and Rise of the PDS in Eastern Germany* (Birmingham: Birmingham University Press, 2002), pp. 148–153.

7. Dan Hough, 2002, pp. 153–160; Christian von Ditfurth, *Ostalgie oder linke Alternative? Meine Reise durch die PDS* (Cologne: Kiepenheuer and Witsch, 1998), p. 238.

8. Lothar Bisky, speech to the Rostock Party Conference, 3 April 1998, *PDS Pressedienst*, 15–16, 17 April, p. 11.

9. PDS, *Europawahlprogramm der Partei des Demokratischen Sozialismus* (Berlin: PDS, 1999), p. 43; *Neues Deutschland*, 'Der PDS reichen 100,000 Mann', 17 May 2000, p. 1.

10. PDS, 1999, p. 42.

11. *Neues Deutschland*, 'Für eine 100,000 Personen-Armee', 19 May 2000, p. 14.

12. Thoralf Staud, 'Ankunft im Modernen: Die PDS braucht ein neues Programm und einen neuen Chef', *Die Zeit*, 6 April 2000, on http://www.zeit.de/archiv/ 2000/15/200015.pds_.xml (viewed on 27 July 2006).

13. It is assumed that such calls for more social justice centre round a better working and social environment for the 'socially disadvantaged'. An underlying presupposition that universal standards of social justice both exist, and are attainable, is evident within the PDS's political rhetoric. But it remains clear that such standards are by no means universally accepted – and the means and methods that different actors propagate in an attempt to achieve 'social justice' are therefore wide, diverse and often plain contradictory. The PDS remains skilled at articulating the worries of Easterners about their social and working environments, just as it is vociferous in its egalitarian, anti-capitalist rhetoric. Yet it (the PDS) is not willing to define its broad understanding of 'social justice' over and above basic calls for equality and more 'fairness'. For an analysis on the theoretical underpinnings of social justice, see David Harvey, 'Class Relations, Social Justice and the Politics of Difference' in Michael Keith and Steve Pile (eds), *Place and the Politics of Identity* (London: Routledge, 1993), pp. 41–66.

14. Infratest Dimap, *Wahlreport Berlin 1999* (Berlin: Infratest Dimap, 1999), p. 12.

15. PDS Mecklenburg-Vorpommern, 'Für eine andere Beschäftigungs- und Wirtschaftspolitik in Mecklenburg-Vorpommern. Beschluß der 4. Tagung des 4. Landesparteitages der PDS Mecklenburg-Vorpommern, Parchim, 15 and 16 February 1997', *PDS Pressedienst*, 21 February 1997, p. 8.

16. *Deutscher Bundestag*: Drucksache 13/10015.

17. Even André Brie, widely perceived as being on the reforming wing of the PDS, has concluded that full employment is both a legitimate and necessary goal. See André Brie, 'Erfordernis, Möglichkeiten, Schwierigkeiten und Inhalt eines Strategiewechsels der PDS', available on http:// sozialisten.de/ politik/publikationen/pressedienst/view_html?zid=7912&bs=7&n=5 (viewed on 31 July 2006). See also *PDS Pressedienst*, 51, 23 December 1999.

18. *Deutscher Bundestag*: Drucksache 13/7417. For more details on the ÖBS see Dan Hough, 2002, pp. 167–169.

19. *Mecklenburg-Vorpommern Landtagsnachrichten* 9 (2), 1999, p. 5.

20. For more on Schröder's links to industrial tycoons, see 'Der "Genosse der Bosse" und sein Draht in die Wirtschaft', *Die Welt*, 3 April 2006. Also

available on http://www.welt.de/data/2006/04/03/869191.html (viewed on 28 July 2006).

21. Richard Stöss and Gero Neugebauer, *Mit einem blauen Auge davon gekommen: Eine Analyse der Bundestagswahl 2002* (Berlin: Otto-Stammer-Zentrum an der FU, Number 7, 2002), p. 20. See also David F. Patton, 'Germany's PDS. The PDS and the Vacuum Thesis: From Regional Milieu Party to Left Alternative?', *Journal of Communist Studies and Transition Politics*, 22 (2), 2006: 206–227.
22. 'Nein zu UN-Militäreinsatzen', *Disput*, 4, April 2000, pp. 24–26.
23. Brie had actually departed to the European Parliament a year before, but he was nonetheless intrinsically linked – regardless of where he physically was – with the policies, attitudes and strategies of Gysi and Bisky.
24. Gysi had periodically threatened to resign in the years previously, sometimes in order to force through motions at party conferences, on other occasions simply to get out of politics, spend more time with his family and look after his health. This time there was no doubt that he was serious. Bisky, meanwhile, admitted that he was 'burnt out' by politics and needed a break away from the daily rigmarole of leading such an, at times, complicated party. See Lothar Bisky, *So viele Träume: Mein Leben* (Berlin: Rowohlt Verlag, 2005).
25. Porsch has since been fired from his position at the University of Leipzig on account of alleged dealings with the Stasi pre-1989. For more information on this case see Raoul Löbbert, 'Das Gespenst der Vergangenheit', *Die Zeit*, 30 August 2004, also available on http://www.zeit.de/2004/36/pds (viewed on 31 July 2006). For a much more sympathetic interpretation of events, see Michael Bartsch, 'Stasi-Keule nun auch gegen Peter Porsch', *Neues Deutschland*, 9 August 2004. Also available on http://sozialisten.de/sozialisten/medienspiegel/view_html/zid22344/bs1/n53 (viewed 31 July 2006). See also Marcel Braumann, 'Die Linke am Pranger – die Nazis im Boot', available on http://www.pdsfraktion-sachsen.de/pvl/abganklage_pp.html (viewed on 31 July 2006).
26. Some commentators have gone further than this. André Brie et al. claimed that 'previous election victories led to an overwhelming sense of self-aggrandisement' within the leadership of the PDS, prompting them to shirk discussions and analyses of future aims, strategies and tactics. See André Brie, Michael Brie and Michael Chrapa, *Für eine moderne sozialistische Partei in Deutschland. Grundprobleme der Erneuerung der PDS* (Berlin: Rosa Luxemburg Foundation, Standpunkte 7, 2002), p. 3.
27. See Joanna McKay, 'From Pariah to Power. The Berlin Election of 2001 and the PDS Question', *German Politics*, 11 (2), 2002: 21–38.
28. André Brie et al., 2002, p. 4.
29. Quoted in Stöss and Neugebauer, 2002, p. 21.
30. André Brie et al., 2002, p. 4.
31. See Infratest Dimap, *Wahl zum 15. Deutschen Bundestag, 22. September 2002* (Berlin: Infratest Dimap, 2002), pp. 37–52.
32. For a clear and succinct analysis of the PDS's 2002 election failure, see Christoph Spehr, *Ohne dramatische Erfolge im Westen gibt es keinen Wiedereintritt für die PDS: Zahlen, Analyse und Thesen zur Bundestagswahl 2002* (Berlin: Rosa-Luxemburg-Stiftung, 2002). Also available on http://rls.gesellschaftsanalyse.de/archiv/texte/cs0209.htm (viewed on 31 July 2006).

33. See for example Richard Hilmer, 'Bundestagswahl 2002: Eine zweite Chance für Rot-Grün', *Zeitschrift für Parlamentsfragen*, 34, 2003, p. 210; Dieter Roth and Matthias Jung, 'Ablösung der Regierung vertagt: Eine Analyse der Bundestagswahl 2002', *Aus Politik und Zeitgeschichte*, B 49–50, 2002, p. 17.
34. Although membership numbers have stabilised at just over 60,000 since 2004, the PDS's membership continues to age at an alarming rate. By the beginning of 2006, 63.4 per cent of PDS members were over 65 years of age and just 6.8 per cent were 40 or under. See http://sozialisten.de/partei /daten/statistiken/struktur.htm (viewed on 11 December 2006).
35. Harald Schoen and Jürgen Falter, 'Die Linkspartei und ihre Wähler', *Aus Politik und Zeitgeschichte*, 51–52, 2005, p. 33.
36. Harald Schoen and Jürgen Falter, 2005, p. 33.
37. Michael Brie, *Nach der Bundestagswahl: Analyse und Prognose* (Berlin: Rosa Luxemburg Foundation, 2005), p. 2.

3   Aims and Ambitions: Policy, Office, Votes and the Left Party

1. See for example speeches and publications by their most notable representatives, Sahra Wagenknecht, Ellen Brombacher and Uwe-Jens Heuer. See also http://sozialisten.de/partei/strukturen/agigs/kpf/index.htm (viewed on 23 August 2006); http://www.sahrawagenknecht.de/de/ (viewed on 23 August 2006).
2. Tim Bale and Richard Dunphy, 'In from the Cold: Left Parties, Policy, Office and Votes in Advanced Liberal Democracies since 1989', paper presented to University of Sussex's Centre for the Study of Parties and Democracy conference on the non-social democratic left and government participation', University of Sussex, 12 September 2006.
3. Robert Michels, *Political Parties. A Sociological Study of the Oligarchical Tendencies of Modern Democracy* (New York: Dover Publications, 1959), p. 32.
4. Robert Michels, 1959, p. 163. For a more detailed application of the Michels's work to the case of the Left Party, see Stuart Graham, *The Party of Democratic Socialism and the Temptations of Parliamentary Democracy* (Birmingham: University of Birmingham, unpublished Ph.D. thesis, 2001).
5. For particular scathing criticisms of Michels's assumptions about the generalisability of his model see Duncan Hallas, 'Towards a Revolutionary Socialist Party', in Duncan Hallas (ed.), *Party and Class* (London: Pluto, 1971). Available on http://marxists.de/party/hallas/party.htm (viewed on 4 August 2006).
6. Richard S. Katz and Peter Mair, 'Changing Models of Party Organisation and Party Democracy: The Emergence of the Cartel Party', *Party Politics*, 1, 1995: 5–28. For a biting critique of their ideas see Herbert Kitschelt, 'Citizens, Politicians, and Party Cartelization: Political Representation and State Failure in Post-Industrial Democracies', *European Journal of Political Research*, 37, 2000: 149–179.
7. Robert Michels, 1959, pp. 70–73.
8. Gordon Hands, 'Robert Michels and the Study of Political Parties', *British Journal of Political Science*, 1, 1971: 155–172.

9. Richard S. Katz and Peter Mair, 'The Ascendancy of the Party in Public Office: Party Organizational Change in Twentieth-Century Democracies', in Richard Gunther, Jose Ramon Montero, and Juan J. Linz (eds), *Political Parties: Old Concepts and New Challenges* (Oxford: Oxford University Press, 2002), pp. 113–135.

10. Peter Gay, *The Dilemma of Democratic Socialism: Eduard Bernstein's Challenge to Marx* (New York: Columbia University Press, 1952), p. ix.

11. For more on interpretivism, see Mark Bevir and R. A. W. Rhodes, 'Interpretive Theory', in David Marsh and Gerry Stoker (eds), *Theory and Methods in Political Science* (London: Palgrave Macmillan, 2002) pp. 131–152.

12. For exceptions see Kate Hudson, *European Communism since 1989* (London: Macmillan, 2000); Anna Bosco, 'Four Actors in Search of a Role: The Southern European Communist Parties', in P. Nikiforos Diamandouros and Richard Gunther (eds), *Parties, Politics and Democracy in the New Southern Europe* (Baltimore: Johns Hopkins University Press, 2001); Stuart Gapper, *From Eastern European Communist Successor to Western European Socialist Party? Germany's Party of Democratic Socialism in a Comparative Context, 1990–2002* (Birmingham: University of Birmingham, unpublished Ph.D. thesis, 2002); Richard Dunphy, *Contesting Capitalism? Left Parties and European Integration* (Manchester: Manchester University Press, 2004); Luke March and Case Mudde, 'What's Left of the Radical Left? The European Radical Left after 1989: Decline and Mutation', *Comparative European Politics*, 3 (1), 2005: 23–49.

13. An important, if little studied, exception to the general trend of electoral decline is AKEL in Cyprus. AKEL remains a *Volkspartei* in a way that no other self-proclaimed radical Left Party does. See Richard Dunphy and Tim Bale, 'Red flag still flying? Explaining AKEL – Cyprus's communist anomaly', *Party Politics*, 12 (4), 2006: 129–146.

14. See Kaare Strøm, 'A Behavioral Theory of Competitive Political Parties', *American Journal of Political Science*, 34/2, (1990): 566–568; Kaare Strøm and Wolfgang C. Müller, 'Political Parties and Hard Choices', in Wolfgang C. Müller and Kaare Strøm (eds), *Policy, Office, or Votes? How Political Parties in Western Europe Make Hard Decisions*, (Cambridge: Cambridge University Press, 1999), pp. 5–9; Stephen B. Wolinetz, 'Beyond the Catch-All Party: Approaches to the Study of Parties and Party Organization in Contemporary Democracies', in Richard Gunther, Jose Montero and Juan Linz (eds), *Political Parties: Old Concepts and New Challenges* (Oxford: Oxford University Press, 2002), pp. 150–153.

15. A potential fourth aim – that of simply holding the party together as a coherent unit – is also sometimes mentioned alongside these three. See Gunnar Sjöblom, *Party Strategies in a Multiparty System* (Lund: Studentlitteratur, 1968). See also Strøm and Müller, 'Political Parties and Hard Choices', p. 31.

16. Michael Laver and Norman Schofield, *Multi-Party Government: The Politics of Coalition in Europe* (Oxford, Oxford University Press, 1990), p. 10.

17. Peter Lösche, 'Lose verkoppelte Anarchie'. Zur aktuellen Situation von Volksparteien am Beispiel der SPD', *Aus Politik und Zeitgeschichte*, B43/1993: 34–45.

18. Elmar Wiesendahl, *Parteien in Perspektive. Theoretische Ansichten der Organisationswirklichkeit politischer Parteien* (Opladen: Westdeutscher Verlag, 1998), pp. 219–249; Elmar Wiesendahl, 'Changing Party Organisations in

Germany: How to Deal with Uncertainty and Organised Anarchy', *German Politics*, 8 (2), 1999: 117.

19. Karl Weick, 'Educational Organizations as Loosely Coupled Systems', *Administrative Science Quarterly*, 21 (1), 1976: 5.
20. Nils Brunsson, *The Organisation of Hypocrisy: Talk, Decisions and Actions in Organisations* (New York: John Wiley and Sons, 1989), p. 27.
21. Robert Harmel and Kenneth Janda, 'An Integrated Theory on Party Goals and Party Change', *Journal of Theoretical Politics*, 6/3 (1994): 269.
22. See Frank L. Wilson, 'The Sources of Party Change: The Social Democratic Parties of Britain, France, Germany and Spain', in Kay Lawson (ed.), *How Political Parties Work: Perspectives form Within* (Westport und London: Praeger, 1994), p. 264; Robert Harmel and Alexander C. Tan, 'Party Actors and Party Change: Does Factional Dominance Matter?', *European Journal of Political Research*, 42/3, (2003): 409–424.
23. Stephen Wolinetz, 2002, p. 155.
24. 'Streitkultur' remains inherently difficult to translate, but is probably best understood as 'culture of debate'.
25. Stephen Wolinetz, 2002, p. 155.
26. Wolfgang Müller and Kaare Strøm, 1999, p. 11. For an excellent discussion of this, see Tim Bale and Richard Dunphy, 2006, pp. 4–5.
27. Wolfgang Müller and Kaare Strøm, 1999, p. 279.
28. Dan Hough, *The Fall and Rise of the* PDS *in Eastern Germany* (Birmingham: Birmingham University Press, 2002), p. 22.
29. Dan Hough, 2002, p. 17. See also Michael Gerth, *Die PDS und die ostdeutsche Gesellschaft im Transformationsprozess. Wahlerfolge und politisch-kulturelle Kontinuitäten* (Hamburg: Dr. Kovac, 2003), p. 139.
30. Angelo Panebianco, *Political Parties: Organisation and Power* (Cambridge: Cambridge University Press, 1988), pp. 247–250.
31. Abram de Swann, *Coalition Theories and Cabinet Formation* (Amsterdam: Elsevier, 1973); William H. Riker, 'Implications from the Disequilibrium of Majority Rule for the Study of Institutions', *American Political Science Review*, 74, 1980: 432–446; Michael Laver and Norman Schofield, 1990; Michael Laver and Kenneth Shepsle, 'Government Coalitions and Intraparty Politics', *British Journal of Politics Science*, 20 (4), 1990: 489–507; Ian Budge and Hans Kerman, *Parties and Democracy: Coalition Formation and Government Functioning in Twenty States* (Oxford: Oxford University Press, 1990).
32. Lawrence Dodd, *Coalitions in Parliamentary Government* (Princeton: Princeton University Press, 1976).
33. William M. Downs, *Coalition Government Subnational Style* (Columbus: Ohio State University Press, 1998), p. 20. See also Robert Axelrod, *Conflict of Interest* (Chicago: Markham, 1970) and George Tsebelis, *Nested Games: Rational Choice in Comparative Politics* (Berkeley: University of California Press, 1990).
34. Michael Laver, 'Theories of Coalition Formation and Local Government Coalitions', in Colin Mellors and Bert Pijnenburg (eds), *Political Parties and Coalitions in European Local Government* (London: Routledge, 1989), p. 16.
35. See for example William Riker, *The Theory of Political Coalitions* (New Haven: Yale University Press, 1962); Michael Leiserson, 'Factions and Coalitions in One-Party Japan', *American Political Science Review*, 62, 1968: 770–787;

Michael Leiserson, 'Game Theory and the Study of Coalition Behaviour', in Sven Groennings, E. W. Kelly and Michael Leiserson (eds), *The Study of Coalition Behaviour* (New York: Holt, Rinehart and Winston, 1970); Robert Axelrod, 1970; Abram de Swann, 1973; Laver and Shepsle, 1990; David Austen-Smith and Jeffery Banks, 'Stable Governments and the Allocation of Party Portfolios', *American Political Science* Review, 82, 1990: 891–906; Norman Schofield, 'Political Competition and Multiparty Coalition Governments', *European Journal of Political Research*, 23, 1993: 1–33.

36. See Klaus von Beyme, 'Governments, Parliaments and the Structure of Power in Political Parties', in Hans Daalder and Peter Mair (eds) *Western European Party Systems: Continuity and Change* (London: Sage, 1983); Laver and Schofield, 1990, p. 70.

37. For more analysis see William Downs, 1998, pp. 24–25.

38. Norman Schofield, 1993, p. 3; Michael Laver and Kenneth Shepsle, 1990.

39. William Downs, 1998.

40. William Downs, 1998, p. 163.

41. This compares with only 44 per cent of provincial councillors in Belgium and 60 per cent of French sub-national politicians. See William Downs, 1998, pp. 195–196.

42. William Downs, 1998, p. 274.

43. For an analysis of rising levels of regionalisation in the German party system, see Charlie Jeffery and Dan Hough, 'Germany: An Erosion of Federal-Länder Linkages?' in Dan Hough and Charlie Jeffery (eds), *Devolution and Electoral Politics* (Manchester: Manchester University Press, 2006).

4 Haven't We Been Here Before? Comparing the Left Party and the Greens

1. It is interesting to note here that by as early as 1992 even more politically conservative analysts, such as Hans-Joachim Veen (formerly of the CDU's Konrad Adenauer Foundation), were arguing that the Greens were 'almost' an established, politically acceptable party rather than an anti-system, anti-democratic one. See Hans-Joachim Veen and Jürgen Hoffman, *Die Grünen zu Beginn der neunziger Jahre. Profil und Defizite einer fast etablierten Partei* (Bonn and Berlin: Bouvier Verlag, 1992).

2. See for example Werner Hülsberg, *The German Greens: A Social and Political Profile* (London and New York: Verso, 1988); Rudolf van Hüllen, *Ideologie und Machtkampf bei den Grünen* (Bonn: Bouvier, 1990); E. Gene Frankland and Donald Schoonmaker, *Between Protest and Power: The Green Party in Germany* (Boulder, CO and Oxford: Westview Press, 1992); Hubert Kleinert, *Aufstieg und Fall der Grünen: Analyse einer alternativen Partei* (Bonn: Verlag J.H.W. Dietz Nachf., 1992); Thomas Poguntke, *Alternative Politics: The German Green Party*, (Edinburgh: Edinburgh University Press, 1993); Andrei S. Markovits and Philip S. Gorski, *The German Left: Red, Green, and Beyond* (New York: Oxford University Press, 1993); Joachim Raschke, *Die Grünen: Wie sie wurden, was sie sind* (Cologne: Bund-Verlag, 1993); Thomas Scharf, *The German Greens: Challenging the Consensus* (Oxford and Providence: Berg, 1994); Paul Tiefenbach, *Die Grünen: Verstaatlichung einer Partei*

(Cologne: PapyRossa, 1998); Tad Shull, *Red and Green: Ideology and Strategy in European Political Ecology* (Albany: State University of New York Press, 1999); Jon Burchell, *The Evolution of Green Politics: Development and Change within European Green Parties* (San Francisco: Earthscan Publications Limited, 2002).

3. For more on anti-establishment parties see Andreas Schedler, 'Anti-Political-Establishment Parties' *Party Politics* 2 (3), 1996: 291–312; Amir Abedi, *Anti-Political Establishment Parties: A Comparative Analysis* (London: Routledge, 2004).

4. Charles Lees, 'The Red-Green Coalition', *German Politics* 8 (2), 1999: 174–194; See also Charles Lees, *The Red-Green Coalition in Germany. Politics: Personalities and Power* (Manchester: Manchester University Press, 2000a), p. 7.

5. On extreme right elements within the early environmental movement and Green Party see Jonathan Olsen, *Nature and Nationalism. Right-Wing Ecology and the Politics of Identity in Contemporary Germany* (New York: St. Martin's/Palgrave Macmillan, 1999).

6. For documentation on the founding Greens party congresses and assessments of these from former Green activists, see Michael Schroeren (ed.), *Zehn bewegte Jahren* (Vienna: Ueberreuter, 1990).

7. *Fundis* was a term coined by Joschka Fischer but rejected by the main group of regime-participation opponents who preferred the term 'Radical Ecologists'. A good discussion of these terms is provided by Björn Johnsen, *Von der Fundamentalopposition zur Regierungsbeteiligung. Die Entwicklung der Grünen in Hessen 1982–1985* (Marburg: Schüren, 1988), pp. 12–13. See also Thomas Poguntke, 1993, pp. 102–105.

8. On red-green coalitions generally see Wolfram Bickerich (ed.), *SPD und Grüne: Das neue Bündnis?* (Hamburg: Spiegel-Buch, 1985); Jörg Mettke (ed.), *Die Grünen: Regierungspartner von Morgen?* (Hamburg: Spiegel-Buch, 1982); Richard Menge, *Links der Mitte: Welche Chancen hat Rot-Grün?* (Marburg: Schüren Presseverlag, 1993); Charles Lees, 'Paradise Postponed: An Assessment of Ten Years of Governmental Participation by the German Green Party' in Stephen C. Young (ed.), *The Emergence of Ecological Modernisation: Integrating the Environment and the Economy?* (London and New York: Routledge, 2000b), pp. 189–208.

9. This is to say, red-green at the *Land* level. Already by 1981 red-green coalitions existed at the local level in various states.

10. On coalition negotiations in Hesse, see 'Was abnehmen', *Der Spiegel*, 30 September 1985, pp. 101–102; 'Das war's,' *Der Spiegel*, 21 October 1985, pp. 31–32.

11. See 'Stumm vor Zorn,' *Der Spiegel*, 31 March 1986, pp. 79–80.

12. The AL in Berlin was formed in the late 1970s. Although there was also a 'Green Party' in Berlin, the strength of the pre-existing AL convinced the national Green Party leadership to dissolve the local Green Party and absorb the AL into the national Greens. Thus, the Berlin organisation (just like the Hamburg organisation) has always been quite distinctive within the party.

13. As Charles Lees has noted, 'if it [the SPD] chose, it could profile the more socially conservative and authoritarian side of its ideological profile in

order to bargain with the CDU, or it could pursue a more post-materialist, New Left-oriented agenda in order to bargain with the AL.' Charles Lees, 2000a, p. 44.

14. On the red-green coalition in Berlin generally, and on the situation of the AL specifically, see Gudrun Heinrich, *Rot-Grün in Berlin. Die Alternative Liste in der Regierungsverantwortung 1989–1990* (Marburg: Schüren, 1993).

15. Richard Menge, 1993, p. 69.

16. On this, see E. Gene Frankland and Donald Schoonmaker, 1998, p. 154.

17. On cabinet portfolios in the 1990 red-green government see Rainer Hinrichs, 'Professionaliersung durch Regierungsbeteiligung', in Winfried Thaa and Dieter Salomon (eds), *Grüne an der Macht. Widerstände und Chancen grün-alternativer Regierungsbeteiligungen* (Cologne: Bund-Verlag, 1994), pp. 88–106.

18. Charles Lees, 2000a, p. 74.

19. See the discussion in Rainer Hinrichs, 1994, pp. 88–89; Charles Lees, 2000a, pp. 74–76.

20. Rainer Hinrichs, 1994, p. 88.

21. 'Jeder hat seine Talente, *Der Spiegel*, 28 January 1991, pp. 92–94.

22. For a discussion of internal changes within the Greens, see Richard Menge, 1993.

23. 'Blitzflink ohne Widerspruch,' *Der Spiegel*, 18 March 1991, pp. 30–32.

24. For further discussion of the Greens problems in Hesse in the 1990s, see Charles Lees, 2000a; 'Schwarzbau unter Schutz,' *Der Spiegel*, 8 March 1993, pp. 53–56; 'Wo bleibt Fischer?' *Der Spiegel*, 12 February 1998, p. 18; 'Vom Laster überfahren. Herber Schlag für die Grünen,' *Der Spiegel*, 14 June 1995, p. 18.

25. See Petra Kelly, 'Wir müssen die Etablierten entblößen, wo wir können,' in Jörg Mettke (ed.), 1982.

26. Thomas Poguntke, 'Green Parties in National Governments: From Protest to Acquiescence?' in Ferdinand Müller-Rommel and Thomas Poguntke (eds), *Green Parties in National Governments* (London: Routledge, 2002), pp. 133–145. See also Margit Mayer and John Ely (eds), *The German Greens. Paradox between Movement and Party* (Philadelphia: Temple University Press, 1999), pp. 224–228.

27. Cited in Björn Johnsen, 1988, p. 59.

28. The Greens were only able to remain in the *Bundestag* because of a special electoral law that divided the country into two parts. Strictly speaking, the Greens failed to clear the 5 per cent hurdle in the west, while Alliance 90 did surmount this in the east. Running as two separate parties almost certainly hurt 'Alliance 90/the Greens' and their electoral failure undoubtedly hastened the merger of the two parties.

29. A proposal to abandon the rule preventing the simultaneous holding of party office and parliamentary mandate failed by a narrow margin at Neumünster. However, this rule was finally abolished in the late 1990s. On reforms at Neumünster, see E. Gene Frankland, 'The Fall, Rise, and Recovery of Die Grünen', in Dick Richardson and Chris Rootes (eds), *The Green Challenge. The Development of Green Parties in Europe* (London: Routledge, 1995), pp. 23–44.

30. Paul Tiefenbach, 1998.
31. On the question of how external shocks affect leadership changes see Robert Harmel and Lars Svåsand, 'Party Leadership and Party Institutionalisation: Three Phases of Development', *West European Politics*, 16 (2), 1993: 69–83.
32. Charles Lees, 2000a, pp. 19–23.
33. The first Hesse red-green coalition, for example, only became possible with the ascendancy of a *Realo* group that eventually came to dominate the party, diminishing inter-party strife. For a discussion of this see Björn Johnsen, 1988, pp. 15–40.
34. In Berlin, according to one high-ranking member of the AL, the AL did not even seriously try to get a high-profile ministry, such as justice because 'we simply didn't back ourselves to be successful'. Cited in Gudrun Heinrich, 1993, p. 34.
35. Cited in Charles Lees, 1999, p. 182.
36. First, co-operation/toleration between the SPD and Greens/Left Party appeared randomly at the local level before state-level toleration agreements were reached. Because local politics is much more personalised and de-ideologised than politics at the state level, it cannot be said that these local political arrangements serve as 'models' in any comprehensive sense. Nevertheless, in both the case of the Greens and in the case of the Left Party these local arrangements represented a certain 'breach' in the wall. In other words, they provided some examples of co-operation between the established parties and the new party at a time when the national SPD was categorically ruling out any co-operation with the Greens or Left Party.
37. As Andrei S. Markovits and Philip S. Gorski (1993, p. 216) note, during this later phase 'realists had become so fixated on the "question of power", narrowly conceived as "red-green", that they had neglected to develop concrete policy positions'.
38. See Michael Koß and Dan Hough, 'Between a Rock and Many Hard Places: The PDS and Government Participation in the Eastern German Länder,' *German Politics* 15 (1), 2006: 88–91.

5   The Left Party in Mecklenburg-Western Pomerania

1. Helmut Holter, 'Mehrheiten gewinnen durch eine Politik für Mehrheiten', *Pressedienst*, 48, 2000. Available on http://sozialisten.de/politik/publikationen/pressedienst/view_html?zid=8800&bs=7&n=17 (viewed on 22 November 2006).
2. Interview with Gerd Walther MdL, 1 July 2005, Schwerin.
3. Interview with Barbara Borchardt MdL, 8 July 2005, Schwerin.
4. Interview with Gerd Walther MdL, 1 July 2005, Schwerin.
5. The 2006 election proved to be an exception to this rule with the FDP (9.6 per cent) and NPD (7.3 per cent) gaining seats in parliament. Between 1994 and 2006 there had been just the three parties in parliament. For more detailed analysis on the 2006 election see Viola Neu, *Landtagswahl in Mecklenburg-Vorpommern und Abgeordnetenhauswahl in Berlin am 17. September 2006* (Bonn: Konrad-Adenauer-Stiftung, 2006). Available on http://www.kas.de/db_files/dokumente/7_dokument_dok_pdf_9129_1.pdf (viewed on 22 November 2006).
6. Ernst-Michael Brandt, 'Wir sind das Volk', *Die Woche*, 30 June 1994.

7. See Peter Ritter, 'Regierungsbeteiligung der Linkspartei.PDS in Mecklenburg-Vorpommern; Maßstäbe, praktische Ansätze, Ergebnisse', Cornelia Hildebrandt and Michael Brie (eds), *Die Linke in Regierungsverantwortung: Analysen, Erfahrungen, Kontroversen* (Berlin: Rosa Luxemburg Foundation, 2006), p. 55.

8. 'SPD stellt der PDS Bedingungen', *Frankfurter Rundschau*, 27 September 1997. See also Ingo Preusker, 'Der dritte Mann', *Wochenpost*, 25 April 1996.

9. See Thoralf Cleven, 'PDS-Chef kam mit blauem Auge davon', *Ostsee Zeitung*, 17 February 1997 and Georg Fehst, 'Helmut Holter will Lösungen für die Leute im Land', *Disput*, 4, 2003. Available on http://www.sozialisten.de/politik/publikationen/disput/view_html?zid=2788&bs=1&n=2 (viewed on 22 November 2006).

10. Thoralf Cleven, 'PDS möchte Konservative in Schwerin ablösen', *Ostsee Zeitung*, 12 August 1996.

11. Closing down nuclear reactors is a long time goal of most left-of-centre politicians and to hear any Left Party, Green or SPD politician say anything to the contrary goes against one of the core tenets of left/centre-left wing ideology in the Federal Republic.

12. Interview with Helmut Holter MdL, 5 August 2005, Schwerin.

13. Interview with Barbara Borchardt MdL, 8 July 2005, Schwerin.

14. Thoralf Cleven, 'Im PDS-Kummerkasten steckt die SPD', *Ostsee Zeitung*, 20 June 1997.

15. Catherina Muth was forced to resign after having been caught shoplifting in January 1999. Muth's resignation came at a particularly difficult moment for the Left Party as two other prominent members of the parliamentary party resigned at around the same time, deputy leaders Gabriele Schulz and Torsten Koplin admitting to having Stasi links. To make matters even worse, Kerstin Kassner, an MdL from the island of Rügen, was also fighting accusations of tax evasion. See Diethart Goos, 'Schweriner PDS steht vor Scherbenhaufen', *Die Welt*, 14 January 1999. Also available on http://www.welt.de/data/1999/01/14/623018.html (viewed on 22 November 2006).

16. Andreas Frost, 'Schweriner PDS lässt die Muskeln spielen', *Tagesspiegel*, 11 March 1999.

17. Andreas Baum, 'Der Fehlstart des Bettvorlegers', *Frankfurter Rundschau*, 12 October 1998.

18. Brigitte Fehrle, 'Vorwärts, und vergessen', *Berliner Zeitung*, 2 November 1998.

19. Klaus Walter and Jan Freitag, 'Von Aufruhr keine Spur', *Ostsee Zeitung*, 4 November 2002, p. 3. Holter's position within the party was not assisted when the Mecklenburg-Western Pomerania Court of Auditors accused him of running his department in a 'sloppy fashion'. Dieter Wenz, 'Rot-rotes Auslaufmodell', *Frankfurter Allgemeine Zeitung*, 2 May 2003, p. 10.

20. See AG Bilanz, 'Zur bisherigen Regierungsbeteiligung der PDS Mecklenburg-Vorpommern', *Pressedienst*, 51 (2000), available at http://sozialisten.de/politik/publikationen/pressedienst/view_html?zid=8879&bs=7&n=24 (viewed on 20 November 2006).

21. Wolfgang Rex, 'Im Kern eine positive Bilanz', *Neues Deutschland*, 27 October 2000, p. 5.

22. See Klaus Walter and Jan Freitag, 'Von Aufruhr keine Spur', 2002.

23. Stefan Bockhahn, 'Licht und Schatten und der Rat, Schwerpunkte zu setzen. Die APO-Gruppe in Mecklenburg-Vorpommern' *Disput*, 10, 2004, available

at http://sozialisten.de/politik/publikationen/disput/view_html? zid= 24353 &bs=1&n=5 (viewed on 20 November 2006).

24. One possible explanation for this may lie in the membership profile in Mecklenburg-Western Pomerania. Many Left Party members are former SED functionaries – particularly in the former county towns (*Bezirkshauptstädte*) of Rostock, Neubrandenburg and Schwerin – and it is these 'normal' members who are likely to be restorative ideologues or who possess, at the very least, traditionalist tendencies that lead them to be inherently sceptical of financial consolidation strategies. See Gudrun Heinrich, *Kleine Koalitionspartner in Landesregierungen. Zwischen Konkurrenz und Kooperation* (Opladen: Leske und Budrich 2002), p. 222.

25. Interview with Barbara Borchardt MdL, 8 July 2005, Schwerin.

26. Interview with Barbara Borchardt MdL, 8 July 2005, Schwerin.

27. Interview with Birgit Schwebs MdL, 1 July 2005, Schwerin.

28. See Edeltraut Felfe, Erwin Kischel and Peter Kroh (eds), *Warum? Für wen? Wohin? 7 Jahre PDS Mecklenburg-Vorpommern in der Regierung* (Schkeuditz: GNN Verlag, 2005).

29. Felfe does list nine achievements of the coalition, ranging from the introduction of 700/800 school social workers to the introduction of a subsided care allowance (*Landespflegegeld*) and from the preservation of a number of cultural programmes to the fight to against the so-called *Bombodrom*. See Edeltraut Felfe, 'Warum? Für wen? Wohin? 7 Jahre PDS Mecklenburg-Vorpommern in der Regierung', in Cornelia Hildebrandt and Michael Brie (eds), 2006, p. 55.

30. Felfe is quick to dismiss accusations that Left Party participation in *Land* governments should be rejected per se. Edeltraut Felfe, 2006, p. 54.

31. Edeltraut Felfe, 2006, p. 54.

32. Edeltraut Felfe, 2006, p. 53.

33. Interview with former leader of the GDR, former MEP and Honorary President of the Left Party Hans Modrow, 29 June 2005, Berlin.

34. Frank Berg and Thomas Koch, *Politikwechsel in Mecklenburg-Vorpommern?* (Berlin: Rosa Luxemburg Foundation, 2001a).

35. Frank Berg and Thomas Koch, *Die Mitte-Links-Koalition in Mecklenburg-Vorpommern. Teil II: Parteien- und Politikstilanalysen* (Berlin: Rosa Luxemburg Foundation, 2001b), p. 95.

36. Frank Berg and Thomas Koch, 2001b, pp. 95–96.

37. Dieter Wenz, 'Wir fühlten uns an DDR-Zeiten erinnert', *Frankfurter Allgemeine Zeitung*, 18 August 1998.

38. Dan Hough, 2002, pp. 167–169.

39. For a detailed list of what these demands were see Peter Ritter in Cornelia Hildebrandt and Michael Brie (eds), 2006, pp. 46–47.

40. Frank Berg and Thomas Koch, 2001b, p. 29.

41. Dieter Wenz, 'Schwerin, die höchste Hochburg', *Frankfurter Allgemeine Zeitung*, 13 December 1997. See also *Mecklenburg-Vorpommern* Landtagsnachrichten 9 (2), 1999, p. 5.

42. *Mecklenburg-Vorpommern Landtags Nachrichten* 9 (2), 1999, p. 5.

43. Jonathan Olsen: 'Seeing Red: The SPD-PDS Coalition Government in Mecklenburg-West Pomerania,' *German Studies Review*, XXIII (3), October 2000: 570–571.

44. Interview with Gerd Walther MdL, 1 July 2005, Schwerin.
45. See the heated debate in the Schwerin parliament on this issue. Available on http://www.landtag-mv.de/dokumentenarchiv/plenarprotokolle/3_Wahlperiode/plpr03-0017.pdf (viewed on 22 November 2006).
46. Peter Ritter in Cornelia Hildebrandt and Michael Brie (eds), 2006, p. 47.
47. Viola Neu and Verena Lieber, *PolitikKompass: Analyse der Landtagswahl in Mecklenburg-Vorpommern* (Bonn: Konard-Adenauer-Stiftung, 2002), pp. 36–37. Also available on http://www.kas.de/db_files/dokumente/arbeitspapiere/7_dokument_dok_pdf_986_1.pdf (viewed on 22 November 2006).
48. Viola Neu and Verena Lieber, 2002, p. 14.
49. Peter Ritter in Cornelia Hildebrandt and Michael Brie (eds), 2006, p. 47.
50. 'Die Beibehaltung einer wohnortnahen und qualitativ hochwertigen stationären medizinischen Versorgung'.
51. Peter Ritter in Cornelia Hildebrandt and Michael Brie (eds), 2006, p. 48.
52. See AG Bilanz, 'Zur bisherigen Regierungsbeteiligung der PDS Mecklenburg Vorpommern'; Stefan Bockhahn, 'Licht und Schatten und der Rat, Schwerpunkte zu setzen. Die APO-Gruppe in Mecklenburg-Vorpommern', 2000.
53. Peter Ritter in Cornelia Hildebrandt and Michael Brie (eds), 2006, p. 48.
54. Interview with Marianne Linke, minister for Social Affairs, 2002–2006, 20 July 2005, Schwerin.
55. Klaus Walter and Jan Freitag, 'Von Aufruhr keine Spur', 2002.
56. Birgit Schwebs, 'Regierungsbeteiligung der Linkspartei.PDS in Mecklenburg-Vorpommern; Maßstäbe, praktische Ansätze, Ergebnisse', in Cornelia Hildebrandt and Michael Brie (eds), 2006, p. 64.
57. Interview with Gerd Walther MdL, 1 July 2005, Schwerin.
58. Interview with Gerd Walther MdL, 1 July 2005, Schwerin.
59. Ringstorff even went on record by saying that had red-red enjoyed a larger majority in the Schwerin parliament then 'the decision we made on prospective coalition partners would have been different'. 'Rot-Schwarz in Nordost?', *Neues Deutschland*, 30 September/1 October 2006, p. 2.
60. Peter Ritter, 'Gemeinsam für mehr Gerechtigkeit', *Disput*, October 2006. Also available on http://www.sozialisten.de/politik/publikationen/disput/view_html? zid=34344&bs=1&n=7 (viewed on 22 November 2006).

6 The Left Party in Berlin

1. Areas such as Kreuzberg, Prenzlauer Berg and, latterly, Friedrichshain in the centre of Berlin are three of the few Alliance 90/Green bastions of electoral support in the whole country.
2. See Harald Wolf, *Zwei entscheidende Jahre. Plädoyer für die Fortsetzung der Koalition über 2006 hinaus* (Berlin: PDS, 2004). Available on http://www.pds-berlin.de/partei/deba/2004/0409226wolf.html (viewed on 27 November 2006).
3. The Left Party *Basis* in Berlin only appears to kick up a fuss when issues of interpreting the past arise. The most obvious example of this was the considerable disagreement about the wording of a section in the preamble to the 2001 coalition agreement where the GDR was defined as an *'Unrechtsstaat'*. See Daniel Hough and Jonathan Olsen, 'The PDS and Participation in

Eastern German Land Governments', *gfl-journal*, 3, 2004: 136. Evidence that the Left Party leadership in Berlin feels it has generated a considerable degree of independence can be seen in biting comments by some of the leading Left Party politicians. Stefan Liebich, for example, provocatively remarked that it would be nice if the rank and file spent the same amount of time and energy analysing contemporary problems and challenges as it did analysing the past. Stefan Richter, '… da halten sich Chancen und Risiken in der Waage', interview with Stefan Liebich in *Disput*, 2 (2002). Also available on http://sozialisten.de/politik/publikationen/disput/view_html?zid=2512&bs =1&n=3 (viewed on 4 December 2006).

4. See for example Gero Neugebauer's comments in Robin Alexander, 'Dabei sein ist alles', *Tageszeitung*, 29 June 2002, p. 31.

5. See a recently published strategy paper by Berliner Benjamin Hoff and colleagues. Benjamin-Immanuel Hoff, Horst Kahrs and Gerry Woop, 'Aspekte eines linken Crossover-Diskurses', *spw-Zeitschrift für sozialistische Politik und Wirtschaft*, 145 (4), 2005: 49–52. They are not alone in claiming this; Berlin MdL Elke Breitenbach and Katina Schubert also claim 'that we are striving to participate in governments at the *Land* level and are therefore compelled to formulate practical policies to implement'. See Elke Breitenbach and Katina Schubert, *Opposition und Regierung – Partei und Bewegung – Widersprüche?*, *Utopie kreativ*, 165/166, 2004: 725.

6. Interview with Annegret Gabelin, deputy leader of the Berlin Left Party, 15 July 2005, Berlin. Green and SPD members in eastern Berlin have, on occasion, supported Left Party candidates for mayoral positions since as early as 1995.

7. Robert Michels, 1959, pp. 70–73.

8. Interview with Michael Nelken MdA, 21 June 2005, Berlin.

9. Interview with Harald Wolf, Senator for the Economy, 13 January 2006, Berlin.

10. Interview with Gernot Klemm MdA, 1 July 2005, Berlin.

11. 'Berliner PDS will Machtwechsel', *Berliner Zeitung*, 2 December 1996.

12. Joanna McKay, 2002, p. 22.

13. Heinrich Bortfeldt, 'Die PDS am Ende?', *Deutschland Archiv*, 36 (5), 2003: 745.

14. Stefan Richter, 2002. See also Andreas Spannbauer, 'Eher dafür als dagegen', *Die Tageszeitung*, 1 December 2001, p. 36; Oliver Hoischen, 'Hart am Leben orientierter Linker', *Frankfurter Allgemeine Zeitung*, 22 January 2002; Berliner Seiten, p. 3.

15. See Ulrich Kalinowski, 'Vom Berg besteigen und den Mühen der Ebene', *Disput*, 2, 2002. Also available on http://sozialisten.de/politik/publikationen/ disput/view_html?zid=2513&bs=1&n=4 (viewed on 3 December 2006).

16. Elke Breitenbach and Katina Schubert, 2004, p. 722.

17. Interview with Left Party parliamentarian, 15 July 2005, Berlin.

18. Interview with Delia Hinz MdA, 20 July 2005, Berlin.

19. Interview with Udo Wolf MdA, 22 June 2005, Berlin.

20. One can, for example, become a member of the Reforming Left; this is not possible in the Forum (as it is exactly that; a discussion forum). Interview with Gernot Klemm MdA, 1 July 2005, Berlin.

21. Interview with Left Party parliamentarian, 1 July 2005, Berlin.

22. Interview with Left Party parliamentarian, 1 July 2005, Berlin.

23. Tobias Miller, 'Wir wollen Magdeburger Verhältnisse', *Berliner Zeitung*, 24 November 1997.
24. Interestingly, the Berlin SPD believed that the Greens were too dependent on their rather awkward rank and file. This is something that the SPD does not need to fret about with the Left Party. See Andreas Rabenstein, 'Kinnhaken von der Berliner Basis', *Welt am Sonntag*, 20 June 2004, p. 76.
25. 'Berliner PDS will einen rot-grünen Senat tolerieren', *Berliner Morgenpost*, 28 February 1999.
26. Karsten Hintzmann, 'Rot-rote Gedankenspiele der PDS', *Berliner Morgenpost*, 23 January 2001, p. 26.
27. Michael Gerth, 2003, p. 125.
28. Interview with Udo Wolf MdA, 22 June 2005, Berlin. See also Carola Freundl and Harald Wolf, *Vor der Kür kommt die Pflicht: Arbeitspapier zu den politischen Aufgaben der PDS-Fraktion bis 2004* (Berlin: PDS, 2001).
29. Rolf Reißig, *Mitregieren in Berlin. Die PDS auf dem Prüfstand* (Berlin: Rosa-Luxemburg-Stiftung, Texte 22, 2004), p. 10.
30. Dan Hough and Jonathan Olsen, 2004, pp. 132–134.
31. In reality, the Left Party's savings plans actually went much further than did those of the Greens, the SPD or the CDU. Uwe Rada, 'PDS spart am besten', *Die Tageszeitung*, 25 June 2001, p. 19.
32. Rolf Reißig and Michael Brie, *Restriktionen und Optionen linkssozialistischer Politik in Regierungsverantwortung. Das Beispiel Berlin* (Berlin: Rosa Luxemburg Foundation, 1, 2005), p. 3.
33. Rolf Reißig and Michael Brie, 2005, p. 4.
34. See 'Einstimmig gefasster Beschluss des Berliner Landessprecherrates der Kommunistischen Plattform der Linkspartei.PDS im Februar 2006', *Die PDS braucht die Regierungsbeteiligung nicht – aber diese Gesellschaft braucht die PDS als Oppositionskraft*, at http://www.antikapitalistische-linke.de/article/ 38._die_pds_braucht_die_regierungsbeteiligung_nicht___aber_diese_ gesellshaft_braucht_die_pds_als_oppositionskraft____.html (viewed on 6 January 2007).
35. Interview with Left Party parliamentarian, 1 July 2005, Berlin.
36. Rolf Reißig and Michael Brie, 2005, p. 3.
37. Anna Lehmann, 'PDS-Spitze hat Konto überzogen', *Tageszeitung*, 5 April 2004, p. 22.
38. Ulrich Zawatka-Gerlach, 'Der Watschenmann wird noch gebraucht', *Tagesspiegel*, 10 May 2004, p. 10.
39. Stefan Liebich, 'Drei Zahlen – milliardenschwer: Zur Haushaltsstrategie der Berliner PDS', *Disput*, 10, 2003. Also available on http://sozialisten.de/ politik/publikationen/disput/view_html?zid=2896&bs=1&n=0 (viewed on 3 December 2006).
40. Interview with Left Party parliamentarian, 1 July 2005, Berlin.
41. Rolf Reißig, 2004, p. 13.
42. Interview with Udo Wolf MdA, 22 June 2005, Berlin.
43. Interview with Left Party parliamentarian, 1 July 2005, Berlin.
44. Principally the Wolf brothers, Udo and Harald. Interview with Udo Wolf MdA, 22 June 2005, Berlin.
45. 'Der lachende Vierte ist die PDS', *Berliner Zeitung*, 5 December 2001.

46. For an initial attempt at assessing the policy outputs of the Berlin coalition, see Rolf Reißig, 2004, pp. 17–49.
47. Wolfgang Rex, 'Mehr einfallen lassen als SPD oder Grüne', *Neues Deutschland*, 15 November 2004, p. 15. Stefan Mentschel, 'PDS-Glaubwürdigkeit bedroht', *Neues Deutschland*, 16 October 2003, p. 18.
48. Interview with Michael Nelken MdA, 21 June 2005, Berlin.
49. Interview with Martina Michels MdA, 21 June 2005, Berlin; Interview with Carl Wechselberg MdA, 20 July 2005, Berlin.
50. See for example Sabine Beikler, 'Die heimliche Opposition', *Tagesspiegel*, 16 June 2003, p. 14; Christine Richter, 'PDS: Das Studium darf nichts kosten', *Berliner Zeitung*, 8 December 2003, p. 20.
51. Rolf Reißig, 2004, pp. 47–50.
52. Sabine Beikler, 'Profil schärfen, Streit vermeiden', *Tagesspiegel*, 28 September 2004, p. 10; Wolfgang Rex, 'Mehr einfallen lassen als SPD oder Grüne', *Neues Deutschland*, 15 November 2004.
53. The parliamentary party is also quite prepared to follow Wolf along this course. The lone voice of scepticism was one of the Left Party's two MPs in the *Bundestag*, Gesine Lötzsch. See Sabine Beikler, 'Die heimliche Opposition', *Tagesspiegel*, 16 June 2003.
54. Arne Boecker, 'Koalitionskrise in Mecklenburg-Vorpommern', *Süddeutsche Zeitung*, 27 May 2005, p. 6.
55. Karsten Hintzmann, 'Rot-rote Gedankenspiele der PDS', *Berliner Morgenpost*, 23 January 2001.
56. Interview with Hans Modrow, 29 June 2005, Berlin. See also Hans Modrow, 'Zum Geleit', in Edeltraut Felfe et al. (eds), 2005, p. 10.
57. The 'social structure atlas' is essentially an instrument to assist in planning public health provision within Berlin.
58. Rolf Reißig and Michael Brie, 2005, p. 4.
59. Rolf Reißig and Michael Brie, 2005, p. 3.
60. Rolf Reißig, 2004, p. 26.
61. Mechthild Küpper, 'Berliner Einheit in Lafontaines Gegenwind', *Frankfurter Allgemeine Zeitung*, 20 November 2006, p. 4. There were also plenty of critical voices at the programme convention of the Left Party and WASG in October 2006. See Mechthild Küpper, 'Abschied vom Avantgardekozept', *Frankfurter Allgemeine Zeitung*, 2 October 2006, p. 4. See also 'Parteitag ebnet den Weg zur Fusion', *Spiegel*, 20 November 2006. Available on http://www.spiegel.de/politik/deutschland/0,1518,449419,00.html (viewed on 3 December 2006).
62. Rolf Reißig, 2004, p. 21.
63. Mechthild Küpper, 'Die Fusion hat immer Recht', *Frankfurter Allgemeine Zeitung*, 19 September 2006, p. 2.
64. Mechthild Küpper, 'Höhere Steuereinnahmen retten Rot-Rot über die nächsten fünf Jahre', *Frankfurter Allgemeine Zeitung*, 3 November 2006, p. 3.
65. Angelo Panebianco, 1988, pp. 247–250.

7 The Left Party in Opposition

1. We concentrate exclusively on the eastern party branches for the simple reason that the western branches are (much) smaller in terms of both members

and of influence within the party and, of course, they are all a long way from entering western *Landtage*, let alone western *Land* governments. For analysis of the Left Party's position in western Germany see Viola Neu, *Am Ende der Hoffnung: Die PDS im Westen* (Bonn: Konrad Adenauer Foundation, 2000); Jonathan Olsen, 'The PDS in Western Germany: An Empirical Study of Local PDS Politicians', *German Politics*, 11 (1), April 2002: 147–172; Joanna McKay, 'The PDS Tests the West: The Party of Democratic Socialism's Campaign to become a Pan-German Socialist Party', *Journal of Communist Studies and Transition Politics*, 20 (2), June 2004: 50–72; Meinhard Meuche-Mäker, *Die PDS im Westen 1990–2005: Schlussfolgerungen für eine neue Linke* (Berlin: Dietz, 2005); Florian Weis, 'Die PDS in den westlichen Bundesländern: Anmerkungen zu keiner Erfolgsgeschichte', *Utopie kreativ*, 173, March 2005: 257–265; Michael Koß, 2007.

2. Although the Left Party in Saxony-Anhalt has not, strictly speaking, been in government it acted as a support party to, firstly, an SPD–Green administration and then an SPD minority government for eight years between 1994 and 2002. For reasons of clarity and consistency we therefore leave the Saxony-Anhalt case to one side for now. For more on the role and function of support parties see Tim Bale and Torbjörn Bergman, 'A Taste of Honey is Worse Than None at All? Coping with the Generic Challenges of Support Party Status in Sweden and New Zealand', *Party Politics*, 12 (2), 2006: 189–209.

3. Gero Neugebauer, 'Die PDS in Brandenburg – wohin des Wegs?', *Perspektive*, 21 (13), 2001: 55–57.

4. Michael Gerth, 2003, p. 85.

5. Michael Mara, 'Die PDS sucht ihr Oppositionsprofil', *Tagesspiegel*, 21 March 2000.

6. Interview with a member of the Left Party's parliamentary party in Brandenburg, 23 June 2005, Potsdam. See also 'PDS Brandenburg hat eine neue Vorsitzende', *Frankfurter Allgemeine Zeitung*, 22 February 1999.

7. Lothar Bisky and Kornelia Wehlan, 'Brandenburger Weg ist endgültig zu Ende', *Pressedienst*, 45, 1999. Available on http://sozialisten.de/politik/publikationen/pressedienst/view_html/n22/bs7/zid7840 (viewed on 11 December 2006).

8. Anita Tack's election to party leader caused considerable disquiet within the central office of the Left Party in Brandenburg that eventually led to a complete breakdown of relations between Tack and Left Party activists working there. When – following a series of decidedly bizarre events – a fax appeared in the *Parteizentrale* that had a falsified Tack signature on it, the usually relaxed and easy-going Lothar Bisky talked of 'left-wing bandits' within the Brandenburg Left Party. For more on some of Tack's rather unique problems see Gudrun Mallwitz, 'Politbüro Tack', *Berliner Morgenpost*, 5 December 1999.

9. Michael Mara, 'Die PDS sucht ihr Oppositionsprofil', *Tagesspiegel*, 21 March 2000.

10. See 'Wir brauchen Optionen', Interview with Ralf Christoffers, *Der Spiegel*, 13 August 2001, p. 58. 'Muss es mit der CDU sein? Offener Brief von Ralf Christoffers', *Pressedienst* 34, 2001. Available on http://www.dielinkspartei.de/politik/publikationen/pressedienst/view_html?zid=9546&bs=4&n=10 (viewed on 11 December 2006). Isabel Daniel, 'Wiederbelebte Option',

Freitag, 22 June 2001. Available on http://www.freitag.de/2001/26/ 01260502.php (viewed on 12 December 2006).

11. See Gudrun Mallwitz, 'PDS will aufs Regieren vorbereitet sein', *Berliner Morgenpost*, 9 March 2002, p. 27. Matthias Platzeck's rise to the top of the Brandenburg SPD to replace long-time leader Manfred Stolpe was also likely to have had a considerable impact on the course that the Left Party chose to take. Stolpe had always rejected co-operation with the Left Party, largely as he feared accusations about his own links to the Stasi would be aired again, while Platzeck was seen as being much more open to such ideas. 'Die PDS und die Koalitionsfrage', *Tagesspiegel*, 10 August 1999; Stefan Berg, 'Mann aus dem Kreml', *Der Spiegel*, 23 August 2004, p. 30. Even Ralf Christoffers had previously rejected notions of co-operating with an SPD led by Manfred Stolpe. Ralf Christoffers, 'Brandenburg: Politikfähigkeit der Großen Koalition in Frage zu stellen', *Pressemitteilung der brandenburgischen PDS*, 22 April 2002. Available on http://www.pds-brandenburg.de/archiv/2002/april/2204_02.htm (viewed on 11 December 2006).

12. Christoph Seils, 'In Sachsen toben Flügelkämpfe und legen den Landesverband lahm', *Berliner Zeitung*, 24 September 1997. Available on http://www.berlinonline.de/berliner-zeitung/archiv/.bin/dump.fcgi/ 1997/0924/politik/0044/index.html (viewed on 11 December 2006).

13. Sven Siebert, 'PDS will Fünf-Prozent-Hürde für Bonn in Sachsen nehmen', *Leipziger Volkszeitung*, 24 November 1997. Weckesser was – alongside fellow Saxon Christine Ostrowski – the author of the 'Letter from Saxony' in which the authors called for the Left Party to seek alliances with the SPD and Greens and to transform itself into an eastern German version of the Bavarian CSU. Unsurprisingly these demands met with little support within the party. See Dan Hough, 2002, p. 35.

14. This is one of the key reasons that Ernst was able to take over the leadership in the first place. Although Ernst is not seen as a particularly effective leader, this very weakness is seen as being an asset as it ensured that the balance Porsch created – and continues to maintain – between the Dresden and Leipzig groups of Left Party MdLs remains intact. Sven Heitkamp, 'Conny Ernst entzweit die Gemüter in Sachsen', *Leipziger Volkszeitung*, 26 July 2001, p. 4.

15. 'Die PDS in Koalitionslaune', *Frankfurter Allgemeine Zeitung*, 24 February 1997.

16. Michael Mara, 'Die PDS denkt sich ins Mitregieren hinein', *Tagesspiegel*, 14 January 1997.

17. Michael Mara, 'Mit Schönbohm wird es für uns leichter', *Tagesspiegel*, 16 October 1998.

18. Christoph Seils, 'Interne Kritik an sächsischer PDS-Fraktion', *Berliner Zeitung*, 21 September 1999. Available on http://www.berlinonline.de/berliner-zeitung/archiv/.bin/dump.fcgi/1999/0921/politik/ 0044/index.html (viewed on 11 December 2006).

19. Sven Heitkamp, 2001, p.4.

20. Michael Bartsch, 'Regierungspläne vertagt', *Neues Deutschland*, 2 July 2001, p. 5.

21. See Andreas Novak, 'Auf Kuschelkurs zum rot-roten Sieg', *Sächsische Zeitung*, 16 July 2003, p. 6; Gunnar Saft, 'Rote Schattenkrieger: PDS benennt Wahlka mpfspitze', *Sächsische Zeitung*, 26 January 2004, p. 8; Hendrik Lasch, 'Zwischen Profil und Partnersuche', *Neues Deutschland*, 29 November 2004, p. 4.

22. Cornelia Ernst, 'Wichtig ist, dass die PDS es aushält, weiter Regierung wie Opposition zu sein. Offener Brief des Landesvorstandes Sachsen an die PDS Berlin', *Pressedienst*, 3, 2002. Available on http://www.sozialisten.de/politik/publikationen/pressedienst/view_html?zid=9932&bs=4&n=11 (viewed on 11 December 2006).

23. Cornelia Ernst and Peter Porsch, 'Keine Alternative zur Überwindung der Stagnation der PDS von innen heraus', *Pressedienst*, 39, 2002. Available on http://sozialisten.de/politik/publikationen/pressedienst/ view_html/n5/pp1/bs4/zid10755 (viewed on 11 December 2006).

24. While leader of the Brandenburg Left Party Christoffers irritated the rank and file by speculating about possible avenues of co-operation with the CDU and was widely seen taking up positions on economic matters that were worryingly (for the Left Party) near to those of the Christian Democrats. See 'Wir brauchen Optionen', *Der Spiegel*, 13 August 2001, p. 59.

25. See Andrea Beyerlein, 'Kampf um Bisky-Nachfolge beginnt', *Berliner Zeitung*, 9 July 2003, p. 24.

26. Christoffers frequently advocated a pragmatic course that had more akin with the working procedures of the Left Party in Mecklenburg-Western Pomerania. According to Christoffers, for instance, 100 million euro could perhaps be moved into the education budget and 25,000 new jobs created by offering loan guarantees to companies. 'Partner für große Koalition nicht erkennbar', *Neues Deutschland*, 21 June 2004, p. 18.

27. Gerlinde Schneider, 'Märkische PDS will "22 plus XXL"', *Neues Deutschland*, 22 March 2004, p. 16.

28. Christoph Seils, 'Gebremste Kandidatin', *Frankfurter Rundschau*, 13 September 2004, p. 3.

29. Interview with Left Party Parliamentarian, 21 June 2005, Potsdam.

30. Thomas Nord, 'Brandenburg: Für weiteren Sozialabbau steht die PDS nicht zur Verfügung', *Pressemitteilung der brandenburgischen PDS*, 29 September 2004. Available on http://www1.pds-brandenburg.de/web/pressemitteilungen/2004/09/000493/ (viewed on 11 December 2006).

31. Oskar Niedermayer, 'Die brandenburgische Landtagswahl vom 19. September 2004. Reaktionen der Wähler auf Hartz IV', *Zeitschrift für Parlamentsfragen*, 36 (1), 2005, p. 76.

32. Kerstin Kaiser only managed to win support from 69 per cent of the delegates when she was elected parliamentary party leader in October 2005. Gudrun Mallwitz, 'Linkspartei.PDS: Kerstin Kaiser neue Chefin der Landtagsfraktion', *Die Welt*, 19 October 2005. Available on http://www.welt.de/data/2005/10/19/791096.html (viewed on 11 December 2006).

33. Andrea Beyerlein, 'PDS vor dem sechsten Führungswechsel', *Berliner Zeitung*, 17 December 2004, p. 22; 'IM-Debatte auf dem Parteitag', *Berliner Zeitung*, 21 February 2005, p. 21.

34. For more analysis on the generational conflict in Saxony see Michael Koß and Dan Hough, 'Between a Rock and Many Hard Places – the PDS and Government Participation in the Eastern German Länder', *German Politics*, 15 (1), 2006: 90–91.

35. It is not clear where the term 'Young Brigade' actually comes from. Some within the party point an accusatory finger at Ronald Weckesser, the Dresden MdL and long-time opponent of many of the Youth Brigade's members.

Others, including Weckesser himself, are adamant that it is a term invented by Gunnar Saft from the *Sächsische Zeitung*. Interview with Ronald Weckesser MdL, 7 July 2005, Dresden.

36. The Young Brigade is frequently portrayed as a coherent and well-drilled unit. It is not. Its members may have similar political styles but there is a significant amount of diversity in both long-term aims and methods of achieving them.

37. Interview with Julia Bonk MdL, 14 July 2005, Dresden.

38. 'Neuer Streit um alte Linie im PDS-Programm', *Leipziger Volkszeitung*, 12 March 2004, p. 4.

39. Gunnar Saft, 'Betonliste und Eigentor', *Sächsische Zeitung*, 10 May 2004, p. 7.

40. 'PDS- Politiker fechten eigene Wahlliste an', *Leipziger Volkszeitung*, 7 October 2004, p. 4.

41. Mechthild Küpper, 'Hartz IV als Glaubwürdigkeitstest', *Frankfurter Allegemeine Zeitung*, 5 August 2004, p. 4.

42. Cornelia Ernst, 'Die nächsten Aufgaben der PDS in Sachsen. Rede auf dem PDS-Landesparteitag am 28 November 2004 in Chemnitz', *Pressedienst*, 50, 2004. Available on http://sozialisten.de/politik/publikationen/pressedienst/view_html?zid=25196&bs=1&n=12 (viewed on 11 December 2006). Interestingly, this observation comes from a speech that Ernst gave at a party conference rather than in an interview, indicating that it was directed more at the Left Party's own supporters than at its electorate.

43. Interview with Left Party Parliamentarian, 21 June 2005, Potsdam.

44. 'Bisky: PDS will zurzeit nicht regieren', *Berliner Zeitung*, 4 January 2003, p. 22.

45. Interview with Dagmar Enkelmann MdB, 21 July 2005, Bernau.

46. Interview with Torsten Krause MdL, 24 June 2005, Potsdam.

47. See Linkspartei.PDS-Fraktion im Landtag Brandenburg, *Für ein zukunftsfähiges und solidarisches Brandenburg* (Potsdam: Linkspartei.PDS-Fraktion im Landtag Brandenburg, 2006).

48. 'PDS entdeckt den Realismus', *Tagesspiegel*, 11 October 2006. Available on http://www.tagesspiegel.de/brandenburg/archiv/11.10.2006/2828142.asp (viewed on 11 December 2006).

49. 'Noch kein grünes Signal für Rot-Rot', *Neues Deutschland*, 4/5 November 2006, p. 18.

50. 'Bundesvorstand rüffelt Sachsen-PDS', *Sächsische Zeitung*, 9 September 1999.

51. Bernd Honnigfort, 'Die Entdeckung des Himmels', *Frankfurter Rundschau*, 7 June 2000.

52. Interview with Katja Kipping MdB, Deputy Leader of the Left Party, 14 July 2005, Dresden.

53. Michael Gerth, 2003, p. 78.

54. PDS-Fraktion im Sächsischen Landtag, *Aleksa. Alternatives Landesent wicklungskonzept für den Freistaat Sachsen*, (Dresden: PDS-Fraktion im Sächsischen Landtag, 2004). Benjamin Hoff argues that in spite of this qualitative jump forward the Saxon Left Party's development plan for the state nonetheless remained more vague than that of those developed by Left Party branches elsewhere. See Benjamin-Immanuel Hoff, *Die Linkspartei.PDS in der sächsischen Landespolitik*, (Berlin: Rosa Luxemburg Foundation, 2006). Available on http://www.rosalux.de/cms/fileadmin/rls_uploads/pdfs/Sachsenstudie_01.pdf (viewed on 11 December 2006).

55. For more on this see Benjamin-Immanuel Hoff, 2006, pp. 22–23.
56. 'CDU soll wie Linkspartei privatisieren', *Die Welt*, 20 March 2006. Available on http://www.welt.de/data/2006/03/20/862467.html (viewed on 11 December 2006).
57. Saxon pragmatists Christine Ostrowski and Ronald Weckesser were not slow to answer Lafontaine's criticisms in an open letter. See 'PDS-Streit über Neoliberalismus', *Frankfurter Allgemeine Zeitung*, 17 March 2006, p. 4.
58. See for example Frank Käßner, 'Sächsische Linkspartei wollte harte Drogen freigeben', *Die Welt*, 10 August 2005. Available on http://www.welt.de/data/2005/08/10/757824.html (viewed on 11 December 2006).
59. Interview with Julia Bonk MdL, 14 July 2005, Dresden.
60. *Jugendwahlprogramm der PDS Sachsen zur Landtagswahl 2004* (Dresden: Die Linke.PDS, 2004). Available on http://www.pds-jugend-sachsen.de/wahlen/jwp/drogen.html (viewed on 11 December 2006).
61. Reiner Burger, 'Rausch ohne Reue', *Frankfurter Allgemeine Zeitung*, 11 August 2005, p. 3.
62. Interview with Left Party Parliamentarian, 21 June 2005, Potsdam; Interview with Karin Weber MdL, 21 June 2005, Potsdam.
63. Interview with Left Party Parliamentarian, 21 June 2005, Potsdam.
64. See Richard Rose, *Lesson-Drawing in Public Policy: A Guide to Learning Across Time and Space* (Chatham, NJ: Chatham House, 1993); David Dolowitz and David Marsh, 'Learning from Abroad: The Role of Policy Transfer in Contemporary Policy-Making', *Governance*, 13 (1), 2000: 5–24; Wade Jacoby, *The Enlargement of the European Union and NATO: Ordering from the Menu in Central Europe* (Cambridge: Cambridge University Press, 2004); Dan Hough, 'Introduction', in Dan Hough, William E. Paterson and James Sloam (eds), *Learning from the West: Policy Transfer and Programmatic Change in the Communist Successor Parties of East Central Europe* (London: Routledge, 2006), pp. 1–15.
65. Interview with Karin Weber MdL, 21 June 2005, Potsdam.
66. Interview with Karin Weber MdL, 21 June 2005, Potsdam.
67. See Matthias Micus, 'Die Quadratur des Kreises. Parteiführung in der PDS', in Daniela Forkmann and Michael Schlieben (eds), *Die Parteivorsitzenden der Bundesrepublik Deutschland 1949–2004* (Wiesbaden: Verlag für Sozialwissenschaften, 2006), p. 292.
68. Interview with Torsten Krause MdL, 24 June 2005, Potsdam.
69. Benjamin-Immanuel Hoff, Horst Kahrs and Gerry Woop, 'Aspekte eines linken Crossover-Diskurses', *spw-Zeitschrift für sozialistische Politik und Wirtschaft*, 145 (4), 2005: 49–52.
70. For more on CDU's difficulties see 'Die CDU handelte in der E-Mail-Affäre rechtswidrig', *Tagesspiegel*, 7 September 2006. Available on http://www.tagesspiegel.de/brandenburg/archiv/07.09.2006/2759960.asp (viewed on 12 December 2006); 'CDU Brandenburg entlässt Landesgeschäftsführer', *Tagesspiegel*, 1 November 2006. Available on http://www.tagesspiegel.de/brandenburg/nachrichten/cdu-brandenburg-nelte/79169.asp (viewed on 12 December 2006). 'E-Mail-Affäre: Ermittlungen gegen Petke werden eingestellt', *Märkische Allgemeine*, 1 December 2006. Available on http://www.maerkischeallgemeine.de/cms/beitrag/10829517/2242247/ (viewed on 12 December 2006).

8   From the PDS to the Left Party

1. Florian Weis, 2005, p. 257.
2. Patrick Moreau, 1998, p. 220.
3. For one noticeable exception to this see Christine Ostrowski and Ronald Weckesser's 'Letter from Saxony'. See Klaus Harting, 'Die PDS schielt nach der Macht', *Die Zeit*, 17 January 1997. Also available on http://www.zeit.de/archiv/1997/04/pds.txt.19970117.xml?page=all (viewed on 17 December 2006). For a good summary of these arguments see Michael Koß, 2007.
4. Meinhard Meuche-Mäker, 2005, pp. 14–16.
5. Meinhard Meuche-Mäker, 2005, p. 63.
6. Eva Sturm, 2000, p. 229.
7. For more on the Ingolstadt Manifesto see Gero Neugebauer and Richard Stöss, 1996, p. 94 and Eva Sturm, 2000, p. 208.
8. Meinhard Meuche-Mäker, 2005, p. 23.
9. For more on the so-called vacuum thesis see David Patton, 2006, pp. 206–227.
10. For more on these 'theses' see Eva Sturm, 2000, p. 330.
11. Meinhard Meuche-Mäker, 2005, pp. 69–82.
12. Terminology becomes particularly difficult here. The PDS changed its name to the Left Party in the run-up to the 2005 federal election. However, the party permitted each *Landesverband* to decide whether it wished to campaign on the new name (*Die Linkspartei*) or to keep the initials PDS in the title too (Die Linkspartei.PDS). Furthermore, WASG was now negotiating with the 'Left Party' in the attempt to form a 'new' party that was, most confusingly of all, to be called exactly the same thing! During the rest of this chapter we try to use the 'correct' name of the party at the time of the events discussed, but where we believe this simply causes extra confusion we have used Left Party.
13. Lothar Bisky, cited in Falk Heunemann, *Die Kooperation der PDS und der WASG zur Bundestagswahl 2005* (Jena: Fakultät für Sozial- und Verhaltenswissenschaften, Institut für Politikwissenschaft, Friedrich-Schiller-Universität, 2006), unpublished MA thesis.
14. Bodo Ramelow, cited in 'Das übliche Tohuwabohu,' *Der Spiegel*, 6 August 2004, p. 27.
15. WASG, cited in Falk Heunemann, 2006, p. 18. It may just be a typing mistake on WASG's part but the capital of Mecklenburg-Western Pomerania is, of course, not actually Rostock but Schwerin!
16. See 'Oskar, der Rettungsanker', *Der Spiegel*, 29 September 2003.
17. For a further discussion of these scenarios see Falk Heunemann, 2006, pp. 19–20.
18. 'Ex-SPD-Chef Lafontaine fordert den Kanzler heraus', *Bild*, 24 May 2005, p. 2.
19. For a further discussion of the impact of Lafontaine's public statements on the PDS see Falk Heunemann 2006, pp. 49–50.
20. Gregor Gysi quoted in 'Ein Himmelfahrtskommando', *Der Spiegel*, 30 May 2005, p. 57.
21. Figures here are cited from 'Abschied vom Avantgardeknozept'. *Frankfurter Allgemeine Zeitung*, 2 October 2006, p. 4.
22. Quoted in Nadine Schley, 'WASG tun?', *Die Zeit*, 23 June 2005, p. 14.
23. Mechthild Küpper, 'Fusionieren oder Regieren', *Frankfurter Allgemeine Zeitung*, 25 September 2006, p. 4.

24. On the PDS's initial general reaction to the WASG – and Helmut Holter's in particular – see 'Lyrik und Schwindel,' *Der Spiegel*, 17 June 2005, p. 49.
25. Quoted in 'Die werden sich zerlegen,' *Der Spiegel*, 24 June 2005, p. 37.
26. Mechthild Küpper, 25 September 2006, p. 4.
27. Horst Dietzel, Jana Hoffman, and Gerry Woop, *Studie zum Vergleich der Parteiprogramme von PDS und WASG* (Berlin: Rosa-Luxemburg-Stiftung, 2005). On the problems posed by the different party programmes of PDS and WASG, see Udo Baron and Manfred Wilke, 'Operation Vereinigung,' *Die Politische Meinung*, 439, June 2006: 67–74.
28. Indeed, critics accused the Berlin and Mecklenburg-Western Pomerania WASG organisations of having been taken over by SAV members adopting a classic Communist infiltration strategy. See 'Kuckuck im roten Nest,' *Der Spiegel*, 10 March 2006, p. 44.
29. In addition to the Communist Platform, a number of groups within the WASG and PDS (such as the 'Initiative Rixdorf', the 'Socialist Left' and the 'Network Left Opposition') surfaced to voice their displeasure at the PDS in Berlin and to argue for a sharper left-wing course for the new Party. See 'Initiative Rixdorf für eine Neue Linke' at http://www.initiative-rixdorf.de (viewed on 17 December 2006); 'Für eine antikapitalistische Linke: Diskussionspapier für die Programmdebatte von PDS und WASG', *Neues Deutschland*, 31 March 2006; 'Netzwek linker Opposition' at http://www. netzwerk-linke-opposition.de/ (viewed on 17 December 2006).
30. 'Kuckuck im roten Nest', *Der Spiegel*, 10 March 2006, p. 44.
31. '"Eiertanz" statt Hochzeitswalzer. Interview mit Harald Wolf', *Tageszeitung*, 30 June 2005, p. 28. Available on http://www.taz.de/pt/2005/06/30/a0271.1/ text (viewed on 17 December 2006).
32. On the vote of the Berlin WASG, and the intervention of Hüseyin Aydin, see 'Linkes Projekt versinkt im Fusions-Chaos', *Der Spiegel*, 26 February 2006; 'Großes Foul links außen', *Der Spiegel*, 8 March 2006; 'Hüseyin Aydin appelliert an die Mitglieder der Berliner WASG', *WASG Nachrichten*, 2 March 2006. Available on http://www.w-asg.de/28+M570d9bd27f8.html (viewed on 17 December 2006).
33. See Pascal Beucker and Frank Überall, 'Ab Montag wird angefochten', *Tageszeitung*, 16 September 2005. Also available on http://www.taz.de/pt/ 2005/09/16/ a0099.1/text.ges,1.
34. On these developments see Jan Thomsen, 'Konflikt um WASG Berlin verschärft sich', *Berliner Zeitung*, 17 May 2006. Available at http://www.berli-nonline.de/berliner-zeitung/archiv/.bin/dump.fcgi/2006/0517/ lokales/0044/index.html (viewed on 17 December 2006).
35. 'WASG-Basis stimmt für Ehe mit Linkspartei', *Märkische Oderzeitung*, 2 April 2006. Available at http://www.moz.de/index.php/Moz/Article/category/ Nachrichten/id/106728 (viewed on 17 December 2006).
36. 'Berliner Parteirebellen siegen vor Gericht', *Der Spiegel*, 31 May 2006.
37. 'Chaos' seemed to be *Der Spiegel's* preferred word for this period of the merger process. See 'Chaos statt Revolution', *Der Spiegel*, 3 February 2006, pp. 44–45; 'Chaos bei der Linken', *Der Spiegel*, 14 May 2006.
38. 'Linkspartei plant schon ohne WASG', *Der Spiegel*, 28 April, 2006.
39. The entire transcript of the interview is available on the Left Party's web site. See 'Es gibt noch genügend Schwungmasse, und wir sind in der Pflicht' at

http://sozialisten.de/sozialisten/medienspiegel/view_html/zid33693/bs1/n2 (viewed on 17 December 2006).

40. 'Programmatische Eckpunkte auf dem Weg zu einer neuen Linkspartei in Deutschland'. Available at http://sozialisten.de/sozialisten/parteibildung/protokolle/programm/view_html?zid=31907&bs=1&n=1 (viewed on 17 December 2006). On the discussion involving this document, see Julia Müller, 'Synopse der Diskussion um die Programmatischen Eckpunkte zur Bildung einer neuen Linkspartei', available at http://www.rosalux.de/cms/fileadmin/rls_uploads/pdfs/synopseUS.pdf (viewed on 17 December 2006).
41. 'Bundessatzung der Partei DIE LINKE', available on http:// sozialisten.de/ sozialisten/parteibildung/pdf/gruendungsdokumente/061022_entwurf_ bundessatzung-B.pdf (viewed on 17 December 2006).
42. On the citizens' initiatives in the GDR see Christiane Olivio, *Creating a Democratic Civil Society in Eastern Germany: The Case of the Citizen Movements and Alliance 90* (Palgrave Macmillan/Macmillan: New York and London, 2001).
43. Markovits and Gorski, 1993, pp. 254–255.
44. Further details of the merger process can be found in Thomas Poguntke and Rüdiger Schmitt-Beck, 'Still the Same with a New Name? Alliance 90/Die Grünen after the Fusion', *German Politics*, 3 (1), April 1994: 91–113 and Detlef Jahn, 'Unifying the Greens in a United Germany', *Environmental Politics*, 3 (2), Summer 1994: 312–318.
45. Frankland and Schoonmaker, 1992, p. 226.
46. See Detlef Jahn, 1994, pp. 312–318.
47. 'Die Partei ist westdeutsch', *Der Spiegel*, 9 March 1996, p. 41.

9 Conclusion

1. Wolfgang C. Müller and Kaare Strøm, 1999.
2. Lafontaine resigned not just as finance minister in Schröder's government, but also from all other political offices. Many within the SPD felt completely betrayed by Lafontaine who appeared to be more interested in profiling himself than in seriously trying to run the country. See 'Oskar bravo', *The Economist*, 18 March 1999.
3. Jürgen Seidel, 'Linkspartei übt wieder Opposition', *Neues Deutschland*, 18 December 2006. Available on http://www.nd-online.de/artikel.asp? AID=102224&IDC=2 (viewed on 18 December 2006).
4. See Christoph Seils, 'Nächtlicher Bücherkauf', *Die Zeit*, 20 November 2006. Available on http://www.zeit.de/online/2006/47/Ladenschluss-Berlin?page= all (viewed on 15 December 2006).
5. 'Christoffers schließt PDS-CDU-Koalition langfristig nicht aus', *Der Tagesspiegel*, 11 August 2001. Available on http://www.tagesspiegel.de/ brandenburg/archiv/11.08.2001/ak-br-447846.html (viewed on 18 December 2006); Christian Panster, 'Wir pfeifen auf Schönbohm', *die Tageszeitung*, 29 August 2006, p. 7; 'Volksstimme-Interview mit Wulf Gallert: "Die soziale Frage ist das A und O"', *Magdeburger Volksstimme*, 19 December 2006. Available on http://www.volksstimme.de/vsm/nachrichten/sachsen_anhalt/?&em_cnt= 209517 (viewed on 19 December 2006).
6. Anna Bosco, 2001, p. 387.
7. Anna Bosco, 2001, p. 385.
8. Tim Bale and Richard Dunphy, 2006, pp. 26–27.

Bibliography

PDS literature and literature produced by organisations affiliated to the PDS

Berg, Frank and Thomas Koch, *Politikwechsel in Mecklenburg-Vorpommern?* (Berlin: Rosa Luxemburg Foundation, 2001a).

Berg, Frank and Thomas Koch, *Die Mitte-Links-Koalition in Mecklenburg-Vorpommern. Teil II: Parteien- und Politikstilanalysen* (Berlin: Rosa Luxemburg Foundation, 2001b).

Braumann, Marcel, 'Die Linke am Pranger – die Nazis im Boot', available on http://www.pdsfraktion-sachsen.de/pvl/abganklage_pp.html.

Brie, André, Michael Brie and Michael Chrapa, *Für eine moderne sozialistische Partei in Deutschland. Grundprobleme der Erneuerung der PDS* (Berlin: Rosa Luxemburg Foundation, Standpunkte 7, 2002).

Brie, Michael, *Nach der Bundestagswahl: Analyse und Prognose* (Berlin: Rosa Luxemburg Foundation, 2005).

Christoffers, Ralf, 'Brandenburg: Politikfähigkeit der Großen Koalition in Frage zu stellen', *Pressemitteilung der brandenburgischen PDS*, 22 April 2002.

Dietzel, Horst, Jana Hoffman, and Gerry Woop, *Studie zum Vergleich der Parteiprogramme von PDS und WASG* (Berlin: Rosa Luxemburg Foundation, 2005).

Felfe, Edeltraut, 'Warum? Für wen? Wohin? 7 Jahre PDS Mecklenburg-Vorpommern in der Regierung', in Cornelia Hildebrandt and Michael Brie (eds), *Die Linke in Regierungsverantwortung: Analysen, Erfahrungen, Kontroversen* (Berlin: Rosa Luxemburg Foundation, 2006).

Freundl, Carola and Harald Wolf, *Vor der Kür kommt die Pflicht: Arbeitspapier zu den politischen Aufgaben der PDS-Fraktion bis 2004* (Berlin: PDS, 2001).

Hildebrandt, Cornelia and Michael Brie (eds), *Die Linke in Regierungsverantwortung: Analysen, Erfahrungen, Kontroversen* (Berlin: Rosa Luxemburg Foundation, 2006).

Hoff, Benjamin-Immanuel, *Die Linkspartei. PDS in der sächsischen Landespolitik*, (Berlin: Rosa Luxemburg Foundation, 2006).

Hoff, Benjamin-Immanuel, Horst Kahrs and Gerry Woop, 'Aspekte eines linken Crossover-Diskurses', *spw-Zeitschrift für sozialistische Politik und Wirtschaft*, 145 (4), 2005: 49–52.

Jugendwahlprogramm der PDS Sachsen zur Landtagswahl 2004 (Dresden: Die Linkspartei. PDS, 2004).

Linkspartei.PDS-Fraktion im Landtag Brandenburg, *Für ein zukunftsfähiges und solidarisches Brandenburg* (Potsdam: Linkspartei.PDS-Fraktion im Landtag Brandenburg, 2006).

Müller, Julia, 'Synopse der Diskussion um die Programmatischen Eckpunkte zur Bildung einer neuen Linkspartei', available at http://www.rosalux.de/cms/fileadmin/rls_uploads/pdfs/synopseUS.pdf.

Nick, Harry, *Alternativen '98? Die Wahlprogramme von SPD, PDS und Bündnis 90/Die Grünen im Vergleich* (Berlin: Diskussionsangebot der PDS, Grundsatzkommission der PDS, 1998).

Nord, Thomas, 'Brandenburg: Für weiteren Sozialabbau steht die PDS nicht zur Verfügung', *Pressemitteilung der brandenburgischen PDS*, 29 September 2004.

PDS, *Europawahlprogramm der Partei des Demokratischen Sozialismus* (Berlin: PDS, 1999).

PDS-Fraktion im Sächsischen Landtag, *Aleksa. Alternatives Landesentwicklungskonzept für den Freistaat Sachsen*, (Dresden: PDS-Fraktion im Sächsischen Landtag, 2004).

PDS Parteivorstand, *Das Rostocker Manifest. Für einen zukunftsfähigen Osten in einer gerechten Republik* (Berlin: Parteivorstand der Partei des Demokratischen Sozialismus, 1998).

Reißig, Rolf, *Mitregieren in Berlin. Die PDS auf dem Prüfstand* (Berlin: Rosa Luxemburg Foundation, Texte 22, 2004).

Reißig, Rolf and Michael Brie, *Restriktionen und Optionen linkssozialistischer Politik in Regierungsverantwortung. Das Beispiel Berlin* (Berlin: Rosa Luxemburg Foundation, 2005).

Ritter, Peter, 'Regierungsbeteiligung der Linkspartei.PDS in Mecklenburg-Vorpommern; Maßstäbe, praktische Ansätze, Ergebnisse', in Cornelia Hildebrandt and Michael Brie (eds), *Die Linke in Regierungsverantwortung: Analysen, Erfahrungen, Kontroversen* (Berlin: Rosa Luxemburg Foundation, 2006).

Schwebs, Birgit, 'Regierungsbeteiligung der Linkspartei.PDS in Mecklenburg-Vorpommern; Maßstäbe, praktische Ansätze, Ergebnisse', in Cornelia Hildebrandt and Michael Brie (eds), *Die Linke in Regierungsverantwortung: Analysen, Erfahrungen, Kontroversen* (Berlin: Rosa Luxemburg Foundation, 2006).

Spehr, Christoph, *Ohne dramatische Erfolge im Westen gibt es keinen Wiedereintritt für die PDS: Zahlen, Analyse und Thesen zur Bundestagswahl 2002* (Berlin: Rosa Luxemburg Foundation, 2002).

Wolf, Harald, *Zwei entscheidende Jahre. Plädoyer für die Fortsetzung der Koalition über 2006 hinaus* (Berlin: PDS, 2004).

PDS News Service

AG Bilanz, 'Zur bisherigen Regierungsbeteiligung der PDS Mecklenburg Vorpommern', *Pressedienst*, 51, 2000.

Bisky, Lothar and Kornelia Wehlan, 'Brandenburger Weg ist endgültig zu Ende', *Pressedienst*, 45, 1999.

Brie, André, 'Erfordernis, Möglichkeiten, Schwierigkeiten und Inhalt eines Strategiewechsels der PDS', *Pressedienst*, 51, 1999.

Ernst, Cornelia, 'Wichtig ist, dass die PDS es aushält, weiter Regierung wie Opposition zu sein. Offener Brief des Landesvorstandes Sachsen an die PDS Berlin', *Pressedienst*, 3, 2002.

Ernst, Cornelia, 'Die nächsten Aufgaben der PDS in Sachsen. Rede auf dem PDS-Landesparteitag am 28 November 2004 in Chemnitz', *Pressedienst*, 50, 2004.

Ernst, Cornelia and Peter Porsch, 'Keine Alternative zur Überwindung der Stagnation der PDS von innen heraus', *Pressedienst*, 39, 2002.

'Geschichtsaufklärung versachlichen! Erklärung junger PDS-Mitglieder zum Politbüro-Prozess', *Pressedienst*, 36, 1997.

Gysi, Gregor, 'Zur gegenwärtigen Diskussion in unserer Partei', *Pressedienst*, 34, 1996.

Holter, Helmut, 'Mehrheiten gewinnen durch eine Politik für Mehrheiten', *Pressedienst*, 48, 2000.

Modrow, Hans, 'Zum Jahrestag des 13. August 1961. Persönliche Erklärung von Hans Modrow', *Pressedienst*, 35, 1997.

'Muss es mit der CDU sein? Offener Brief von Ralf Christoffers', *Pressedienst*, 34, 2001.

PDS Mecklenburg-Vorpommern, 'Für eine andere Beschäftigungs- und Wirtschaftspolitik in Mecklenburg-Vorpommern. Beschluß der 4. Tagung des 4. Landesparteitages der PDS Mecklenburg-Vorpommern, Parchim, 15 and 16 Februar 1997', *Pressedienst*, 7, 1997.

Disput, PDS Members' Newspaper

Bockhahn, Stefan, 'Licht und Schatten und der Rat, Schwerpunkte zu setzen. Die APO-Gruppe in Mecklenburg-Vorpommern', *Disput*, 10, 2004.

Fehst, Georg, 'Helmut Holter will Lösungen für die Leute im Land', *Disput*, 4, 2003.

Kalinowski, Ulrich, 'Vom Berg besteigen und den Mühen der Ebene', *Disput*, 2, 2002.

Liebich, Stefan, 'Drei Zahlen – milliardenschwer: Zur Haushaltsstrategie der Berliner PDS', *Disput*, 10, 2003.

'Nein zu UN-Militäreinsatzen', *Disput*, 4, 2000.

Richter, Stefan, '...da halten sich Chancen und Risiken in der Waage', interview with Stefan Liebich, *Disput*, 2, 2002.

Ritter, Peter, 'Gemeinsam für mehr Gerechtigkeit', *Disput*, 10, 2006.

Websites

http://www.antikapitalistische-linke.de/article/38._die_pds_braucht_die_regierungsbeteiligung_nicht__aber_diese_gesellschaft_braucht_die_pds_als_oppositionskraft_____.html

http://www.initiative-rixdorf.de

http://www.landtag-mv.de/dokumentenarchiv/plenarprotokolle/3_Wahlperiode/plpr03-0017.pdf

http://www.netzwerk-linke-opposition.de/

http://www.pds-online.de/geschichte

http://www.pds-online.de/geschichte/9808/weizsaecker-brief.htm

http://www.rosalux.de/cms/index.php?id=stiftung

http://www.sahrawagenknecht.de/de/

http://www.sahrawagenknecht.de/de/html/kurzbiografie.php

http://sozialisten.de/download/dokumente/grundsatzdokumente_partei/parteiprogramm1993.pdf

http://sozialisten.de/geschichte/9808/view_html?zid=3359&bs=41&n=40

http://sozialisten.de/partei/strukturen/agigs/index.htm

http://sozialisten.de/partei/strukturen/agigs/kpf/index.htm

http://sozialisten.de/partei/daten/statistiken/struktur.htm

http://sozialisten.de/sozialisten/medienspiegel/view_html/ zid33693/bs1/n2

http://sozialisten.de/sozialisten/parteibildung/pdf/gruendungsdokumente/061022_entwurf_bundessatzung-B.pdf

http://sozialisten.de/sozialisten/parteibildung/protokolle/programm/view_html?zid=31907&bs=1&n=1

Others

'Gysi tritt wegen Bonusmeilen zurück', on http://www.tagesschau.de/aktuell/
meldungen/0,1185,OID9741 22_NAV_REF1,00.html.
http://www.dradio.de/dkultur/sendungen/fazit/482963/
52 interviews with PDS parliamentarians and staff at party offices.

Secondary sources

Abedi, Amir, *Anti-Political Establishment Parties: A Comparative Analysis* (London: Routledge, 2004).

Austen-Smith, David and Jeffery Banks, 'Stable Governments and the Allocation of Party Portfolios', *American Political Science Review*, 82, 1990: 891–906.

Axelrod, Robert, *Conflict of Interest* (Chicago: Markham, 1970).

Bale, Tim and Torbjörn Bergman, 'A taste of honey is worse than none at all? Coping with the generic challenges of support party status in Sweden and New Zealand', *Party Politics*, 12 (2), 2006: 189–209.

Bale, Tim and Richard Dunphy, 'In from the cold: left parties, policy, office and votes in advanced liberal democracies since 1989', paper presented to University of Sussex's Centre for the Study of Parties and Democracy conference on the non-social democratic left and government participation', University of Sussex, 12 September 2006.

Barker, Peter, 'From the SED to the PDS: Continuity or Renewal?' in *German Monitor: The Party of Democratic Socialism. Modern Post-Communism or Nostalgic Populism?* (Amsterdam: Rodopi B.V, volume 42, 1998), pp. 1–17.

Baron, Udo and Manfred Wilke, 'Operation Vereinigung', *Die Politische Meinung*, 439, June 2006: 67–74.

Barthel, Wilfred et al., *Forschungsbericht Strukturen, Politische Aktivitäten und Motivationen in der PDS* (Berlin: Trafo Verlag, 1995).

Bastian, Jens, 'The *Enfant Terrible* of German Politics: The PDS between GDR Nostalgia and Democratic Socialism', *German Politics*, 4 (2), August 1995: 95–111.

Betz, Hans-Georg and Helga A. Welsh, 'The PDS in the New German Party System', *German Politics*, 4 (3), 1995: 92–111.

Bevir, Mark and R. A. W. Rhodes, 'Interpretive Theory', in David Marsh and Gerry Stoker (eds), *Theory and Methods in Political Science* (London: Palgrave Macmillan, 2002), pp. 131–152.

Beyme, Klaus von, 'Governments, Parliaments and the Structure of Power in Political Parties', in Hans Daalder and Peter Mair (eds), *Western European Party Systems: Continuity and Change* (London: Sage, 1983).

Bickerich, Wolfram (ed.), *SPD und Grüne: Das neue Bündnis?* (Hamburg: Spiegel-Buch, 1985).

Bisky, Lothar, *So viele Träume: Mein Leben* (Berlin: Rowohlt Verlag, 2005).

Bisky, Lothar, Uwe-Jens Heuer and Michael Schumann, *Rücksichten: Politische und juristische Aspekte der GDR-Geschichte* (Berlin: VSA, 1993).

Bortfeldt, Heinrich, *Von der SED zur PDS: Wandlung zur Demokratie* (Bonn: Bouvier, 1991).

Bortfeldt, Heinrich, 'Die Ostdeutschen und die PDS', *Deutschland Archiv*, 27 (12), 1994: 1283–1287.

Bortfeldt, Heinrich, 'Die PDS am Ende?', *Deutschland Archiv*, 36 (5), 2003: 738–751.

Bosco, Anna, 'Four Actors in search of a Role: The Southern European Communist Parties', in P. Nikiforos Diamandouros and Richard Gunther (eds), *Parties, Politics and Democracy in the New Southern Europe* (Baltimore: Johns Hopkins University Press, 2001).

Breitenbach, Elke and Katina Schubert, 'Opposition und Regierung – Partei und Bewegung – Widersprüche?', *Utopie kreativ*, 165/166, 2004: 715–725.

Brie, Michael, 'Das politische Projekt PDS – eine unmögliche Möglichkeit', in Michael Brie, Martin Herzig and Thomas Koch (eds), *Die PDS – empirische Befunde und kontroverse Analysen* (Cologne: Papyrossa, 1995).

Brunsson, Nils, *The Organisation of Hypocrisy: Talk, Decisions and Actions in Organisations* (New York: John Wiley and Sons, 1989).

Budge, Ian and Hans Kerman, *Parties and Democracy: Coalition Formation and Government Functioning in Twenty States* (Oxford: Oxford University Press, 1990).

Burchell, Jon, *The Evolution of Green Politics: Development and Change within European Green Parties* (San Francisco: Earthscan Publications Limited, 2002).

de Swann, Abram, *Coalition Theories and Cabinet Formation* (Amsterdam: Elsevier, 1973).

Deutscher Bundestag: Drucksache 13/7417 (Berlin: Deutscher Bundestag, 1997).

Deutscher Bundestag: Drucksache 13/10015 (Berlin: Deutscher Bundestag, 1998).

Ditfurth, Christian von, *Ostalgie oder linke Alternative? Meine Reise durch die PDS* (Cologne: Kiepenheuer and Witsch, 1998).

Dodd, Lawrence, *Coalitions in Parliamentary Government* (Princeton: Princeton University Press, 1976).

Dolowitz, David and David Marsh, 'Learning from Abroad: The Role of Policy Transfer in Contemporary Policy-Making', *Governance*, 13 (1), 2000: 5–24.

Downs, William M., *Coalition Government Subnational Style* (Columbus: Ohio State University Press, 1998).

Dunphy, Richard, *Contesting Capitalism? Left Parties and European Integration* (Manchester: Manchester University Press, 2004).

Dunphy, Richard and Tim Bale, 'Red flag still flying? Explaining AKEL – Cyprus's communist anomaly', *Party Politics*, 13 (1), 2007: 129–146.

Falter, Jürgen W. and Markus Klein, 'Die Wähler der PDS bei der Bundestagswahl 1994. Zwischen Ideologie, Nostalgie und Protest', *Aus Politik und Zeitgeschichte*, B51-52/94: 22–34.

Felfe, Edeltraut, Erwin Kischel and Peter Kroh (eds), *Warum? Für wen? Wohin? 7 Jahre PDS Mecklenburg-Vorpommern in der Regierung* (Schkeuditz: GNN Verlag, 2005).

Frankland, E. Gene, 'The Fall, Rise, and Recovery of Die Grünen', in Dick Richardson and Chris Rootes (eds), *The Green Challenge: The Development of Green Parties in Europe* (London: Routledge, 1995), pp. 23–44.

Frankland, E. Gene and Donald Schoonmaker, *Between Protest and Power: The Green Party in Germany* (Boulder, CO and Oxford: Westview Press, 1992).

Gapper, Stuart, *From Eastern European Communist Successor to Western European Socialist Party? Germany's Party of Democratic Socialism in a Comparative Context, 1990–2002* (Birmingham: University of Birmingham, unpublished Ph.D. thesis, 2002).

Gay, Peter, *The Dilemma of Democratic Socialism: Eduard Bernstein's Challenge to Marx* (New York: Columbia University Press, 1952).

Gerner, Manfred, *Partei ohne Zukunft? Von der SED zur PDS* (Munich: Tilsner Verlag, 1994).

Gerth, Michael, *Die PDS und die ostdeutsche Gesellschaft im Transformationsprozess* (Hamburg: Dr. Kovac, 2003).

Graham, Stuart, *The Party of Democratic Socialism and the Temptations of Parliamentary Democracy* (Birmingham: University of Birmingham, unpublished Ph.D. thesis, 2001).

Hallas, Duncan, 'Towards a Revolutionary Socialist Party', in Duncan Hallas (ed.), *Party and Class* (London: Pluto, 1971).

Hands, Gordon, 'Robert Michels and the Study of Political Parties', *British Journal of Political Science*, 1, 1971: 155–172.

Harmel, Robert and Kenneth Janda, 'An Integrated Theory on Party Goals and Party Change', *Journal of Theoretical Politics*, 6 (3), 1994: 259–284.

Harmel, Robert and Lars Svåsand, 'Party Leadership and Party Institutionalisation: Three Phases of Development', *West European Politics*, 16 (2), 1993: 69–83.

Harmel, Robert and Alexander C. Tan, 'Party Actors and Party Change: Does Factional Dominance Matter?', *European Journal of Political Research*, 42 (3), 2003: 409–424.

Hartleb, Florian, *Rechts- und Linkspopulismus. Eine Fallstudie anhand von Schill-Partei und PDS* (Wiesbaden: VS, 2004).

Harvey, David, 'Class Relations, Social Justice and the Politics of Difference', in Michael Keith and Steve Pile (eds), *Place and the Politics of Identity* (London: Routledge, 1993).

Heinrich, Gudrun, *Rot-Grün in Berlin. Die Alternative Liste in der Regierungsverantwortung 1989–1990* (Marburg: Schüren, 1993).

Heinrich, Gudrun, *Kleine Koalitionspartner in Landesregierungen. Zwischen Konkurrenz und Kooperation* (Opladen: Leske und Budrich, 2002).

Heunemann, Falk, *Die Kooperation der PDS und der WASG zur Bundestagswahl 2005* (Jena: Fakultät für Sozial- und Verhaltenswissenschaften, Institut für Politikwissenschaft, Friedrich-Schiller-Universität, unpublished Masters thesis, 2006).

Hilmer, Richard, 'Bundestagswahl 2002: Eine zweite Chance für Rot-Grün', *Zeitschrift für Parlamentsfragen*, 34, 2003: 187–219.

Hinrichs, Rainer, 'Professionaliersung durch Regierungsbeteiligung', in Winfried Thaa and Dieter Salomon (eds), *Grüne an der Macht. Widerstände und Chancen grün-alternativer Regierungsbeteiligungen* (Cologne: Bund-Verlag, 1994).

Hough, Dan, 'Made in Eastern Germany': The PDS and the Articulation of Eastern German Interests', *German Politics*, 9 (2), 2000: 125–148.

Hough, Dan, *The Fall and Rise of the PDS in Eastern Germany* (Birmingham: Birmingham University Press, 2002).

Hough, Dan and Jonathan Olsen, 'The PDS and Participation in Eastern German Land Governments', *gfl-journal*, 3, 2004: 117–142.

Hough, Dan, *The German Bundestag Election of September 2005* (Brighton: University of Sussex, EPERN Election Briefing No.23, 2005).

Hough, Dan, 'Introduction', in Dan Hough, William E. Paterson and James Sloam (eds), *Learning from the West: Policy Transfer and Programmatic Change in the*

Communist Successor Parties of East Central Europe (London: Routledge, 2006), pp. 1–15.

Hradil, Stefan, 'Die Modernisierung des Denkens. Zukunftspotentiale und "Altlasten" in Ostdeutschland', *Aus Politik und Zeitgeschichte*, B20/95, 1995: 3–15.

Hudson, Kate, *European Communism since 1989* (London: Macmillan, 2000).

Hüllen, Rudolf van, *Ideologie und Machtkampf bei den Grünen* (Bonn: Bouvier, 1990).

Hülsberg, Werner, *The German Greens: A Social and Political Profile* (London and New York: Verso, 1988).

Infratest Dimap, *Wahlreport Berlin 1999* (Berlin: Infratest Dimap, 1999).

Infratest Dimap, *Wahl zum 15. Deutschen Bundestag, 22. September 2002* (Berlin: Infratest Dimap, 2002).

Jacoby, Wade, *The Enlargement of the European Union and NATO: Ordering from the Menu in Central Europe* (Cambridge: Cambridge University Press, 2004).

Jahn, Detlef, 'Unifying the Greens in a United Germany', *Environmental Politics*, 3 (2), Summer 1994: 312–318.

Jeffery, Charlie and Dan Hough, 'Germany: An Erosion of Federal-Länder Linkages?', in Dan Hough and Charlie Jeffery (eds), *Devolution and Electoral Politics* (Manchester: Manchester University Press, 2006).

Johnsen, Björn, *Von der Fundamentalopposition zur Regierungsbeteiligung. Die Entwicklung der Grünen in Hessen 1982–1985* (Marburg: Schüren, 1988).

Katz, Richard S. and Peter Mair, 'Changing Models of Party Organisation and Party Democracy: The Emergence of the Cartel Party', *Party Politics*, 1, 1995: 5–28.

Katz, Richard S. and Peter Mair, 'The Ascendancy of the Party in Public Office: Party Organizational Change in Twentieth-Century Democracies', Richard Gunther, Jose Ramon Montero and Juan J. Linz (eds), *Political Parties: Old Concepts and New Challenges* (Oxford: Oxford University Press, 2002).

Kelly, Petra, 'Wir müssen die Etablierten entblößen, wo wir können', in Jörg Mettke (ed.), *Die Grünen: Regierungspartner von Morgen?* (Hamburg: Spiegel-Buch, 1982).

King, Ian, 'A Damned Close-Run Thing: The German General Election of 2002', *Debatte*, 10 (2), 2002: 123–139.

Kitschelt, Herbert, 'Citizens, Politicians, and Party Cartellization: Political Representation and State Failure in Post-Industrial Democracies', *European Journal of Political Research*, 37, 2000: 149–179.

Klein, Markus and Claudio Caballero, 'Rückwärts in die Zukunft. Die Wähler der PDS bei der Bundestagswahl 1994', *Politische Vierteljahresschrift*, 37 (2), 1996: 229–247.

Kleinert, Hubert, *Aufstieg und Fall der Grünen: Analyse einer alternativen Partei* (Bonn: Verlag J.H.W. Dietz Nachf., 1992).

Koch-Baumgarten, Sigrid, 'Postkommunisten im Spagat: Zur Funktion der PDS im Parteiensystem', *Deutschland Archiv*, 30 (6), 1997: 864–878.

Koß, Michael, 'Durch die Krise zum Erfolg? Die PDS und ihr langer Weg nach Westen', in Tim Spier, Felix Butzlaff, Matthias Micus and Franz Walter (eds), *Die Linkspartei: Zeitgemäße Idee oder Bündnis ohne Zukunft?* (Wiesbaden: VS, 2007).

Koß, Michael, 'Lose verkoppelte Anarchie: Die Linkspartei im deutschen Föderalismus', in Michael Brie and Cornelia Hildebrandt (eds), *Parteien und Bewegungen. Die Linke im Aufbruch* (Berlin: Dietz, 2006).

Koß, Michael and Dan Hough, 'Between a Rock and Many Hard Places: The PDS and Government Participation in the Eastern German Länder', *German Politics* 15 (1), 2006: 73–98.

Lang, Jürgen P., 'Nach den Wahlen 1994: PDS-Strategie im Wandel?', *Deutschland Archiv*, 28(4), 1995: 369–380.

Lang, Jürgen P., *Ist die PDS eine demokratische Partei? Eine extremismustheoretische Untersuchung* (Baden-Baden: Nomos, 2003).

Laver, Michael, 'Theories of Coalition Formation and Local Government Coalitions', in Colin Mellors and Bert Pijnenburg (eds), *Political Parties and Coalitions in European Local Government* (London: Routledge, 1989).

Laver, Michael and Norman Schofield, *Multi-Party Government: The Politics of Coalition in Europe* (Oxford, Oxford University Press, 1990).

Laver, Michael and Kenneth Shepsle, 'Government Coalitions and Intraparty Politics', *British Journal of Politics Science*, 20 (4), 1990: 489–507.

Lees, Charles, 'The Red-Green Coalition', *German Politics* 8 (2), 1999: 174–194.

Lees, Charles, *The Red-Green Coalition in Germany: Politics, Personalities and Power* (Manchester and New York: Manchester University Press, 2000a).

Lees, Charles, 'Paradise Postponed: An Assessment of Ten Years of Governmental Participation by the German Green Party', in Stephen C. Young (ed.), *The Emergence of Ecological Modernisation: Integrating the Environment and the Economy?* (London and New York: Routledge, 2000b).

Leiserson, Michael, 'Factions and Coalitions in One-Party Japan', *American Political Science Review*, 62, 1968: 770–787.

Leiserson, Michael, 'Game Theory and the Study of Coalition Behaviour', in Sven Groennings, E. W. Kelly and Michael Leiserson (eds), *The Study of Coalition Behaviour* (New York: Holt, Rinehart and Winston, 1970).

Lösche, Peter, 'Lose verkoppelte Anarchie'. Zur aktuellen Situation von Volksparteien am Beispiel der SPD', *Aus Politik und Zeitgeschichte*, B43/1993: 34–45.

March, Luke and Case Mudde, 'What's Left of the Radical Left? The European Radical Left after 1989: Decline and Mutation', *Comparative European Politics*, 3 (1), 2005: 23–49.

Markovits, Andrei S. and Philip S. Gorski, *The German Left: Red, Green, and Beyond* (New York: Oxford University Press, 1993).

Mayer, Margit and John Ely (eds), *The German Greens: Paradox between Movement and Party* (Philadelphia: Temple University Press, 1999).

McKay, Joanna, 'From Pariah to Power. The Berlin Election of 2001 and the PDS Question', *German Politics*, 11 (2), 2002: 21–38.

McKay, Joanna, 'The PDS Tests the West: The Party of Democratic Socialism's Campaign to become a Pan-German Socialist Party', *Journal of Communist Studies and Transition Politics*, 20 (2), 2004: 50–72.

Mecklenburg-Vorpommern Landtagsnachrichten 9 (2), 1999.

Menge, Richard, *Links der Mitte: Welche Chancen hat Rot-Grün?* (Marburg: Schüren Presseverlag, 1993).

Mettke, Jörg (ed.), *Die Grünen: Regierungspartner von Morgen?* (Hamburg: Spiegel-Buch, 1982).

Meuche-Mäker, Meinhard, *Die PDS im Westen 1990–2005: Schlussfolgerungen für eine neue Linke* (Berlin: Dietz, 2005).

Michels, Robert, *Political Parties. A Sociological Study of the Oligarchical Tendencies of Modern Democracy* (New York: Dover Publications, 1959).

Micus, Matthias, 'Die Quadratur des Kreises. Parteiführung in der PDS', in Daniela Forkmann and Michael Schlieben (ed.), *Die Parteivorsitzenden der Bundesrepublik Deutschland 1949–2004* (Wiesbaden: VS, 2006).

Minnerup, Günther, 'The PDS and the Strategic Dilemma of the German Left', in Peter Barker (ed.), *German Monitor – The Party of Democratic Socialism. Modern Post-Communism or Nostalgic Populism?* (Amsterdam: Rodopi B.V, 42, 1998).

Modrow, Hans, *Aufbruch und Ende* (Berlin: Konkret Literatur, 1991).

Modrow, Hans, *Ich wollte ein neues Deutschland* (Berlin: Dietz, 1998).

Modrow, Hans, 'Zum Geleit', in Edeltraut Felfe, Erwin Kischel and Peter Kroh (eds), *Warum? Für wen? Wohin? 7 Jahre PDS Mecklenburg-Vorpommern in der Regierung* (Schkeuditz: GNN Verlag, 2005), pp. 7–11.

Moreau, Patrick, *PDS. Anatomie einer postkommunistischen Partei* (Bonn: Bouvier, 1992).

Moreau, Patrick, 'Mit Lenin im Bauch...? Die PDS auf der Suche nach einer Berliner Republik von links', *Politische Studien*, 349, September/October 1996: 27–42.

Moreau, Patrick, *Die PDS: Profil einer antidemokratischen Partei* (Munich: Hanns Seidel Foundation, 1998).

Moreau, Patrick and Jürgen Lang, *Was will die PDS?* (Frankfurt am Main: Ullstein, 1994).

Moreau, Patrick and Jürgen Lang, *Linksextremismus. Eine unterschätzte Gefahr* (Bonn: Bouvier, 1996).

Moreau, Patrick and Viola Neu, *Die PDS zwischen Linksextremismus und Linkspopulismus* (Sankt Augustin bei Bonn: Konrad Adenauer Foundation, Interne Studien 76, 1994).

Müller, Wolfgang C. and Kaare Strøm (eds), *Policy, Office, or Votes? How Political Parties in Western Europe Make Hard Decisions* (Cambridge: Cambridge University Press, 1999).

Müller, Wolfgang C. and Kaare Strøm, 'Conclusions: Party Behaviour and Representative Democracy', in Wolfgang C. Müller and Kaare Strøm (eds), *Policy, Office, or Votes? How Political Parties in Western Europe Make Hard Decisions* (Cambridge: Cambridge University Press, 1999).

Neu, Viola, 'Party of Government in Waiting', *German Comments*, April 1997: 20–27.

Neu, Viola, *Die Potentiale der PDS und der Republikaner im Winter 1997–98* (Bonn: Konrad Adenauer Foundation, 1998).

Neu, Viola, *Die PDS 10 Jahre nach dem Fall der Mauer* (Bonn: Konrad Adenauer Foundation, 1999).

Neu, Viola, *Am Ende der Hoffnung: Die PDS im Westen* (Bonn: Konrad Adenauer Foundation, 2000).

Neu, Viola, *Das Janusgesicht der PDS. Wähler und Partei zwischen Demokratie und Extremismus* (Baden-Baden: Nomos, 2004).

Neu, Viola, *Landtagswahl in Mecklenburg-Vorpommern und Abgeordnetenhauswahl in Berlin am 17. September 2006* (Bonn: Konrad Adenauer Foundation, 2006).

Neu, Viola and Verena Lieber, *PolitikKompass: Analyse der Landtagswahl in Mecklenburg-Vorpommern* (Bonn: Konard Adenauer Foundation, 2002).

Neugebauer, Gero, '1994 im Aufschwung Ost: Die PDS. Eine Bilanz', *Gegenwartskunde*, 43 (4), 1994: 431–444.

Neugebauer, Gero and Richard Stöss, *Die PDS: Geschichte, Organisation, Wähler, Konkurrenten* (Opladen: Leske und Budrich, 1996).

Neugebauer, Gero, 'Die PDS in Brandenburg – wohin des Wegs?', *Perspektive*, 21 (13), 2001: 43–63.

Niedermayer, Oskar, 'Die brandenburgische Landtagswahl vom 19. September 2004. Reaktionen der Wähler auf Hartz IV', *Zeitschrift für Parlamentsfragen*, 36 (1), 2005: 64–80.

Olivio, Christiane, *Creating a Democratic Civil Society in Eastern Germany: The Case of the Citizen Movements and Alliance 90* (Palgrave Macmillan/Macmillan: New York and London, 2001).

Olsen, Jonathan, *Nature and Nationalism: Right-Wing Ecology and the Politics of Identity in Contemporary Germany* (New York: St. Martin's/Palgrave Macmillan, 1999).

Olsen, Jonathan: 'Seeing Red: The SPD-PDS Coalition Government in Mecklenburg-West Pomerania', *German Studies Review*, XXIII (3), October 2000: 557–580.

Olsen, Jonathan, 'The PDS in Western Germany: An Empirical Study of Local PDS Politicians', *German Politics*, 11 (1), April 2002: 147–172.

Oswald, Franz, *The Party that Came Out of the Cold War: The Party of Democratic Socialism in United Germany* (London: Praeger, 2002).

Panebianco, Angelo, *Political Parties: Organisation and Power* (Cambridge: Cambridge University Press, 1988).

Patton, David F., 'Germany's Left Party. The PDS and the Vacuum Thesis: From Regional Milieu Party to Left Alternative?', *Journal of Communist Studies and Transition Politics*, 22 (2), 2006: 206–227.

Poguntke, Thomas, *Alternative Politics: The German Green Party*, (Edinburgh: Edinburgh University Press, 1993).

Poguntke, Thomas, 'Green Parties in National Governments: From Protest to Acquiescence?', in Ferdinand Müller-Rommel and Thomas Poguntke, *Green Parties in National Governments* (London and Portland, OR: Routledge, 2002).

Poguntke, Thomas and Rüdiger Schmitt-Beck, 'Still the Same with a New Name? Bündnis 90/Die Grünen after the Fusion', *German Politics*, 3 (1), April 1994: 91–113.

Raschke, Joachim, *Die Grünen: Wie sie wurden, was sie sind* (Cologne: Bund-Verlag Gmbh, 1993).

Riker, William, *The Theory of Political Coalitions* (New Haven: Yale University Press, 1962).

Riker, William, 'Implications from the Disequilibrium of Majority Rule for the Study of Institutions', *American Political Science Review*, 74, 1980: 432–446.

Roberts, Geoffrey, '"Emigrants in their own Country": German Reunification and its Political Consequences', *Parliamentary Affairs*, 44, 1991: 373–388.

Roberts, Geoffrey, *German Electoral Politics* (Manchester: Manchester University Press, 2006).

Rose, Richard, *Lesson-Drawing in Public Policy: A Guide to Learning Across Time and Space* (Chatham, NJ: Chatham House, 1993).

Roth, Dieter, 'Die Wahlen zur Volkskammer in der DDR. Der Versuch einer Erklärung', *Politische Vierteljahresschrift*, 31, 1990: 369–393.

Roth, Dieter and Matthias Jung, 'Ablösung der Regierung vertagt: Eine Analyse der Bundestagswahl 2002', *Aus Politik und Zeitgeschichte*, 49–50, 2002: 3–17.

Scharf, Thomas, *The German Greens: Challenging the Consensus* (Oxford and Providence: Berg, 1994).

Schedler, Andreas, 'Anti-Political-Establishment Parties', *Party Politics*, 2 (3), 1996: 291–312.

Schoen, Harald and Jürgen Falter, 'Die Linkspartei und ihre Wähler', *Aus Politik und Zeitgeschichte*, 51–52, 2005: 33–40.

Schofield, Norman, 'Political Competition and Multiparty Coalition Governments', *European Journal of Political Research*, 23, 1993: 1–33.

Schroeren, Michael, (ed.), *Zehn bewegte Jahren* (Vienna: Ueberreuter, 1990).

Shull, Tad, *Red and Green: Ideology and Strategy in European Political Ecology* (Albany: State University of New York Press, 1999).

Sjöblom, Gunnar, *Party Strategies in a Multiparty System* (Lund: Studentlitteratur, 1968).

Stöss, Richard and Gero Neugebauer, *Mit einem blauen Auge davon gekommen: Eine Analyse der Bundestagswahl 2002* (Berlin: Otto-Sammer-Zentrum an der FU, 7, 2002).

Strøm, Kaare, 'A Behavioral Theory of Competitive Political Parties', *American Journal of Political Science*, 34 (2), 1990: 566–568.

Strøm, Kaare, and Wolfgang C. Müller, 'Political Parties and Hard Choices', in Wolfgang C. Müller and Kaare Strøm (eds), *Policy, Office, or Votes? How Political Parties in Western Europe Make Hard Decisions*, (Cambridge: Cambridge University Press, 1999).

Sturm, Eva, 'Und der Zukunft zugewandt?' Eine Untersuchung zur 'Politikfähigkeit' der PDS (Opladen: Leske and Budrich, 2000).

Tiefenbach, Paul, *Die Grünen: Verstaatlichung einer Partei* (Cologne: PapyRossa, 1998).

Tsebelis, George, *Nested Games: Rational Choice in Comparative Politics* (Berkeley: University of California Press, 1990).

Veen, Hans-Joachim and Jürgen Hoffmann, *Die Grünen zu Beginn der neunziger Jahre. Profil und Defizite einer fast etablierten Partei* (Bonn und Berlin: Bouvier Verlag, 1992).

Vester, Michael, 'Milieuwandel und regionaler Strukturwandel in Ostdeutschland', in Michael Vester, Michael Hoffman and Irene Zierke (eds), *Soziale Milieus in Ostdeutschland. Gesellschaftliche Strukturen zwischen Zerfall und Neubildung* (Köln: Bund, 1995).

Weick, Karl, 'Educational Organizations as Loosely Coupled Systems', *Administrative Science Quarterly*, 21 (1), 1976: 1–19.

Weis, Florian, 'Die PDS in den westlichen Bundesländern: Anmerkungen zu keiner Erfolgsgeschichte', *Utopie kreativ*, 173, March 2005: 257–265.

Wiesendahl, Elmar, *Parteien in Perspektive. Theoretische Ansichten der Organisationswirklichkeit politischer Parteien* (Opladen: Westdeutscher Verlag, 1998).

Wiesendahl, Elmar, 'Changing Party Organisations in Germany: How to Deal with Uncertainty and Organised Anarchy', *German Politics*, 8 (2), 1999: 108–125.

Wilson, Frank L., 'The Sources of Party Change: The Social Democratic Parties of Britain, France, Germany and Spain', in Kay Lawson (ed.), *How Political Parties Work: Perspectives form Within* (Westport und London: Praeger, 1994).

Wolinetz, Stephen B., 'Beyond the Catch-All Party: Approaches to the Study of Parties and Party Organization in Contemporary Democracies', in Richard Gunther et al. (eds), *Political Parties: Old Concepts and New Challenges*, (Oxford: Oxford University Press, 2002).

Zessin, Helmut, Edwin Schwertner and Frank Schumann, *Chronik der PDS: 1989 bis 1997* (Berlin: Dietz, 1998).

Newspaper articles

Articles by named authors

Alexander, Robin, 'Dabei sein ist alles', *Tageszeitung*, 29 June 2002.

Bartsch, Michael, 'Regierungspläne vertagt', *Neues Deutschland*, 2 July 2001.

Bartsch, Michael, 'Stasi-Keule nun auch gegen Peter Porsch', *Neues Deutschland*, 9 August 2004.

Baum, Andreas, 'Der Fehlstart des Bettvorlegers', *Frankfurter Rundschau*, 12 October 1998.

Beikler, Sabine, 'Die heimliche Opposition', *Tagesspiegel*, 16 June 2003.

Beikler, Sabine, 'Profil schärfen, Streit vermeiden', *Tagesspiegel*, 28 September 2004.

Benjamin, Michael, '7. Oktober – war da nicht was?', *Junge Welt*, 7 October 1999.

Berg, Stefan, 'Mann aus dem Kreml', *Der Spiegel*, 23 August 2004.

Beuscker, Pascal and Frank Überall, 'Ab Montag wird angefochten', *Taz*, 16 September 2005.

Beyerlein, Andrea, 'Kampf um Bisky-Nachfolge beginnt', *Berliner Zeitung*, 9 July 2003.

Beyerlein, Andrea, 'PDS vor dem sechsten Führungswechsel', *Berliner Zeitung*, 17 December 2004.

Boecker, Arne, 'Koalitionskrise in Mecklenburg-Vorpommern', *Süddeutsche Zeitung*, 27 May 2005.

Brandt, Ernst-Michael, 'Wir sind das Volk', *Die Woche*, 30 June 1994.

Bullion, Constanze von, 'Wandlungen eines Dampfplauderers', *Süddeutsche Zeitung*, 3 June 2005.

Burger, Reiner, 'Rausch ohne Reue', *Frankfurter Allgemeine Zeitung*, 11 August 2005.

Cleven, Thoralf, 'PDS möchte Konservative in Schwerin ablösen', *Ostsee Zeitung*, 12 August 1996.

Cleven, Thoralf, 'PDS-Chef kam mit blauem Auge davon', *Ostsee Zeitung*, 17 February 1997.

Cleven, Thoralf, 'Im PDS-Kummerkasten steckt die SPD', *Ostsee Zeitung*, 20 June 1997.

Daniel, Isabel, 'Wiederbelebte Option', *Freitag*, 22 June 2001.

Fehrle, Brigitte, 'Vorwärts, und vergessen', *Berliner Zeitung*, 2 November 1998.

Frost, Andreas, 'Schweriner PDS lässt die Muskeln spielen', *Tagesspiegel*, 11 March 1999.

Goos, Diethart, 'Schweriner PDS steht vor Scherbenhaufen', *Die Welt*, 14 January 1999.

Harting, Klaus, 'Die PDS schielt nach der Macht', *Die Zeit*, 17 January 1997.

Hauser, Otto: 'PDS stimmt für Höppner – heftige Kritik aus Bonn', *Leipziger Volkszeitung*, 27 May 1998.

Heitkamp, Sven, 'Conny Ernst entzweit die Gemüter in Sachsen', *Leipziger Volkszeitung*, 26 July 2001.

Hoffmann, Sabine, 'Die Picknick-Politikerinnen', *Der Spiegel*, 20 December 2002.

Honnigfort, Bernd, 'Die Entdeckung des Himmels', *Frankfurter Rundschau*, 7 June 2000.

Hintzmann, Karsten, 'Rot-rote Gedankenspiele der PDS', *Berliner Morgenpost*, 23 January 2001.

Hoischen, Oliver, 'Hart am Leben orientierter Linker', *Frankfurter Allgemeine Zeitung*, 22 January 2002.

Käßner, Frank, 'Sächsische Linkspartei wollte harte Drogen freigeben', *Die Welt*, 10 August 2005.

Küpper, Mechthild, 'Hartz IV als Glaubwürdigkeitstest', *Frankfurter Allegemeine Zeitung*, 5 August 2004.

Küpper, Mechthild, 'Die Fusion hat immer Recht', *Frankfurter Allgemeine Zeitung*, 19 September 2006.

Küpper, Mechthild, 'Fusionieren oder Regieren', *Frankfurter Allgemeine Zeitung*, 25 September 2006.

Küpper, Mechthild, 'Abschied vom Avantgardekozept', *Frankfurter Allgemeine Zeitung*, 2 October 2006.

Küpper, Mechthild, 'Höhere Steuereinnahmen retten Rot-Rot über die nächsten fünf Jahre', *Frankfurter Allgemeine Zeitung*, 3 November 2006.

Küpper, Mechthild, 'Berliner Einheit in Lafontaines Gegenwind', *Frankfurter Allgemeine Zeitung*, 20 November 2006.

Lasch, Hendrik, 'Zwischen Profil und Partnersuche', *Neues Deutschland*, 29 November 2004.

Lehmann, Anna, 'PDS-Spitze hat Konto überzogen', *Tageszeitung*, 5 April 2004.

Löbbert, Raoul, 'Das Gespenst der Vergangenheit', *Die Zeit*, 30 August 2004.

Mallwitz, Gudrun, 'Politbüro Tack', *Berliner Morgenpost*, 5 December 1999.

Mallwitz, Gudrun, 'PDS will aufs Regieren vorbereitet sein', *Berliner Morgenpost*, 9 March 2002.

Mallwitz, Gudrun, 'Linkspartei.PDS: Kerstin Kaiser neue Chefin der Landtagsfraktion', *Die Welt*, 19 October 2005.

Mara, Michael, 'Die PDS denkt sich ins Mitregieren hinein', *Tagesspiegel*, 14 January 1997.

Mara, Michael, 'Mit Schönbohm wird es für uns leichter', *Tagesspiegel*, 16 October 1998.

Mara, Michael, 'Die PDS sucht ihr Oppositionsprofil', *Tagesspiegel*, 21 March 2000.

Mentschel, Stefan, 'PDS-Glaubwürdigkeit bedroht', *Neues Deutschland*, 16 October 2003.

Miller, Tobias, 'Wir wollen Magdeburger Verhältnisse', *Berliner Zeitung*, 24 November 1997.

Novak, Andreas, 'Auf Kuschelkurs zum rot-roten Sieg', *Sächsische Zeitung*, 16 July 2003.

Oertel, Gabriele, 'Dem Trübsinn ein Ende', *Neues Deutschland*, 19 September 2005.

Panster, Christian, 'Wir pfeifen auf Schönbohm', *Tageszeitung*, 29 August 2006.

Preusker, Ingo, 'Der dritte Mann', *Wochenpost*, 25 April 1996.

Rabenstein, Andreas, 'Kinnhaken von der Berliner Basis', *Welt am Sonntag*, 20 June 2004.

Rada, Uwe, 'PDS spart am besten', *Tageszeitung*, 25 June 2001.

Rex, Wolfgang, 'Im Kern eine positive Bilanz', *Neues Deutschland*, 27 October 2000.

Rex, Wolfgang, 'Mehr einfallen lassen als SPD oder Grüne', *Neues Deutschland*, 15 November 2004.

Richter, Christine, 'PDS: Das Studium darf nichts kosten', *Berliner Zeitung*, 8 December 2003.

Saft, Gunnar, 'Rote Schattenkrieger: PDS benennt Wahlkampfspitze', *Sächsische Zeitung*, 26 January 2004.

Saft, Gunnar, 'Betonliste und Eigentor', *Sächsische Zeitung*, 10 May 2004.

Schley, Nadine, 'WASG tun?', *Die Zeit*, 23 June 2005.

Schneider, Gerlinde, 'Märkische PDS will "22 plus XXL"', *Neues Deutschland*, 22 March 2004.

Seidel, Jürgen, 'Linkspartei übt wieder Opposition', *Neues Deutschland*, 18 December 2006.

Seils, Christoph, 'In Sachsen toben Flügelkämpfe und legen den Landesverband lahm', *Berliner Zeitung*, 24 September 1997.

Seils, Christoph, 'Interne Kritik an sächsischer PDS-Fraktion', *Berliner Zeitung*, 21 September 1999.

Seils, Christoph, 'Gebremste Kandidatin', *Frankfurter Rundschau*, 13 September 2004.

Siebert, Sven, 'PDS will Fünf-Prozent-Hürde für Bonn in Sachsen nehmen', *Leipziger Volkszeitung*, 24 November 1997.

Spannbauer, Andreas, 'Eher dafür als dagegen', *Tageszeitung*, 1 December 2001.

Straud, Toralf, 'Ankunft im Modernen: Die PDS braucht ein neues Programm und einen neuen Chef', *Die Zeit*, 6 April 2000.

Thomsen, Jan, 'Konflikt um WASG Berlin verschärft sich', *Berliner Zeitung*, 17 May 2006.

Walter, Klaus and Jan Freitag, 'Von Aufruhr keine Spur', *Ostsee Zeitung*, 4 November 2002.

Wenz, Dieter, 'Schwerin, die höchste Hochburg', *Frankfurter Allgemeine Zeitung*, 13 December 1997.

Wenz, Dieter, 'Rot-rotes Auslaufmodell', *Frankfurter Allgemeine Zeitung*, 2 May 2003.

Wenz, Dieter, 'Wir fühlten uns an DDR-Zeiten erinnert', *Frankfurter Allgemeine Zeitung*, 18 August 1998.

Zawatka-Gerlach, Ulrich, 'Der Watschenmann wird noch gebraucht', *Tagesspiegel*, 10 May 2004.

Articles by unnamed authors

'Berliner PDS will einen rot-grünen Senat tolerieren', *Berliner Morgenpost*, 28 February 1999.

'Berliner PDS will Machtwechsel', *Berliner Zeitung*, 2 December 1996.

'CDU fordert Ausschluß von PDS-Mitglied: Kritik an Benjamin wegen Äußerungen zur Mauerbau', *Berliner Zeitung*, 26 January 1999.

'Der lachende Vierte ist die PDS', *Berliner Zeitung*, 5 December 2001.

'Bisky: PDS will zurzeit nicht regieren', *Berliner Zeitung*, 4 January 2003.

'IM-Debatte auf dem Parteitag', *Berliner Zeitung*, 21 February 2005.

'Ex-SPD-Chef Lafontaine fordert den Kanzler heraus', *Bild*, 24 May 2005.

'Oskar bravo', *The Economist*, 18 March 1999.

'Up and Away', *The Economist*, 8 August 2002.

'A plan to put Germans back into jobs', *The Economist*, 22 August 2002.

'Die PDS in Koalitionslaune', *Frankfurter Allgemeine Zeitung*, 24 February 1997.

'PDS Brandenburg hat eine neue Vorsitzende', *Frankfurter Allgemeine Zeitung*, 22 February 1999.

'PDS-Streit über Neoliberalismus', *Frankfurter Allgemeine Zeitung*, 17 March 2006.

'Abschied vom Avantgardekouzept', *Frankfurter Allgemeine Zeitung*, 2 October 2006.

'SPD stellt der PDS Bedingungen', *Frankfurter Rundschau*, 27 September 1997.

'Neuer Streit um alte Linie im PDS-Programm', *Leipziger Volkszeitung*, 12 March 2004.

'PDS- Politiker fechten eigene Wahlliste an', *Leipziger Volkszeitung*, 7 October 2004.

'E-Mail-Affäre: Ermittlungen gegen Petke werden eingestellt', *Märkische Allgemeine*, 1 December 2006.

'Volksstimme-Interview mit Wulf Gallert: "Die soziale Frage ist das A und O"', *Magdeburger Volksstimme*, 19 December 2006.

'WASG-Basis stimmt für Ehe mit Linkspartei', *Märkische Oderzeitung*, 2 April 2006.

'Der PDS reichen 100,000 Mann', *Neues Deutschland*, 17 May 2000.

'Für eine 100,000 Personen-Armee', *Neues Deutschland*, 19 May 2000.

'Partner für große Koalition nicht erkennbar', *Neues Deutschland*, 21 June 2004.

'Für eine antikapitalistische Linke: Diskussionspapier für die Programmdebatte von PDS und WASG', *Neues Deutschland*, 31 March 2006.

'Rot-Schwarz in Nordost?', *Neues Deutschland*, 30 September/1 October 2006.

'Noch kein grünes Signal für Rot-Rot', *Neues Deutschland*, 4/5 November 2006.

'Bundesvorstand rüffelt Sachsen-PDS', *Sächsische Zeitung*, 9 September 1999.

'PDS Vorstandsmitglied verteidigt Mauerbau', *Schweriner Volkszeitung*, 25 January 1999.

'Was abhehmen', *Der Spiegel*, 30 September 1985.

'Das war's', *Der Spiegel*, 21 October 1985.

'Stumm vor Zorn', *Der Spiegel*, 31 March 1986.

'Jeder hat seine Talente', *Der Spiegel*, 28 January 1991.

'Blitzflink ohne Widerspruch', *Der Spiegel*, 18 March 1991.

'Schwarzbau unter Schutz', *Der Spiegel*, 8 March, 1993.

'Vom Laster überfahren. Herber Schlag für die Grünen', *Der Spiegel*, 14 June 1995.

'Die Partei ist westdeutsch', *Der Spiegel*, 9 March 1996.

'Wo bleibt Fischer?', *Der Spiegel*, 12 February, 1998.

'Wir brauchen Optionen', Interview with Ralf Christoffers, *Der Spiegel*, 13 August 2001.

'Oskar, der Rettungsanker', *Der Spiegel*, 29 September 2003.

'Das übliche Tohuwabohu', *Der Spiegel*, 6 August 2004.

'Gregor Gysi zum Dritten', *Der Spiegel*, 1 November 2004.

'Ein Himmelfahrtskommando', *Der Spiegel*, 30 May 2005.

'Lyrik und Schwindel', *Der Spiegel*, 17 June 2005.

'Die werden sich zerlegen', *Der Spiegel*, 24 June 2005.

'Chaos statt Revolution', *Der Spiegel*, 3 February 2006.

'Linkes Projekt versinkt im Fusions-Chaos', *Der Spiegel*, 26 February 2006.

'Großes Foul links außen', *Der Spiegel*, 8 March 2006.

'Kuckkuck im roten Nest', *Der Spiegel*, 10 March 2006.

'Linkspartei plant schon ohne WASG', *Der Spiegel*, 28 April, 2006.

'Chaos bei der Linken', *Der Spiegel*, 14 May 2006.

'Berliner Parteirebellen siegen vor Gericht', *Der Spiegel*, 31 May 2006.

'Parteitag ebnet den Weg zur Fusion', *Der Spiegel*, 20 November 2006.

'Die PDS und die Koalitionsfrage', *Tagesspiegel*, 10 August 1999.

'Christoffers schließt PDS-CDU-Koalition langfristig nicht aus', *Tagesspiegel*, 11 August 2001.

'Die CDU handlete in der E-Mail-Affäre rechtswidrig', *Tagesspiegel*, 7 September 2006.

'PDS entdeckt den Realismus', *Tagesspiegel*, 11 October 2006.

'CDU Brandenburg entlässt Landesgeschäftsführer', *Tagesspiegel*, 1 November 2006.

'"Eiertanz" statt Hochzeitswalzer. Interview mit Harald Wolf', *Tageszeitung*, 30 June 2005.

This Week in Germany: 20 January 1995.

'Hüseyin Aydin appelliert an die Mitglieder der Berliner WASG', *WASG Nachrichten*, 2 March 2006.

'CDU soll wie Linkspartei privatisieren', *Die Welt*, 20 March 2006.

'Der "Genosse der Bosse" und sein Draht in die Wirtschaft', *Die Welt*, 3 April 2006.

Index

Agenda 2010 (see also Hartz reforms)
3, 43–44, 91, 113, 125–126, 153
AG Bilanz 88
AG Christinnen und Christen 17
AG JungeGenossInnen 6, 17, 20, 101
Aleksa 128, 132
Antikapitalistische Linke
(Anti-Capitalist Left) 90
APO 67
Association of West German
Communists (BWK) 135
Aufbaugeneration/Altgenossen 20, 32
Autonome 71
Aydin, Hüseyin 145

Bartsch, Dietmar 38
Basic Law 13
Bavaria 41, 137, 142
Berghofer, Wolfgang 16
Benjamin, Michael 19
Berlin Wall 6, 13, 14, 19, 22
Berlin-Brandenburg Fusion
122, 126, 127
Berliner Stadtreinigung 111
Berliner Verkehrsbetriebe 111
BEWAG 72
Bischoff, Joachim 137, 146
Bischoff-Pflanz, Heidi 72
Bisky, Lothar 4, 16, 32, 33, 37–38,
44, 116–188, 119, 120, 121, 122,
123, 126, 137, 140, 145–146,
147, 157
Bismarck, Otto van 15
Blair, Tony 18
Blaul, Iris 75
Bluhm (nee Freundl), Carola
103, 104
Bonk, Julia 129
Börner, Holger 70
Breitenbach, Elke 103, 104, 113
Brie, André 16, 18, 32, 37, 137
Brie, Michael 18, 20, 146
Brandenburg Way 117

Brombacher, Ellen 19
Bundesrat 2, 94, 96, 110, 139
Bundestag 2, 11, 27, 31, 33, 40, 49,
52, 74, 83, 103, 123, 131, 134,
140, 145, 148
Bundesverfassungsschutz 20
Bundeswehr 34
Bush, George 40

CDU 2, 3, 24, 29, 31, 36, 37, 42, 64,
67, 68, 71, 72, 76, 78, 86, 102,
105, 117, 118, 119, 124, 126, 127,
128, 132, 157, 163, 164
Chemnitz 45, 123
Christoffers, Ralf 118, 122, 123, 125
Claus, Roland 19, 38, 40
Clinton, Bill 18
Communist Platform (KPF) 6, 17,
19–20, 25, 28, 32, 89, 104, 117,
133, 135, 161
Constitution (EU) 110, 112, 113
Cottbus Conference 37, 38
CSU 3, 24, 42
Cyprus 54
Czech Republic 41

Daimler-Benz 72
Dehm, Dieter 38, 40, 44, 133, 161
Denmark 54
Direktmandate 39
Doganay, Hakan 144
Dohnanyi, Klaus von 69
Dörre, Karsten 143
Dresden 15–16, 45, 119, 120, 121,
123, 124, 128, 129
Dresden Declaration 29
Drugs policy 129
DVU 5

Eichel, Hans 74
Einsiedel, Count von 26
Emancipatory Left (in *Die Linke*) 60,
89, 98, 113, 123, 128, 129, 159

212 *Index*

Enkelmann, Dagmar   44, 117,
    122, 123
Erfurt Declaration   29
Ernst, Cornelia   119, 121, 123,
    124, 129
Ernst, Klaus   4, 111, 137, 140, 147
Erziehungsgeld   93
European Union   26, 27,
    34, 35, 41, 110

FDP   24, 27, 42, 65, 68, 71, 72, 76,
    78, 95, 157, 163
Federal Election
  1980   68
  1990   67, 74, 77, 82, 156
  1994   26
  1998   7, 17, 31, 34, 38, 127, 135
  2002   40, 41–43, 49, 83, 94, 106,
    121, 136, 156, 161
  2005   1, 3, 4, 12, 39, 49, 112, 128,
    137, 138, 139–141, 148, 152, 154
  2009   46
Felfe, Edeltraut   90–91
Finland   54
Filz   109
Fischer, Joschka   70, 74, 75
Flierl, Thomas   18, 39, 107–108
Forum Zweite Erneuerung (Forum of
    the Second Renewal)   104
Fraktionsvorsitzendenkonferenz   130, 157
France   54, 63
Free German Youth (FDJ)   101
Friedrichshain-Kreuzberg   27

GDR   2–3, 7, 13–23, 25–26, 28, 32,
    33, 37, 45, 47, 72, 100, 101, 153
Gehrcke, Wolfgang   133, 146, 161
Gera Conference   104
German Communist Party (DKP)
    39, 135
Gramkow, Angela   86, 87
Greece   54, 164
Greens   1, 10, 24, 27, 28–29, 34, 36,
    42, 43–44, 48, 50, 51, 64, 65,
    66–83, 95, 99, 100, 103, 113, 141,
    147–152, 154–157, 161, 163
Gysi,   Gregor 1, 2, 3, 4, 11, 15, 16,
    32, 37–38, 40, 42, 44–45, 102,
    104, 105, 106, 112, 148, 153

Händel, Thomas   4, 137
Hanns Seidel Foundation   6
Hartz, Peter   136
Hartz Reforms   3, 43, 122, 125,
    126, 136–137, 138, 144
Hauser, Otto   24
Heuer, Uwe-Jens   19, 158
Heym, Stefan   26
Hilsberg, Stephan   30
Hoff, Benjamin   102, 104, 108
Holter, Helmut   19, 32, 35, 38,
    86–89, 92–93, 94, 141
Honecker, Erich   14
Höppner, Reinhard   28–29
Hungary   41

IG Metall   137
IMs   24
Independent Commission for the
    Investigation of the Property of
    Parties and Mass Organisations in
    the GDR   22–23
Ingolstadt Manifesto   135
Initiative for Labour and Social
    Justice (ASG)   137
Iraq   8, 41
Ireland   54
Italy   54

Jugendbrigade   123
Junge Welt   5

Kaiser, Kerstin   123
Karl-Liebknecht House
    22–23, 24
Kaufmann, Karl-Heinz   23
Kipping, Katja   44, 128, 147
Kirchoff, Paul   3, 4
KITAs   72
Klein, Dieter   18, 146
Klemm, Gernot   102, 104
Knake-Werner, Heidi   103
Kohl, Helmut   14, 22, 23, 24, 28
Konrad Adenauer Foundation   6
Kosovo   94
Krause, Torsten   126, 131
Krehl, Constanze   121
Krenz, Egon   14, 16
Kutzmutz, Rolf   117

Lafontaine, Oskar 1, 3, 23, 29, 45, 111, 129, 133, 135, 138, 139–140, 151, 152, 153, 155, 161, 162
Landowsky, Klaus 105
Langnitschke, Wolfgang 23
Lässig, Barbara 128
Lauter, Reinhard 119
Lederer, Klaus 103, 113
Leipzig 38, 119, 123, 128
Leuchter, Wolfgang 86
Leverkusen Circle 142
Liebich, Stefan 102, 103, 104, 108, 109, 144
Lösing, Sabine 4
Lötzsch, Gesine 2, 103–104
Lühr, Uwe 27
Lüth, Heidemarie 44

Magdeburg Model 29, 32, 39
Marxist Forum 19, 32, 51, 89, 133, 161
Mattern, Ingrid 120, 123
Meckel, Markus 30
Merkel, Angela 3
Methling, Wolfgang 44, 86, 88, 96
Meves, Helge 144, 147
Michels, Martina 101, 109
Michels, Robert 51–52, 54, 101
Modern socialism (in *Die Linke*) 11, 17, 19–20, 32, 61, 99, 100, 102, 103, 108, 111, 112, 113, 116, 119, 127, 128, 129, 130, 136, 141, 158, 159
Modrow, Hans 16, 91
Momper, Walter 71, 72, 74
Mosca, Gaetano 52
Moscow 23
Münster Conference 36–37
Muth, Catherina 87

Nagel, Juliane 129
NATO 34, 37, 76, 82, 94, 155, 156, 159
Nelken, Michail 109
Neumünster 76, 83, 148–149, 156, 157
New Zealand 54
Nuclear Power 67, 68, 69, 70, 73, 74, 76, 82, 87, 156
Neues Deutschland 5, 122

Nord, Thomas 123
North Rhine-Westphalia 137, 138, 139
Norway 54
NPD 5

ÖBS 35, 92, 93, 112, 131
Ostrowski, Christine 19

Pareto, Vilfredo 52
Pau, Petra 2, 19, 27, 38, 39, 44, 102, 103, 104, 105
Petke, Sven 126
Plattform Dritter Weg 18
Pohl, Wolfgang 23
Porsch, Peter 38, 44, 119, 120, 121, 124, 128, 157
'Poverty Report' (Berlin) 110
Pragmatic Reformers (in *Die Linke*) 19, 29, 60, 86, 87, 96, 98, 115, 116, 120, 123, 127, 159
Prütz, Michael 107, 144

Ramelow, Bodo 4, 137, 142, 147
Redler, Lucy 144
Reeh, Martin 144
Reformlinke (Reforming Left in *Die Linke*) 104
Republikaner 71
Restorative Ideologues (in *Die Linke*) 19, 89, 98, 113, 120, 129, 133, 158, 161
Ringstorff, Harald 29, 86, 94, 97
Ritter, Peter 86, 89, 96, 97
Rosa-Luxemburg Foundation 18, 31, 142
Rostock Manifesto 33

Saarbrücken 68
Saarland 42, 138
SAV 144
Saxony-Anhalt 19, 24, 28–29, 32, 39, 69–81, 102–103
Scharping, Rudolf 29
Schleswig-Holstein 27, 68
Schädel, Monty 94
Schatz, Carsten 102
Schill Party 95
Schoenenburg, Arnold 89

Schönbohm, Jörg   3, 4, 126, 132
Schönefeld Airport   122, 127
Schumann, Michael   18, 117, 121, 122
Schröder, Gerhard   2, 3, 8, 10, 31,
    34, 35, 36, 41, 42, 43, 44,
    45, 74, 94, 113, 124, 136,
    137, 138, 139
Schubert, Katina   103
Schwebs, Birgit   96, 97
Schwerin   10, 28, 32, 84, 86, 89, 90,
    92, 98, 108, 135, 163
SED   5, 6, 12–19, 21, 22, 23,
    26, 101, 154
Sitte, Petra   39
Slovakia   41
'Social Democratic Platform'
    (in the PDS)   20
Social Justice   19, 32, 34, 45,
    51, 92, 95, 143, 154
'Social Structure Atlas' (Berlin)   110
'Social Ticket' (Berlin)   107
Sorbs   27
Spain   54, 164
SPD   1, 2, 5–6, 10, 11, 12, 19, 24,
    28–30, 31–32, 34, 35, 36, 38, 39,
    41, 42, 44, 45, 50–51, 52, 61,
    64–65, 66–83, 85–98, 99–114,
    117, 118, 120–121, 122, 123, 124,
    126, 127, 128, 130, 131, 132, 136,
    137, 138, 139, 140, 143, 144, 151,
    153, 155, 157, 158, 159, 161, 163
Stasi   18, 24, 119
Stoiber, Edmund   3, 4
Stolpe, Manfred   36
Streitkultur   57
Ströbele, Hans-Christian   27
Student Account Model
    (Berlin)   107–108
Sweden   54

Tack, Anita   117–118, 120
Taheri, Rouzbeh   39, 107
Thiel, Wolfgang   120
Thuringia   26, 36, 38, 42, 137
Treptow-Köpenick   140
Treuhandanstalt   22–23
Trittin, Jürgen   73
Troost, Axel   4, 137, 146, 147

Unification   12–14, 15, 22, 23, 24,
    26, 76, 153, 154
United Kingdom   61

Ver.di   137
Vietze, Heinz   117–118, 120,
    121, 122, 125
Vivantes   111
Volkskammer   21–22, 148
Volkssolidarität   25

WASG   3, 4, 7, 11, 39, 44, 45, 47,
    107, 109, 111, 112, 133, 136–151,
    154, 155, 160, 161, 162
Wagenknecht, Sahra   17, 19, 32, 39,
    133, 158, 161
Walther, Gerd   97
Wawrzyniak, Halina   102
Wechselberg, Carl   109
Weckesser, Ronald   119, 120,
    123, 128
Werner, Harald   39
Westlinke   6
Wilson, Harold   1
Wolf, Harald   103–104, 109, 110,
    113, 144
Wowereit, Klaus   110

Zillich, Stefan   102
Zimmer, Gabriele   38–40, 44, 105